An Introduction to Logic

AN INTRODUCTION TO LOGIC

by

Morris R. Cohen

&

Ernest Nagel

A HARVEST/HBJ BOOK
HARCOURT BRACE JOVANOVICH
NEW YORK AND LONDON

LMN

Library of Congress Catalog Number: 62-21468

Printed in the United States of America

ISBN   0-15-645125-5

A NOTE ON THE HARVEST EDITION

This edition makes available separately the first part of our book AN INTRODUCTION TO LOGIC AND SCIENTIFIC METHOD. It contains only the Preface, except for the concluding paragraph; the first, or introductory, chapter; and Book I, on *Formal Logic,* but not Book II, on *Applied Logic and Scientific Method,* of the original text first published in 1934. It does not, therefore, embody fully the conception of logic or the pedagogic ideas for presenting the subject that controlled the composition of the complete text, and that are described in the Preface and Chapter I. But it does cover a part of the subject that can be conveniently mastered in a one-semester course; and although it gives greater attention to the traditional analysis of formal arguments than to the techniques of symbolic or mathematical logic (which has had an almost explosive development since the first publication of the full text), it contains sufficient material for making the reader thoroughly acquainted with the basic ideas of deductive logic and demonstrative reasoning.

1962   E. N.

PREFACE

   Though formal logic has in recent times been the object of radical and spirited attacks from many and diverse quarters, it continues, and will probably long continue, to be one of the most frequently given courses in colleges and universities here and abroad. Nor need this be surprising when we reflect that the most serious of the charges against formal logic, those against the syllogism, are as old as Aristotle, who seems to have been fully aware of them. But while the realm of logic seems perfectly safe against the attacks from without, there is a good deal of unhappy confusion within. Though the content of almost all logic books follows (even in many of the illustrations) the standard set by Aristotle's *Organon*—terms, propositions, syllogisms and allied forms of inference, scientific method, probability and fallacies—there is a bewildering Babel of tongues as to what logic is about. The different schools, the traditional, the linguistic, the psychological, the epistemological, and the mathematical, speak different languages, and each regards the other as not really dealing with logic at all.
   No task is perhaps so thankless, or invites so much abuse from all quarters, as that of the mediator between hostile points of view. Nor is the traditional distrust of the peacemaker in the intellectual realm difficult to appreciate, since he so often substitutes an unclear and inconsistent amalgam for points of view which at least have the merit of a certain clarity. And yet no task is so essential, especially for the beginner, when it is undertaken with the objective of adjusting and supplementing the claims of the contending parties, and when it is accompanied by a refusal to sacrifice clarity and rigor in thought.
   In so far as an elementary text permits such a thing, the present text seeks to bring some order into the confusion of tongues concerning the subject matter of logic. But the resolution of the conflicts between various schools which it effects appears in the selection and presentation of material, and not in extensive polemics against any school. The book has been written with the conviction

that logic is the autonomous science of the objective though formal conditions of valid inference. At the same time, its authors believe that the aridity which is (not always unjustly) attributed to the study of logic testifies to the unimaginative way logical principles have been taught and misused. The present text aims to combine sound logical doctrine with sound pedagogy, and to provide illustrative material suggestive of the rôle of logic in every department of thought. A text that would find a place for the realistic formalism of Aristotle, the scientific penetration of Peirce, the pedagogical soundness of Dewey, and the mathematical rigor of Russell—this was the ideal constantly present to the authors of this book.

However inadequately this ideal is embodied in the present text, the embodiment is not devoid of positive doctrine, so presented that at least partial justice is done to supplementary approaches to logic.

1. The traditional view of logic as the science of valid inference has been consistently maintained, against all attempts to confuse logic with psychology, where by the latter is meant the systematic study of how the mind works. Logic, as the science of the weight of evidence in all fields, cannot be identified with the special science of psychology. For such a special science can establish its results only by using criteria of validity employed in other fields as well. And it is clear that questions of validity are not questions of how we happen to think, but of whether that which is asserted is or is not in conformity with certain objective states of fact.

2. On the other hand, the pedagogical applications of psychological logics have not been ignored. We have aimed to present the subject in such a manner that discussion of doctrines new to the student is made continuous with his presumed knowledge at the outset. We have therefore avoided as far as possible the synthetic method of exposition: the method which begins with highly abstract elements and constructs a science out of them. Instead, we have followed what seems to us psychologically a more appropriate method. Illustrations with which a college student may reasonably be supposed to be familiar are usually taken as the text for discussion, and abstract, formal elements are gradually revealed as abstract phases of the subject matter. In this way, we trust, we have removed many of the difficulties which face the young student, and at the same time have indicated to him the important rôle played by logic in all of man's activities.

3. Again, while we have tried to present the significant results of symbolic or mathematical logic to those who have no previous

knowledge of the subject, we have not tried to develop the technique of symbolic manipulation for its own sake. In our opinion,
such a technique, while very valuable, belongs properly to mathematics developed as an organon of science, and not to an elementary
book on logic. Nor do we share the rather hostile attitude towards
the Aristotelian logic expressed by some of the more zealous workers
in the newer fields. We have not been sparing in indicating the
limitations of the traditional presentation of our subject. But we
think that the newer achievements in exact logic have served to
extend as well as to correct the Aristotelian logic. We have thus
given a great deal of attention to traditional views that might well
be left out in a systematic presentation of our present knowledge.
For we think that the discussion and correction of the limitations
of the traditional views has many pedagogical advantages in making our final ideas clear.

4. We do not believe that there is any non-Aristotelian logic in
the sense in which there is a non-Euclidean geometry, that is, a system of logic in which the contraries of the Aristotelian principles
of contradiction and excluded middle are assumed to be true, and
valid inferences are drawn from them. What have recently been
claimed to be alternative systems of logic are different systems of
notation or symbolization for the same logical facts. We have drawn
freely on the natural sciences for illustrations of logical principles,
precisely because the logical structure of these sciences is clearly
more than linguistic. We have therefore frankly indicated the meta-
physical significance of logical principles, and have not failed to
note that the structure of language is itself often a clue to something other than linguistic fact. While maintaining that logic as an
autonomous science must be formal, we have insisted that its principles are not therefore without significant content; on the contrary,
we have taken the position that they are inherently applicable because they are concerned with ontological traits of utmost generality. We think that the category of objective possibility is essential to logical discussion.

In the main, therefore, we view the history of logic as that of a
series of contributions of diverse value by the various schools. If our
point of view is consequently somewhat eclectic, seeking to give the
student a liberal rather than a narrow view of the subject, we have
nevertheless striven hard to maintain clear distinctions as to funda-
mentals. Florence Nightingale transformed modern hospital prac-
tise by the motto: Whatever hospitals do, they should not spread
disease. Similarly, logic should not infect students with fallacies and

confusions as to the fundamental nature of valid or scientific reasoning.

Different instructors will naturally attach more value to different parts of the book. Not all of it can be presented in a one-semester course, and enough material has been included to occupy the student's attention for a full year. In a one-semester course, the authors have found that the substance of Book II, with the inclusion of Chapters III, IV, and VIII of Book I, gives the most satisfactory results. Those not interested in mathematics may omit Chapter VII. Books are tools which wise men use to suit their own ends. One of the authors, who has given courses in elementary logic for over twenty years, has generally treated the contents of Book II (Applied Logic and Scientific Method) before the formal logic of Book I. There are, to be sure, some topics in Book II which presuppose the solutions of Book I. But experience shows that such difficulties are readily surmountable. It is especially the hope of the authors that general readers as well as students of the natural and social sciences will find this book helpful towards an understanding of scientific method.

M. R. C.

E. N.

The continued demand for this book, which has exhausted three printings of it, has given us a chance to correct certain errors and to revise some statements in the interest of greater clarity.

M. R. C.

E. N.

January 7, 1936

CONTENTS

forget

V. HYPOTHETICAL, ALTERNATIVE, AND DISJUNCTIVE
SYLLOGISMS

VI. GENERALIZED OR MATHEMATICAL LOGIC

forget these

CONTENTS

CHAPTER I

THE SUBJECT MATTER OF LOGIC

§ 1. LOGIC AND THE WEIGHT OF EVIDENCE

Most of our daily activities are carried on without reflection, and it seldom occurs to us to question that which generally passes as true. We cannot, however, always remain in a state of unquestioned belief. For our habitual attitudes are frequently challenged by unexpected changes in our environment, if they are not challenged by our own curiosity or by the inquisitiveness of others.

Let us suppose the reader to be seated at his table some late afternoon. The gathering darkness is making his reading difficult. Ordinarily he would turn on the electric light near him and continue with his work. But on this occasion, we suppose, the Shade of Socrates suddenly appears to the busy reader, just as his hand is on the switch, and asks him to please tell what he is doing. The reader has stout nerves, and quickly recovering from his surprise, explains: "I wish to put on the light, and this is the switch. Since your day . . ." "Yes, yes," we can imagine the Shade to interrupt, "I know all about your modern methods and theories of lighting. You needn't take time to tell me about *that*. But I do wish you would tell me how you know that it is the electric switch you were just pointing to." The reader's temper may by this time have been thoroughly ruffled, and after an embarrassed silence, he may reply with pained surprise and some asperity: "Can't you see, Socrates?"— and turn on the light.

What is of interest to us in this imaginary dialogue is that a doubt, however slight, might be raised in the reader's mind about a proposition *This is the electric switch,* which had previously been accepted without question; and that the doubt might be resolved by claiming that any evidence besides *seeing* was superfluous. There are other propositions for which it would be difficult to find any evidence other than a direct seeing, hearing, touching, or smelling. *It is half-past eleven on my watch; My forehead is hot to the touch; This rose I am smelling has a fine fragrance; The shoes I have on are uncomfortable; That is a loud noise.* These are examples of propositions on account of which most of us would lose our tempers if we were pressed to give reasons why we believed them to be true.

Not all propositions, however, are regarded as so obvious. If the Shade should accost the reader entering the office of a life insurance company, and ask him what he is about, the reader might perhaps say: "I am going to buy a life insurance policy." Should the reader be pressed for his motives, a possible answer might be: "I shall die some day, and I wish to provide for my dependents." If Socrates should now demand why the reader believes in the truth of the proposition *I shall die some day,* the answer will no longer be, "Can't you see?" For we cannot literally see our own future death. But a little reflection may suggest the following reply: "All living creatures, O Socrates, must perish some day, and since I too am a living creature, I too shall die some day."

There are propositions, therefore, which we believe to be true because we can find some *other* propositions of whose truth we have no doubt and which we think will serve as *evidence* for the disputed proposition. *The sun is approximately ninety-three million miles away; Caesar crossed the Rubicon; There will be an eclipse of the sun next year in North America; The sum of the angles of a triangle is equal to two right angles.* These are a few propositions in whose truth we may believe because we think others, if not we ourselves, can find supporting propositions for them.

The distinction between propositions which are believed without grounds other than direct observation or apprehension and propositions which are believed because other propositions can be found to serve as evidence for them, cannot always be drawn very sharply. We sometimes believe a proposition to be true partly because we can make direct observations and partly because we can find supporting propositions. If we drop two rocks of unequal weight from the same height at the same time, we believe the proposition, *The two rocks strike the ground at the same time,* not only because we *see* that they do, but because we know a *reason* why they should do so. Moreover, many propositions whose truth seems very clear to us are in fact false. For we often see what we expect to see rather than that which actually happens. Many remarkable advances in knowledge have resulted from our questioning the truth of propositions which we previously regarded as "self-evident." And a critical study of human beliefs reveals how much "interpretation" is present in what at first sight seems like "immediate knowledge." But it is not necessary for our present purpose to settle the question as to what propositions, if any, can be known to be true "immediately."

All that we now require is the recognition of the general need of evidence for what we or others believe or question. In scientific or historic research, in courts of law, and in making up our minds as to all sorts of practical issues, we are constantly called upon to pass on diverse considerations offered in support of various propositions at issue. Sometimes we find such considerations to be irrelevant and to constitute no evidence at all, even though we have no doubt as to their truth, while other propositions we regard as conclusive or demonstrative proof of a point at issue. Between these two extremes we have situations in which there is some testimony or circumstance that points to a given conclusion but is not sufficient to exclude some alternative possibility. For most occasions we are satisfied with a preponderance of evidence, that is, if there is more evidence in favor of a proposition than against it; but in some cases, for example, when as jurymen we pass on the guilt of one accused of a crime, we are required to act affirmatively only if there is no reasonable doubt left, that is, no doubt which a "reasonably" prudent man would act on in the course of his affairs.

Logic may be said to be concerned with the question of the adequacy or probative value of different kinds of evidence. Traditionally, however, it has devoted itself in the main to the study of what constitutes proof, that is, complete or conclusive evidence. For, as we shall see, the latter is necessarily involved in determining the weight of partial evidence and in arriving at conclusions that are said to be more or less probable.

§ 2. CONCLUSIVE EVIDENCE OR PROOF

Let us consider the proposition *There are at least two persons in New York City who have the same number of hairs on their heads,* and let us symbolize it by q. How could its truth be established? An obvious way would be to find two individuals who actually do have the same number of hairs. But this would require an extremely laborious process of examining the scalps of perhaps six million people. It is not a feasible method practically. We may be able to show, however, that the proposition q follows from or is necessitated by other propositions whose truth can be established more easily. In that event, we could *argue* for the truth of the proposition q, in virtue of its being *implied* by the others, and in virtue of the established truth of the propositions offered as evidence. Let us try this method.

Suppose it were known by an actual count that there are five thousand barber shops in New York City. Would the proposition *There are five thousand barber shops in New York City* be satisfactory evidence for q? The reader will doubtless reply, "Nonsense! What has the number of barber shops to do with there being two persons with an identical number of scalp hairs?" In this way the reader expresses the judgment (based on previous knowledge) that the number of barber shops is no evidence at all for the equality in the number of hairs. Not all propositions are *relevant*, even if true, to the truth of a proposition in question.

Let us now consider the proposition *The number of inhabitants in New York City is greater than the number of hairs that any one of its inhabitants has on his head*. We shall denote this proposition by p. Is the truth of p sufficient to establish the truth of q? The reader might be inclined to dismiss p, just as he dismissed the information about the number of barber shops, as irrelevant. But this would be a mistake. We can show that if p is true, q must be true also. Thus suppose, taking small numbers for purposes of illustration, that the greatest number of hairs that any inhabitant of New York City has is fifty, and that there are fifty-one people living in New York City, no one of whom is completely bald. Let us assign a number to each inhabitant corresponding to the number of hairs that he has. Then the first person will have one hair, the second person two hairs, and so on, until we reach the fiftieth person, who will have, at most, fifty hairs. There is one inhabitant left and, since we have assumed that no person has more than fifty hairs, he will necessarily have a number of hairs that is the same as that possessed by one of the other fifty persons. The argument is perfectly general, as a little reflection shows, and does not depend on the number fifty we have selected as the maximum number of hairs. We may, therefore, conclude that our proposition p, *The number of inhabitants in New York City is greater than the number of hairs that any one of its inhabitants has on his head*, implies proposition q, *There are at least two persons in New York who have the same number of hairs on their heads*. The two propositions have been shown to be so related that it is impossible for the first (called the *evidence* or *premise*) to be true, and the second (called the *conclusion* or *that which is to be proved*) to be false.

Other instances of conclusive evidence can be multiplied indefinitely. Thus we can prove that a missing individual is dead by showing that he sailed on a boat destroyed at sea by an explosion that prevented anyone from being saved. So we can prove that our neighbor, Mr. Brown, has no right to vote by showing that he is not yet twenty-one years of age and that the law prohibits such individuals from voting.

Mathematics is, of course, a field in which proof is essential. A distinction, however, must be noted in this respect between applied and pure mathematics. In the former, as in the examples already mentioned, we assume that certain propositions, for example, the laws of mechanics, are *true;* and we prove the *truth* of other propositions by showing that they necessarily follow or are mathematically deducible from those assumed. In pure mathematics, on the other hand, we restrict ourselves to demonstrating that our primary assumptions necessarily imply or entail the theorems which are deduced from them, and ignore the question whether our conclusions as well as our axioms or postulates are in fact true.

It might be of some advantage to use the word "proof" for the former procedure (by which we conclude a proposition to be *true*), and to designate by "deduction" or "demonstration" the procedure which only establishes an *implication* or *necessary connection* between a premise and its conclusion irrespective of the truth or falsity of either. Such a terminology would permit us to say that a proposition is *proved* when, and only when, a premise *implies* that proposition and that premise is itself *true.* But so habitual is the usage which speaks of "proving" theorems in pure mathematics that it would be vain to try to abolish it. It is therefore safer to continue to speak of "proof" in pure mathematics, but to recognize that what we prove there are always implications, that is, that *if* certain propositions are true, certain others must be true. And this, after all, is the phase of all proof in which logic is primarily interested.

In all cases, then, of complete evidence or proof the conclusion is implied by the premises, and the reasoning or inference from the latter to the former is called *deductive.* We *infer* one proposition from another *validly* only if there is an objective relation of *implication* between the first proposition and the second. Hence, it is essential to distinguish *inference,* which is a temporal process, from *implication,* which is an objective relation between propositions. An implication may hold even if we do not know how to infer one proposition from another. Thus an inference to be valid requires that there be an implication between propositions. On the other hand, the being of an implication does not depend upon the occurrence of the psychological process of inferring.

§ 3. THE NATURE OF LOGICAL IMPLICATION

In every attempt at a complete proof of propositions of practical importance we thus find two questions involved:

1. Are the propositions offered as evidence true?

2. Are the conclusions so related to the evidence or premises that the former necessarily follow from and may thus be properly deduced from the latter?

The first question raises what is called a factual or material issue; and the answer to it cannot be assigned entirely to logic withou* making the latter include all the sciences and all common knowledge. Logic as a distinctive science is concerned only with the second question—with the relation of *implication* between propositions. Thus the specific task of logic is the study of the conditions under which one proposition necessarily follows and may therefore be deduced from one or more others, regardless of whether the latter are in fact true.

As any number of propositions can be combined into one, every instance of implication or logical sequence can be said to hold between two propositions, which might be most accurately designated as the *implicating* and the *implied,*[1] but are generally called *antecedent* and *consequent,* as well as *premise* and *conclusion.* We must, however, note that in using the terms "antecedent" and "consequent," or the expression, "It logically follows," we are referring to an abstract relation which, like that between whole and part, does not directly refer to any temporal succession. The logical consequences of a proposition are not phenomena which follow it in time, but are rather parts of its meaning. While our apprehension of premises sometimes precedes that of their conclusion, it is also true that we often first think of the conclusion and then find premises which imply it.

Let us consider this relation of implication a little more closely.

---

[1] In grammar they are known as the *protasis* and *apodosis* of a subjunctive sentence.

Logical Implication Does Not Depend on the Truth of Our Premises.

The specific logical relation of implication may hold (1) between false propositions or (2) between a false and a true one, and (3) may fail to hold between true propositions.

1. Consider the argument *If Sparta was a democracy and no democracy has any kings, it follows that Sparta had no king.* The falsity of the proposition, *Sparta was a democracy,* does not prevent it from having certain implications nor from determining definite logical consequences.

No argument is more common in daily life than that which draws the logical implications of hypotheses contrary to fact. If there were no death there would be no cemeteries, funeral orations, and so on. All our regrets are based on drawing the consequences of propositions asserting what might have been but did not in fact happen.

> "Had we never loved sae kindly,
> Had we never loved sae blindly,
> Never met or never parted,
> We had ne'er been broken-hearted!"

It is a great error to suppose, as many have unthinkingly done, that in the reasoning we call scientific we proceed only from facts or propositions that are true. This view ignores the necessity for deduction from false hypotheses. In science as well as in practical choices, we are constantly confronted with alternative hypotheses which cannot all be true. Is the phenomenon of burning to be explained by the emission of a substance called phlogiston or by the combination with one called oxygen? Does magnetism act at a distance like gravitation, or does it, like sound, require a medium? We generally decide between such conflicting propositions by deducing the consequences of each and ruling out as false that hypothesis which leads to false conclusions, that is, to results which do not prevail in the field of observable fact. If false hypotheses had no logical consequences we should not thus be able to test their falsity.

That a proposition has definite logical consequences even if it is false follows also from the fact that these logical consequences or implications are part of its meaning. And we must know the meaning of a proposition before we can tell whether it is true. But in all cases (whether a proposition is true or false) the test as to whether there is a logical implication between one proposition and another is the impossibility of the former being true and the latter being false.

2. There is a widespread impression to the effect that false prem- ises must logically lead to propositions that are false. This is a seri- ous error, probably due to a thoughtless confusion with the true principle that if the consequences are false the premises must be false. But that true consequences may be implied by (or logically follow from) false premises can be seen from the following simple examples:

If all Mexicans are citizens of the United States and all Virgin- ians are Mexicans, it logically follows that all Virginians are citi- zens of the United States. If all porpoises are fishes and all fishes are aquatic vertebrates, it necessarily follows that porpoises are aquatic vertebrates. (The same conclusion follows if all porpoises are mollusks and all mollusks are aquatic vertebrates.) For again the relation between the antecedents and the consequents is such as to rule out the possibility of the former being true and the latter at the same time false.

Of course if a premise is false, the conclusion is *not proved* to be true even though the conclusion is implied by the premise. But it is of the utmost importance to realize that a proposition is not neces- sarily false, or proved to be so, if an argument in its favor is seen to rest on falsehood. A good cause may have bad reasons offered in its behalf.

3. We have already seen that the proposition *There are five thousand barber shops in New York City,* even if true, is irrele- vant to and cannot prove or logically imply the proposition *There are at least two persons in New York City who have the same number of hairs on their heads.* Let us, however, take an instance in which the absence of logical connection or implication is perhaps not so obvious. Does the proposition *Perfect beings can live to- gether without law and men are not perfect* imply *Men cannot live together without law?* Reflection shows that nothing in the premise rules out the *possibility* of there being men who, though not perfect, live together without law. We may be able, on other grounds, to prove that our conclusion is true, but the evidence here offered is not sufficient. There is no necessary connection shown between it and that which is to be proved.

Logical Implication Is Formal.

The fact that the logical implications of a proposition are the same whether it happens to be true or not, and that the validity of such implications is tested by the *impossibility* of the premise being true and its consequences false, is closely connected with what is called the formal nature of logic.

What do we mean by *formal?* The reader has doubtless had occasion to fill out some official blank, say an application for some position, a lease, a draft, or an income-tax return. In all these cases the unfilled document is clearly not itself an application, lease, draft, or tax return; but every one of these when completed is characterized by conforming to the pattern and provisions of its appropriate blank form. For the latter embodies the character or fixed order which all such transactions must have if they are to be valid. A form is, in general, something in which a number of different objects or operations agree (though they differ in other respects), so that the objects may be varied and yet the form remain the same. Thus any social ceremony or act which diverse individuals must perform in the same way if they occupy a given position or office, is said to be formal. Similarly, logical implication is formal in the sense that it holds between all propositions, no matter how diverse, provided they stand to each other in certain relations. Consider any of the foregoing instances of proof, such as *Brown is a minor; all minors are ineligible to vote; therefore Brown is ineligible to vote.* The implication here does not depend on any peculiarity of Brown other than the fact that he is a minor. If any other person is substituted for Brown the argument will still be valid. We can indicate this truth by writing X *is a minor, all minors are ineligible to vote, therefore* X *is ineligible to vote,* where X stands for anyone of an indefinitely large class. Reflection shows that we can also replace the word "minor" with any other term, say, "felon," "foreigner," without invalidating the argument. Thus if X *is a* Y, *and all* Y's *are ineligible to vote, then* X *is ineligible to vote,* no matter what we substitute for Y. We can now take the third step and realize that the logical implication is not only independent of the specific character of the objects denoted by X and Y, but that the term "ineligible to vote" might be replaced by anything else (*provided it is the same in premise and conclusion*). Thus we get the formula: *If* X *is* Y *and all* Y's *are* Z's, *then* X *is a* Z as true in all cases no matter what X, Y, and Z denote. On the other hand it would be an error to assert that if *All Parisians are Europeans and all Frenchmen are Europeans,* it follows that *All Parisians are Frenchmen.* For if in the generalized form of this argument, *All* X's *are* Y's, *and all* Z's *are* Y's, *therefore all* X's *are* Z's, we substitute "Belgians" for "Parisians," we get an argument in which the premises are true but the conclusion false. Similarly we can assert the implication that

If Socrates is older than Democritus and Democritus is older than Protagoras, then Socrates is older than Protagoras. For this will hold no matter what persons are substituted for these three, provided we keep the form, X *is older than* Y *and* Y *is older than* Z *implies* X *is older than* Z. On the other hand, from the proposition: A *is to the right of* B, *and* B *is to the right of* C, it does not necessarily follow that A *is to the right of* C. For if three men are sitting in a circle *A* can be said to be to the left of *C* even though he is to the right of *B* and the latter to the right of *C*. It is the object of logical study to consider more detailed rules for distinguishing valid from invalid forms of argument. What we need to note at present is that the correctness of any assertion of implication between propositions depends upon their form or structure. If any form can be filled by premises which are true and conclusions which are false, that form is invalid, and the assertion of an implication in any such case is incorrect.

Two observations must be added to the foregoing:

1. The more general statement or formula is not a constraining force or imperative existing before any special instance of it. An argument is valid in virtue of the implication between premises and conclusion in any particular case, and not in virtue of the general rule, which is rather the form in which we have abstracted or isolated what is essential for the validity of the argument. For the objects which enter into propositions are related in a certain way, and a form is an arrangement; hence an implication which holds for one arrangement of objects will not hold for another.

2. This formal character of implication (and thus of valid inference) does not mean that formal logic ignores the entire meaning of our propositions. For without the latter we can have only meaningless marks or sounds—not significant assertions or information having logical consequences. However, the fact that logic is concerned with necessary relations in the field of possibility makes it indifferent to any property of an object other than the function of the latter in a given argument. Formal properties must be common to all of a class.

Logical Implication as Determination

We have thus far considered the nature of logical implication from the point of view which regards it as an element in all proof or conclusive evidence. We may, however, also view it as entering into every situation or problem in which certain given conditions are sufficient to determine a definite result or situation. Take, for instance, the familiar problem: How long is the interval between the successive occasions when the hands of a clock are together? When the relative velocities of these hands are given, the value of the resulting interval is uniquely determined by the relation of logical implication—though if we are untrained in algebra, it may take us a long time before we see how to pass from the given conditions as premises to the conclusion or solution which they determine. The process of exploring the logical implications is thus a form of research and discovery. It should be noted, however, that it is not the business of logic to describe what happens in one's mind as one discovers rigorous or determinate solutions to a problem. That is a factual question of psychology. Logic is relevant at every step only in determining whether what *seems* an implication between one proposition and another is indeed such. Logic may, therefore, be also defined as the science of implication, or of valid inference (based on such implication). This may seem a narrower definition of logic than our previous one, that logic is the science of the weight of evidence. For implication as we have discussed it seems restricted to conclusive evidence. Reflection, however, shows that deductive inference, and hence the implication on which it ought to be based, enters into all determination of the weight of evidence.

§ 4. PARTIAL EVIDENCE OR PROBABLE INFERENCE

We have so far discussed the relation between premises and conclusion in case of rigorous proof. But complete or conclusive evidence is not always available, and we generally have to rely on partial or incomplete evidence. Suppose the issue is whether a certain individual, Baron X, was a militarist, and the fact that most aristocrats have been militarists is offered as evidence. As a rigorous proof this is obviously inadequate. It is clearly possible for the proposition *Baron X was a militarist* to be false even though the proposition offered as evidence is true. But it would also be absurd to assert that the fact that most aristocrats are militarists is altogether irrelevant as evidence for Baron X having been one. Obviously one who continues to make inferences of this type (Most X's are Y's, Z is an X, therefore Z is a Y) will in the long run be more often right than wrong. An inference of this type, which from true premises gives us conclusions which are true in most cases, is called *probable*. And the etymology of the word (Latin *probare*) indicates that such evidence is popularly felt to be a kind of proof even though not a conclusive one.

The reader will note that where the evidence in favor of a proposition is partial or incomplete, the probability of the inference may be increased by additional evidence. We shall in a later chapter consider with some detail when and how we can measure the degree of probability, and what precautions must be taken in order that our inferences shall have the maximum probability attainable. Here we can only briefly note that deductive inference enters as an element in such determination. To do this, let us consider first the case where a probable argument leads to a *generalization* or *induction,* and secondly, the case where such argument leads to what has been called a *presumption of fact.*

Generalization or Induction

Suppose we wish to know whether a certain substance, say, benzoate of soda, is generally deleterious. Obviously we cannot test this on everybody. We select a number of persons who are willing to take it with their food and whom we regard as typical or representative specimens of human beings generally. We then observe whether the ingestion of this substance produces any noticeable ill effect. If in fact all of them should show some positive ill effect we should regard that as evidence for the general proposition *Benzoate of soda is deleterious.* Such generalizations, however, frequently turn out to be false. For the individuals selected may not be typical or representative. They may have all been students, or unusually sensitive, or used to certain diets, or subject to a certain unnoticed condition which does not prevail in all cases. We try to overcome such doubt by using the inferred rule as a premise and deducing its consequences as to other individuals living under different conditions. Should the observed result in the new cases agree with the deduction from our assumed rule, the probability of the latter would be increased, though we cannot thus eliminate all doubt. On the other hand, should there be considerable disagreement between our general rule and what we find in the new cases, the rule would have to be modified in accordance with the general principle of deductive reasoning. Thus while generalizations from what we suppose to be typical cases sometimes lead to false conclusions, such generalizations enable us to arrive frequently at conclusions which are true in proportion to the care with which our generalization is formulated and tested.

Presumption of Fact

The second form of probable inference (which we have called presumption of fact) is that which leads us to deduce a fact not directly observable. Suppose that on coming home we find the lock on the door forced and a letter incriminating a prominent statesman missing. We believe in the general rule that violators of the law will not hesitate to violate it still further to save themselves from punishment. We then infer that the prominent statesman or his agents purloined the letter. This inference is obviously not a necessary one. Our evidence does not preclude the possibility that the letter was stolen by someone else. But our inference is clearly of the type that often leads to a right conclusion; and we increase this probability, when we show that if someone else than the one interested in the contents of the letter had stolen it, other valuables would have disappeared, and that this is not the fact.

Let us take another case. Suppose, for instance, we notice one morning that our instructor is irritable. We may know that headaches are accompanied by irritability. Consequently we may conclude that our instructor is suffering from a headache. If we examine this argument we find that the evidence for our conclusion consists of a proposition asserting the existence of a particular observable state of affairs (the instructor is irritable) and of another proposition asserting a rule or principle which may be formulated either as *All headaches are accompanied by irritability,* or *Many cases of irritability are due to headaches.* In neither case does our conclusion *The instructor has a headache* follow necessarily. His irritability may in fact be due to some other cause. But our inference is of the type that will lead to a true conclusion in a large number of cases, according to the extent to which irritability is connected with headaches. And we test the truth of the latter generalization (or induction) by deducing its consequences and seeing whether they hold in new situations.

This form of inference is so widespread, not only in practical affairs but even in advanced natural science, that illustration from the latter realm may be helpful. Various substances like oxygen, copper, chlorine, sulphur, hydrogen, when they combine chemically do so according to fixed ratios of their respective weights; and when the same amount of one substance, say chlorine, combines with different amounts of another substance, say oxygen, to form different compounds, it does so in ratios that are all small integral multiples of one. (This is the *observed event.*) We know also that if each of these substances were composed of similar atoms, or mechanically indivisible particles, the substances would combine in such integral ratios of their weights. (This is the *general rule.*) We conclude, then, that these substances are composed of atoms. (This is the *inferred fact.*) From the point of view of necessary implication the inference in this case is invalid. For it is possible that the observable facts may be due to an altogether different general cause than the assumed atomic constitution of matter. But our evidence has a very high degree of probability because we have used the general proposition (Matter has an atomic structure) as a premise from which to deduce all sorts of consequences that have been found true by direct observation and experiment—consequences which have also been shown to be inconsistent with other known assumptions.

This is also the character of the evidence for such everyday generalizations as that bread will satisfy our hunger, that walking or taking some conveyance will get us to our destination. These generalizations are not universally true. Accidents unfortunately happen. Bread may disagree with us, and he who walks or rides home may land in the hospital or in the morgue. All of our life, in fact, we depend on using the most probable generalizations. If our friend should refuse to walk on wooden or concrete floors because it has not been absolutely proved that they might not suddenly disintegrate or explode, we should feel some concern about his sanity. Yet it is unassailably true that so long as we lack omniscience and do not know all of the future, all our generalizations are fallible or only probable. And the history of human error shows that a general consensus, or widespread and unquestioned feeling of certainty, does not preclude the possibility that the future may show us to be in error.

§ 5. IS LOGIC ABOUT WORDS, THOUGHTS, OR OBJECTS?

Logic and Linguistics

While it seems impossible that there should be any confusion between a physical object, our "idea" or image of it, and the word that denotes it, the distinction is not so clear when we come to complexes of these elements, such as the government or literature of a country. As the logical inquiry into the implication of propositions is not directly concerned with physical or historical fact, the view naturally arises that it is concerned exclusively with words. The etymology of the word "logic" (as in "logomachy") supports this view. The great English philosopher Hobbes speaks of logic and reason as "nothing but reckoning, that is, adding and subtracting, of the consequences of general names agreed upon." [2] We must not, however, confuse the fact that words or symbols of some sort are necessary for logic (as for all the advanced sciences) with the assertion that valid reasoning is *nothing but* a consequence of the act of naming. For we can change the names of things, as we do when we translate from one language into another, without affecting the logical connections between the objects of our reasoning or "reckoning." The validity of our reasoning depends on the consistency with which we use whatever language we have, and such consistency means that our words must faithfully follow the order and connection of the items denoted by them. Logic, like physics or any other science, starts from the common social fact usually recorded by lexicographers that certain words have certain meanings, that is, that they denote certain things, relations, or operations. But a knowledge of such usage in English, or in any other language, will not enable us to solve all questions as to the adequacy of evidence, for example, the validity of the proof by Hermite and Lindemann that π (the ratio between the circumference and the diameter of a circle) cannot be accurately expressed by rational numbers in finite form.

While the direct subject matter of logic cannot be restricted to words, or even to the meaning of words as distinguished from the meaning or implication of propositions, logic is closely connected with general grammar, and it is not always easy to draw a sharp line between the grammatical and the logical writings of philosophers like Aristotle, Duns Scotus, and C. S. Peirce. We have already mentioned that logic starts by taking the ordinary meaning of words for granted, and we shall later see how just discrimination in the meanings of words helps us to avoid logical fallacies. It must, however, be added that in the general study of the meaning of words (called semantics) we are dependent on logic. The information conveyed by words depends both logically and psychologically on propositions, or the information conveyed by sentences.

Perhaps the most significant distinction between logic and that part of linguistics called grammar can be put thus: The norm or correctness with which grammar is concerned is conformity to certain actual usages, while the norm or correctness of logic is based on the possibilities in the nature of things which are the objects of our discourse. Grammar is primarily a descriptive social science, describing in some systematic manner the way in which words are

[2] *Leviathan*, Pt. I, Chap. 5.

used among certain peoples. It is only incidentally normative, as the description of fashions in clothes is. It is assumed that certain styles, the King's English [3] or the usage of the "best people," is preferable. Many differences of linguistic form may not correspond to any difference of meaning, for example, the differences between the ablative and dative cases in Latin, or such differences as those between "proved" and "proven," "got" and "gotten" in English. But as language is sometimes used to convey significant information, as well as to express emotions, it is impossible for grammarians to ignore logical distinctions. As ordinary experience does not require great accuracy and subtle insight into the nature of things, ordinary language is not accurate. Logic is necessary to correct its vagueness and ambiguity.

In general, though words are among the important objects of human consideration, it is not true that all propositions are about words. Most propositions are about objects like the sun and the stars, the earth and its contents, our fellow-creatures and their affairs, and the like; and the implication between propositions, which is the subject matter of logic, has to do with the possible relations between all such objects. It is only as words are necessary instruments in our statement or expression of a proposition that logic must pay critical attention to them, in order to appreciate their exact function and to detect errors in inference.

Logic and Psychology

An old tradition defines logic as the science of the laws of thought. This goes back to a time when logic and psychology were not fully developed into separate sciences clearly distinguished from other branches of philosophy. But at present it is clear that any investigation into the laws or ways in which we actually think belongs to the field of psychology. The logical distinction between valid and invalid inference does not refer to the way we think—the process going on in someone's mind. The weight of evidence is not itself a temporal event, but a relation of implication between certain classes or types of propositions. Whether, for instance, it necessarily follows from Euclid's axioms and postulates that the area of no square can be exactly equal to that of a circle is a question of what is necessarily involved in what is asserted by our propositions; and how anyone actually thinks is irrelevant to it. Of course thought (and not mere sense perception) is necessary to apprehend such im-

[3] The English kings from the eleventh to the fourteenth century were of course Frenchmen.

plications. But thought is likewise necessary to apprehend that the propositions of any science are true. That, however, does not make physics a branch of psychology—unless we deny that these sciences have different subject matters, in other words, unless we deny that physical objects and our apprehension of them are distinguishable and not identical. Similarly, our apprehension of the logical implication on which our inferences are based may be studied as a psychological event, but the relation directly apprehended is not itself a psychological event at all. It is a relation between the forms of propositions and indirectly one between the classes of possible objects asserted by them.

The realization that logic cannot be restricted to psychological phenomena will help us to discriminate between our science and rhetoric—conceiving the latter as the art of persuasion or of arguing so as to produce the feeling of certainty. People often confuse the two because the word "certainty" is sometimes used as a characteristic of what is demonstrated and sometimes as the feeling of unquestioning assurance. But such feeling of certainty may exist apart from all logic, and the factual persuasiveness of arguments is more often brought about by properly chosen words, which through association have powerful emotional influences, than through logically unassailable arguments. This is not to belittle the art of rhetoric or to accuse it of always using fallacious arguments. The art of persuasion, or getting others to agree with us, is one that almost all human beings wish to exercise more or less. Harmonious social relations depend on it. But strictly logical argumentation is only one of the ways, and not always the most effective way, of persuading those who differ from us. Our emotional dispositions make it very difficult for us to accept certain propositions, no matter how strong the evidence in their favor. And since all proof depends upon the acceptance of certain propositions as true, no proposition can be proved to be true to one who is sufficiently determined not to believe it. Hence the logical necessity revealed in implication, as in pure mathematics, is not a description of the way all people actually think, but indicates rather an impossibility of certain combinations of the objects asserted. The history of human error shows that the assertion, "I am absolutely certain," or, "I cannot help believing," in regard to any proposition is no adequate evidence as to its truth.

In general, the canons of logical validity do not depend upon any investigation in the empirical science of psychology. The latter, indeed, like all other sciences, can establish its results only by conformity to the rules of logical·inference. But a study of psychology is of great help to logic, if for no other reason than that only a sound knowledge of psychology can help us to avoid unavowed but false psychological assumptions in logical theory.

Logic and Physics

If logic cannot be identified with linguistics or psychology, neither is it the same as physics or natural science. The propositions whose relations logic studies are not restricted to any special field, but may be about anything at all—art, business, fairy tales, theology, politics; and while the logical relation of implication is involved in physical science, it is not the primary object of the latter.

The fact that propositions may be about nonexistent objects does not militate against the objectivity of the relation of implication. This relation is objective in the sense that it does not depend upon our conventions of language or on any fiat of ours to think in a certain way. This may perhaps become more obvious if we consider the procedure of pure mathematics. In this field, as we have already indicated, we inquire only as to the implication of our initial propositions, without regard to their truth or to whether their subjects are existent or nonexistent, real or imaginary. And yet research in mathematics of the kind that has been going on for over two thousand years is as bound or determined by the nature of the material (logical implication) as is any geographical exploration of the earth or astronomical study of the movements of the stars.

No linguistic fiat or resolution to think differently can change the truths discovered or deduced in such fields as the theory of prime numbers. And this is true of all rigorous logical deduction.

Logic and the Metaphysics of Knowledge

The essential purpose of logic is attained if we can analyze the various forms of inference and arrive at a systematic way of discriminating the valid from the invalid forms. Writers on logic, however, have not generally been content to restrict themselves to this. Especially since the days of Locke they have engaged in a good deal of speculative discussion as to the general nature of knowledge and the operations by which the human mind attains truth as to the external world. We shall try to avoid all these issues —not because they are not interesting and important, but because they are not necessary for the determination of any strictly logical issues. Indeed, the answers to the questions of metaphysics, rational psychology, or epistemology (as they are variously called) are admittedly too uncertain or too questionable to serve as a basis for the science of all proof or demonstration. We wish, however, to dispose of one of these questions, which may trouble the reader: How can false propositions, or those about nonexistent objects, have implications that are objectively necessary?

This seeming paradox arises from a naïve assumption—that only actually existing things have determinate objective characters. It is rather easy to see that the world of science, the world about which there is true knowledge, cannot be restricted to objects actually existing but must include all their possible functions and arrangements. Consider such elementary propositions as *Carbon burns, Ice melts at 32° F., Metals conduct heat and electricity,* and the like. These all refer to classes or kinds of possibilities of the ideally continuous or recurrent existences we call carbon, ice, or metal. Now whatever actually exists is only one of an indefinite number of possibilities. The actual is a flying moment passing from the future which is not yet to the past which no longer is. Logic may be conceived as ruling out what is absolutely impossible, and thus determining the field of what in the absence of empirical knowledge is abstractly possible. History and the sciences of natural existence rule out certain possible propositions as false, for example: There are frictionless engines, free bodies, perfectly rigid levers, and so on. They are ruled out because they are incompatible with propositions which we believe to be true of the actual world. But the actual world at any one time is only one of a number of possible arrangements of things. A proposition proved false on one set of assumptions may be proved true on another. Thus while logical relations alone are not sufficient to determine which existence is actual, they enter into the determination of every arrangement of things that is at all possible. The essential properties which determine the value of $100 remain the same whether we do or do not possess that amount.

§ 6. THE USE AND APPLICATION OF LOGIC

Like any other science, logic aims at attaining truth in its own special field and is not primarily concerned with the values or uses to which these truths can be put. Bad men may be logically consistent. But correct inference is such a pervasive and essential part of the process of attaining truth (which process in its developed form we call *scientific method*) that a study of the way in which logic enters into the latter is a natural extension of our science, just as pure mathematics is extended and developed by its practical application. This will engage our attention in Book II of this volume. Even at this stage, however, we may note some of the ways in which formal, deductive logic aids us in arriving at true propositions.

1. It is obvious that it is often difficult, if not impossible, to determine the truth of a proposition directly, but relatively easy to establish the truth of another proposition from which the one at issue can be deduced. Thus we have observed how difficult it would be to show by actual count that there are at least two people in New York City who have exactly the same number of scalp hairs. But it is fairly easy to show that the number of inhabitants in New York City exceeds the maximum number of hairs on a human head. For the study of the physiology of hair follicles, as well as random samplings of human heads, enables us to establish that there are not more than five thousand hairs to a square centimeter. Anthropological measurements lead to the conclusion that the maximum area of the human scalp is much under one thousand square centimeters. We may conclude, therefore, that no human being has more than five million scalp hairs. And since the population of New York City is close to seven million, there must be more inhabitants in New York City than any human head has hairs. It follows, in virtue of our previous demonstration, that there must be at least two individuals in that city who are precisely alike in the number of hairs on their heads.

2. Many of our beliefs are formed to meet particular problems, and we are often shocked to find these beliefs inconsistent with one another. But they can be integrated, and their bearings on one another made clear, by exploring deductively their mutual relations. Thus it is deductive reasoning which enables us to discover the incompatibility between the following propositions: *Promise-breakers are untrustworthy; Wine-drinkers are very communicative; A man who keeps his promises is honest; No teetotalers are pawnbrokers; All communicative persons are trustworthy; Some pawnbrokers are dishonest.*

3. Deductive reasoning enables us to discover what it is to which we must, in consistency, commit ourselves if we accept certain propositions. Thus if we admit that two straight lines cannot inclose an area, as well as some other familiar geometric propositions, we must also admit, as we soon discover, that the sum of the angles of any triangle cannot be greater than two right angles.

The full meaning of what it is we believe is discovered by us when we examine deductively the connections between the diverse propositions which we consider. For the propositions which we may be inclined to accept almost without question may have implications altogether surprising to us and requiring us to modify our hasty acceptance of them as premises.

In pointing out these uses of deductive inference, it is not denied that men may and do successfully employ it without any previous theoretical study of logic, just as men learn to walk without studying physiology. But a study of physiology is certainly valuable in preparing plans for training runners. Any competent electrician can adjust our electric lights, but we think it necessary that an engineer who has to deal with new and complicated problems of electricity should be trained in theoretical physics. A theoretical science is the basis of any rational technique. In this way logic, as a theoretical study of the kinds and limitations of different inferences, enables us to formulate and partially mechanize the processes employed in successful inquiry. Actual attainment of truth depends, of course, upon individual skill and habit, but a careful study of logical principles helps us to form and perfect techniques for procuring and weighing evidence.

Logic cannot guarantee useful or even true propositions dealing with matters of fact, any more than the cutler will issue a guarantee with the surgeon's knife he manufactures that operations performed with it will be successful. However, in offering tribute to the great surgeon we must not fail to give proper due to the quality of the knife he wields. So a logical method which refines and perfects intellectual tools can never be a substitute for the great masters who wield them; none the less it is true that perfect tools are a part of the necessary conditions for mastery.[4]

[4] More mature readers will do well to go over Appendix A carefully before undertaking Chapter II.

BOOK I

FORMAL LOGIC

CHAPTER II

THE ANALYSIS OF PROPOSITIONS

§ 1. WHAT IS A PROPOSITION?

In the last chapter logic was defined as dealing with the relation of implication between propositions, that is, with the relation between premises and conclusions in virtue of which the possible truth and falsity of one set limits the possible truth and falsity of the other. Both premises and conclusions are thus propositions; and for the purposes of logic, a *proposition* may be defined as anything which can be said to be true or false. But we shall understand this definition more clearly if we also indicate what a proposition is not.

1. A proposition is not the same thing as the sentence which states it. The three sentences, "I think, therefore, I am," "*Je pense, donc je suis*," "*Cogito, ergo sum*," all state the same proposition. A sentence is a group of words, and words, like other symbols, are in themselves physical objects, distinct from that to which they refer or which they symbolize. Sentences when written are thus located on certain surfaces, and when spoken are sound waves passing from one organism to another. But the proposition of which a sentence is the verbal expression is distinct from the visual marks or sound waves of the expression. Sentences, therefore, have a physical existence. They may or may not conform to standards of usage or taste. But they are not true or false. Truth or falsity can be predicated only of the propositions they signify.

2. It should be noted, however, that while the proposition must not be confused with the symbols which state it, no proposition can be *expressed* or *conveyed* without symbols. The structure of the proposition must, therefore, be expressed and communicated by an appropriate structure of the symbols, so that not every combination of symbols can convey a proposition. "John rat blue Jones," "Walk-

ing sat eat very," are not symbols expressing propositions, but simply nonsense, unless indeed we are employing a code of some sort. Only certain arrangements of symbols can express a proposition. That is why the study of symbolism is of inestimable value in the correct analysis of the structure of propositions. And that is why, although grammatical analysis is not logical analysis, the grammar of a language will often clarify distinctions which are logical in nature.

3. A proposition, we have said, is something concerning which questions of truth and falsity are significant. Consequently when Hamlet declares, "Oh, from this time forth, My thoughts be bloody, or be nothing worth!" or when he asks, "Why wouldst thou be a breeder of sinners?" he is not asserting propositions *except implicitly*. For wishes, questions, or commands cannot as such be true or false. It should be noted, however, that the intelligibility of wishes, questions, and commands rests upon assumptions that certain states of affairs prevail. And such assumptions involve propositions. For consider the question, "Why wouldst thou be a breeder of sinners?" It obviously assumes, among other propositions, that the person addressed exists, is capable of breeding children, and that such children are certain to be sinners. Similarly, the exhortation, "My thoughts be bloody, or be nothing worth!" assumes that the speaker is capable of having ideas, that these ideas can be murderous, that they may have some kind of value, and so forth. Moreover, a command or wish may be put in the form of a declaration, which generally expresses a proposition, for example, *I wish you would come; I shall be pleased if you come; You will be sorry if you do not come.* To the extent that the declarations state something that may be true or false they are propositions.

4. Propositions are often confounded with the mental acts required to think them. This confusion is fostered by calling propositions "judgments," for the latter is an ambiguous term, sometimes denoting the mental act of judging, and sometimes referring to that which is judged. But just as we have distinguished the proposition (as the objective meaning) from the sentence which states it, so we must distinguish it from the act of the mind or the judgment which thinks it.

5. Nor must propositions be identified with any concrete object, thing, or event. For propositions are at most only the abstract and selected relations between things. When we affirm or deny the proposition *The moon is nearer to the earth than the sun,* neither the moon alone, nor the earth, nor the sun, nor the spatial distance

between them is the proposition. The proposition is the relation asserted to hold between them. The relations which are the objects of our thought are elements or aspects of actual, concrete situations. These aspects, while perhaps not spatially and temporally *separable* from other characters in the situation, are *distinguishable* in meaning. That is why sense experience never yields knowledge without a reflective analysis of what it is we are experiencing. For knowledge is *of* propositions. And propositions can be known only by discriminating within some situation relations between abstract features found therein.

(6) While a proposition is defined as that which is true or false, it does not mean that we must *know* which of these alternatives is the case. *Cancer is preventable* is a proposition, though we do not know whether it is true.

A difficulty is nevertheless suggested: We may not be able to tell whether a given sentence does or does not express a proposition. Consider, for example, the expression, "Three feet make a yard." Are we raising questions of truth and falsity in asserting it? It must be acknowledged that the sentence has the appearance of expressing a proposition. But if we analyze what is usually meant by it, we find it expresses a *resolution* rather than something which is capable of being true. We *resolve* to use a unit of measure so that it will be made up of three feet. But the resolution as such cannot have truth or falsity predicated of it. Such resolutions, which often take the form of definitions, are expressed in ways analogous to the way propositions are expressed; but they must be distinguished from the latter.

The question whether the word "yard" is actually used in the sense defined is of course a factual one, and the answer may be true or false. But such propositions are about linguistic usages and not about the objects denoted by the words.

(7) A related difficulty arises from the fact that we popularly speak of propositions as sometimes true and sometimes false, whereas our definition of propositions excludes this possibility and assumes that if a proposition is true it must always be true. Nothing is more common in discussion between candid people than their remark, "What you say is sometimes true, but not always so." This applies to such statements as "Religion preaches love of one's fellow men"; "It is difficult to resist temptation"; "A gentle answer turneth away wrath." We may, however, remove this difficulty by recognizing that if these propositions assert that something is *universally* the case, then the existence of an exception only proves

that they are false. Such an assertion as "Religion sometimes preaches hate of one's neighbors" does not assert the absurdity that a universal proposition *Religion always preaches hate of one's neighbors* is sometimes true.

We can perhaps see this more clearly in the following case. *The present governor of Connecticut is Dr. Cross* seems to be a proposition true for certain years, but surely not always. This, however, is an inadequate analysis. For the phrase "the present governor" clearly presupposes a date; and as we complete our expression by including explicitly the date, we obtain expressions for different propositions, some of which are true and some false. In general, our everyday statements seldom contain all the qualifications necessary to determine whether what we say is true or false. Some of their qualifications we understand, others are not thought of. The incomplete expression is neither true nor false. And when we say that it is sometimes true and sometimes false, we can mean only that our expressions may be completed in some ways which express true propositions and in some ways which express false ones.

§ 2. THE TRADITIONAL ANALYSIS OF PROPOSITIONS

Terms: Their Intension and Extension

According to Aristotle, all propositions either assert or deny something of something else. That about which the assertion is made is called the *subject*, and that which is asserted about the subject is called the *predicate*. The subject and predicate are called the *terms* of the proposition; the proposition is the synthesis or unity of the terms by means of the *copula*, which is always some part of the verb "to be."

This analysis cannot readily be applied to very simple propositions such as *It is raining; There was a parade* and the like. The "It" and the "There" clearly do not denote subjects, of which "raining" and "a parade" are attributes. Nevertheless, there is a certain amount of truth in Aristotle's analysis, if we hold on to the distinction between *terms* and *propositions,* but drop the requirement that there must be just two terms. *It is raining* or *There was a parade* are properly said to be propositions, because they conform to his test, to wit, they are either true or false. "Raining" or "a parade" are not propositions, because they are not either true or false. When we hear the words "raining" or "a parade" we ask, "What about it?" Only when *assertions* are made about these objects can questions of truth or falsity be raised.

These objects, then, as *terms* enter as elements of propositions. A term may be viewed in two ways, either as a class of objects (which may have only one member), or as a set of attributes or characteristics which determine the objects. The first phase or aspect is called the *denotation* or *extension* of the term, while the second is called the *connotation* or *intension*. Thus the extension of the term "philosopher" is "Socrates," "Plato," "Thales," and the like; its intension is "lover of wisdom," "intelligent," and so on.

Although the intension and extension of a term are distinct aspects, they are inseparable. All words or symbols except pure demonstrative ones (those which serve to point out, like a gesture, or "this") signify some attributes in virtue of which they may be correctly applied to a delimited set of objects; and all general terms are capable of being applied to some object, even though at any given time no object may in fact possess the attributes necessary to include it in the extension of the term. *Why* a term is applied to a set of objects is indicated by its intension; the set of objects *to which* it is applicable constitutes its extension.

With many of the difficult problems of extension and intension we shall not concern ourselves. It will be convenient, however, to distinguish between several senses in which the term *intension* is frequently employed. It is necessary to do so if we wish to avoid elementary confusions.

1. The *intension of a term* is sometimes taken to mean the sum total of the attributes which are present to the mind of any person employing the term. Thus to one person the term "robber" signifies: "taking property not lawfully his, socially undesirable, violent," and so forth; to another person it may signify: "taking property with value greater than ten dollars not lawfully his, physically dangerous person, the result of bad disposition," and so on. The intension of a term so understood is called the *subjective intension*. The subjective intension varies from person to person, and is of psychological rather than of logical significance.

2. The *intension of a term* may signify the set of attributes which are essential to it. And by "essential" we mean the necessary and sufficient condition for regarding any object as an element of the term. This condition is generally selected by some convention, so that intension in this sense is called *conventional intension* or *connotation*. The conventional intension of a term, as we shall see later, constitutes its definition.

3. The *intension of a term* may signify *all* the attributes which the objects in the denotation of a term have in common, whether

these attributes are known or not. This is called the *objective in-tension* or *comprehension.* Thus, if the conventional intension of "Euclidean triangle" is "a plane figure bounded by three straight lines," a part of the objective intension is: "a plane figure with three angles, a plane figure whose angle sum is two right angles," and so on.

It is the conventional intension of a term which is logically important. The denotation of a term clearly depends upon its connotation. Whether we may apply the word "ellipse" to some geometric figure is determined by the attributes included in the connotation of the term. From the point of view of knowledge already achieved, the understanding of the connotation of a term is prior to its denotative use: we must know the connotation of "amoeba" before we can apply it. In the order of the *development* of our knowledge, it is doubtful whether there is such a priority. Philosophers have been unable to resist the temptation of regarding either the intension or the extension of a term prior in every respect, and much ink has been shed over the question. It is reasonable to suppose, however, that the development of our knowledge concerning intension and extension, since they are inseparable aspects of the meaning of a term, go hand in hand. A group of objects, such as pieces of iron, bronze, tin, may be selected for certain special purposes in virtue of their possessing some prominent features in common, like hardness, opacity, fusibility, luster. Such objects may then be denoted by a common term, "metal." These striking features may then be taken as criteria for including other objects in the denotation of this term. But greater familiarity with such objects may lead us to note qualities more reliable as signs of the presence of other qualities. We may then group objects together in spite of superficial differences, or group objects differently in spite of superficial resemblances. The conventional intension of the term "metal" may thus become gradually modified. The assigning of the satisfactory conventional intension (or definition) to a term denoting objects with familiar common traits is a difficult task, and is a relatively late achievement of human thought.

Consider now the terms: "figure," "plane figure," "rectilinear plane figure," "quadrilateral," "parallelogram," "rectangle," "square." They are arranged in order of subordination, the term "figure" denoting a class which includes the denotation of "plane figure," and so on. Each class may be designated as the *genus* of its subclass, and the latter as a *species* of its genus. Thus the *denotation*

of these terms *decreases:* the extension of "parallelogram" includes
the extension of "rectangle," but not conversely, and so on. On the
other hand, the *intension* of the term *increases:* the intension of
"rectangle" includes the intension of "parallelogram," but not conversely. Reflection upon such series of terms has led to the rule:
*When a series of terms is arranged in order of subordination, the
extension and intension vary inversely.*

But this formulation of the relation of extension to intension is
not accurate. In the first place, "vary inversely" must not be understood in a strict numerical sense. For in some cases the addition of
a single attribute to the intension of a term is accompanied by a
greater change in its extension than in other cases. Thus the extension of "man" is reduced much more by the addition of the
attribute "centenarian" than by the addition of the attribute
"healthy." And in the second place, variation in the intension may
be accompanied by no change in the extension. Thus, the extension of the term "university professor" is the same as the extension
of "university professor older than five years." It is clear, moreover,
that the relation of inverse variation must be taken between the *conventional* intension of a term, and its denotation in a specified universe of discourse. The law of inverse variation must, therefore, be
stated as follows: *If a series of terms is arranged in order of increasing intension, the denotation of the terms will either remain
the same or diminish.*

The Form of Categorical Propositions

According to the traditional doctrine all propositions can be analyzed into a subject and a predicate joined by a copula, either
from the intensional or from the extensional point of view. *All
cherries are luscious* may on the first view be interpreted to mean
that the attribute of "being luscious" is part of the group of
attributes which define the nature of cherries. On the second view,
this proposition means that the objects called cherries are included
in the denotation of the term "luscious." [1]

The traditional view recognizes other forms of propositions,
called *conditional,* which it tries to reduce to the categorical form.
We shall examine below these conditional forms, as well as other
ways of analyzing propositions. Here we shall only note that on the

[1] The reader should note, however, that in the traditional analysis which
we shall follow in this section the emphasis will be on the *extensional* interpretation.

traditional view all propositions are analyzable in just this way and only in this way.[2]

Propositions which do not obviously present a subject-predicate form must, then, be changed to exhibit that form. Thus *Germany lost the war* must be expressed as *Germany is the loser of the last war,* where "Germany" is the subject, "the loser of the last war," the predicate, and "is," of course, the copula. The proposition *Ten is greater than five* must be analyzed into "ten" as subject, "a number greater than five" as predicate, and "is" as copula.

It is not difficult to exhibit any proposition as *verbally* conforming to the subject-predicate type, but such verbal identity often obscures fundamental logical distinctions. The chief criticism which modern logic has made of the traditional analysis is that the latter has lumped together (as categorical) propositions which have significant differences in form.

The reader may perhaps wonder what is the significance of this quarrel over the manner in which propositions should be analyzed. The answer is simple. The analysis of propositions is undertaken for the purpose of discovering what inferences may be validly drawn from them. Consequently, if there is a plurality of propositional forms, and such form or structure determines the validity of an inference, an increased refinement of analysis may help us to attain a more accurate view of the realm of possible inference.

Another reason for analyzing the structure of propositions is to devise some *standard* or *canonical* ways of representing what it is we wish to assert. We wish to find certain canonical formulations of propositions of a given type, in order that the process of inference shall be expedited. Thus in elementary algebra it is extremely convenient to write the quadratic equation $5x^2 = 3x - 5$ in the standard form $5x^2 - 3x + 5 = 0$. For if we do so, since we already

---

[2] The view that all propositions are of the subject-predicate form has been associated historically with certain philosophical interpretations of the nature of things. The subject, on this view, is regarded as a *substance* in which various qualities inhere, and the task of all inquiry is to discover the inhering predicates in some concrete subject. According to Leibniz, for instance, there is an ultimate plurality of substances or monads, each of which is pregnant with an illimitable number of properties. These monads cannot be said to stand to one another in any relation, for if they did one monad would have to be a *predicate* of another, and therefore not self-subsistent. According to others, like Bradley, there is just *one* substance, so that all predication is the affirmation of something of *all reality* conceived as a single, unique individual. Neither of these extreme positions was adopted by Aristotle. He maintained that the ultimate subject of predication is some concrete, individual substance, and that there is an irreducible plurality of such, but that these substances are systematically related.

know the roots of a general quadratic in the standard form $ax^2 + bx + c = 0$, it is very simple to find the numerical answers to our problems. Moreover, if we adopt a standard form for writing equations, it is much easier to compare different equations and note their resemblances. Similar considerations apply in logic. For if we can once establish criteria of validity for inferences upon propositions stated in a standard form, all subsequent testing of inferences becomes almost mechanical.

Much care must be taken, however, in reducing a proposition expressed in one verbal form to the standard form, lest some part of its original meaning be neglected. In reducing a line of Keats's poetry, for example, into a canonical form it is not easy to believe that every shade of meaning of the original has been retained.

Quantity

Categorical propositions have been classified on the basis of their *quantity* and their *quality*. In the proposition, *All steaks are juicy*, something is affirmed of *every* steak, while in the proposition, *Some steaks are tough,* information is supplied about an *indefinite* part of the class of steaks. Propositions which predicate something of *all of a class* are designated as *universal*, while those which predicate something of an *indefinite part* of a class are *particular*. The particles "all" and "some" are said to be *signs of quantity*, because they indicate of how large a part of the subject the predicate is affirmed. The distinction between them is more accurately stated if "all" is called the sign of a *definite* class, and "some" the sign of an *indefinite* part of a class. For in everyday usage, the signs of quantity are ambiguous. Thus in the proposition *Some professors are satirical* it would ordinarily be understood that a *part, but not the whole,* of the class of professors are satirical; here "some" means "some but not all." On the other hand, *Some readers of this book have no difficulty in understanding it* would generally be understood to mean that a portion of the readers, *not excluding the entire class,* had no difficulty with it; here "some" means "some and perhaps all." We shall obviate such ambiguity by agreeing that in logic "some" will be taken in the latter sense; that is, as not necessarily excluding "all."

A different sort of ambiguity occurs in the use of the word "all." Sometimes it denotes all of a finite and enumerated collection, as in the proposition *All the books on this shelf are on philosophy.* Sometimes, however, as in *All men are mortal* the "all" means "all possible," and cannot be taken, without distortion of intended meaning, to indicate merely an enumeration of the men who do in fact exist or have already existed. We shall find this distinction of paramount importance in the discussion of induction and deduction. Many mistaken views concerning the former are the outcome of ignoring it.

Is the proposition *Thaïs was a courtesan in Alexandria* universal or particular? The reader may be tempted to say it is the latter. But that would be an error, for he would then be using "particular" in a sense different from the one employed in classifying propositions. On the basis of the definition of universal propositions as those which affirm something of *all* of the subject, this proposition must be regarded as a universal. This would be even more obvious if, as we suggest, the terms *definite* and *indefinite* were used instead of *universal* and *particular*. However, since in such propositions we are affirming something of a single individual, traditional logic has sometimes designated them as *singular*. But singular propositions must be classified as universal on the traditional analysis. However, a more subtle analysis cannot be content with such a conclusion. Even untutored people feel dimly that there is a difference *in form* between *Dr. Smith is a reassuring person* and *All physicians are reassuring persons* although traditional logic regards both as universal. Modern logic corroborates this feeling by showing clearly that these propositions do in fact illustrate different logical forms. Nevertheless, for many purposes no harm results if, with traditional logic, we regard both as having the same structure.

Quality

A second classification of categorical propositions is concerned with their *quality*. In the proposition *All snakes are poisonous* the predicate is affirmed of the subject. The proposition is therefore said to be *affirmative*. In *No democracies are grateful* something is denied of the subject. The proposition is therefore said to be *negative*. If we think of a categorical proposition as a relation between classes of individuals, an affirmative proposition asserts the *inclusion* of one class or part of a class in another, while a negative proposition asserts the *exclusion* of one class or part of a class from another. It follows that the negative particle, the sign of quality, must be understood to characterize the copula, not the subject or the predicate.

How should we classify *All citizens are not patriots*? It seems to be a negative proposition, and the sign of quantity seems to indicate it as universal. But while it *may* be interpreted as asserting

that *No citizens are patriots* it may also be understood as denying that *All citizens are patriots* or as asserting that *Some citizens are not patriots.* Expressions employing "all . . . not" as in the
foregoing, or as in *All that glitters is not gold* are essentially ambiguous. In such cases, we must determine what is meant, and then
state it in an unambiguous form.

On the basis of quantity and quality we may therefore distinguish four forms of categorical propositions. *All teetotalers are
short-lived* is a universal affirmative, and is symbolized by the
letter *A*. *No politicians are rancorous* is a universal negative, and is
symbolized by *E*. *Some professors are soft-hearted* is a particular
affirmative, and is symbolized by *I*. *Some pagans are not foolish* is
a particular negative, and is symbolized by *O*. The letters *A* and *I*
have been used traditionally for affirmative propositions: they are
the first two vowels in *affirmo*, while *E* and *O* symbolize negative
propositions: they are the vowels in *nego*.

Exclusive and Exceptive Propositions

In the propositions *The wicked alone are happy, Only the lazy
are poor, None but savages are healthy,* something is predicated
of something else in an exclusive fashion. They are therefore called
exclusive propositions. Traditional logic reduces such propositions
to the canonical form for categoricals. For example, *The wicked
alone are happy* asserts the same thing as *All happy individuals
are wicked. None but the brave deserve the fair* asserts the same
as *All who deserve the fair are brave. None but Seniors are eligible*
asserts the same as *All those eligible are Seniors.*

In the propositions *All students except freshmen may smoke,
All but a handful were killed, No child may enter unless accompanied by a parent* the predicate is denied of some part of the denotation of the subject. They are therefore called *exceptive* propositions. They may also be stated in the standard form for categoricals. For exceptive propositions may always be expressed as exclusive ones. Thus *All students except freshmen may smoke* can be
reduced to *Freshmen alone among students may not smoke.* Consequently, the above exceptive proposition can be stated as the
following *A* proposition *All students who may not smoke are
freshmen.*

Distribution of Terms

We shall now introduce a new technical term. We will say a
term of a proposition is *distributed* when reference is made to *all*

the individuals denoted by it; on the other hand, a term will be said to be *undistributed* when reference is made to an *indefinite part* of the individuals which it denotes.

Let us now determine which terms in each of four types of categoricals are distributed. It is evident that in universal propositions the subject term is always distributed, while in particular propositions the subject is undistributed. How about the predicate terms? In *All judges are fair-minded* is reference made to all the individuals denoted by "fair-minded"? Clearly not, because the proposition supplies no information whether *all* fair-minded individuals are judges or not. Hence the predicate in *A* propositions is undistributed. A similar conclusion is true for *I* propositions. We may therefore conclude that affirmative propositions do not distribute their predicates.

Does the same state of affairs obtain for negative propositions? Consider *No policemen are handsome.* This proposition asserts not only that every individual denoted by "policemen" is excluded from the class denoted by "handsome," but also that all individuals of the latter class are also excluded from the former. Consequently, the predicate in *E* propositions is distributed. A similar conclusion holds for *O* propositions. Thus in *Some of my books are not on this shelf* an indefinite part of the subject class is excluded from the *entire* class denoted by the predicate. The reader will see this clearly if he asks himself what part of the shelf indicated he would have to examine in order to assure himself of the truth of the proposition. Obviously it is not enough to examine only a *part* of the books on the shelf; he must examine *all* the books on the shelf. The predicate is therefore distributed.

We may summarize our inquiry by noting that universal propositions distribute the subject, while particular propositions do not distribute the subject. On the other hand, the predicate is distributed in negative propositions, but undistributed in affirmative ones.

The concept of distribution of terms plays an important part in traditional logic, and is the fundamental idea in the theory of the syllogism. The reader is therefore advised to familiarize himself with it thoroughly. We may note in passing, however, that the subject-predicate analysis of propositions, together with the idea of distribution, sometimes leads to inelegant results. Thus on the traditional analysis *Socrates was snub-nosed* is a universal; its subject must be distributed, since snub-nosedness is predicated of the entire individual Socrates. Nevertheless, while in other universal propositions like *All children are greedy* a corresponding particular proposition may be obtained in which "children" is undistributed, no such corresponding proposition can be found for singular ones. For under no circumstances may the term "Socrates" be undistributed. We shall find other respects in which universal and singular propositions do not receive symmetrical development in traditional logic.

Diagrammatic Representation

The structure of the four types of categorical propositions can be exhibited in a more intuitive fashion if we adopt certain conventional diagrammatic representations. Many methods of doing this have been devised, some having different purposes in mind. The earliest is due to Euler, a Swiss mathematician of the eighteenth century. We shall first explain a slight modification of his method.

Let us agree to the following conventions. A circle drawn in solid line will indicate a distributed term; a circle drawn (in part or in whole) in dotted line will represent an undistributed term. A circle drawn inside another will indicate the inclusion of one class in another; two circles entirely outside each other will indicate the mutual exclusion of two classes; and two overlapping circles will represent either an indefinite partial inclusion or an indefinite partial exclusion.

The four relations between the classes "street-cleaners" and "poor individuals" which characterize the four categorical propositions (in which the former class is subject) may then be diagrammed as follows.

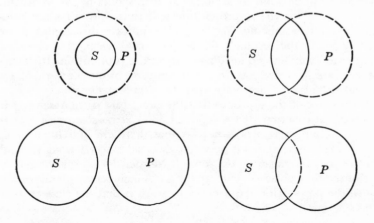

The S circle represents the class "street-cleaners" (the subject), and the P circle the class "poor individuals" (the predicate).

It is often useful to employ another method of representing the categorical propositions, which is due to the English logician John Venn. We first notice that every proposition tacitly refers to some context within which it is significant. Thus *Hamlet killed Polonius* refers to Shakespeare's play. Let us call the domain of reference the *universe of discourse* and represent it diagrammatically by a rectangle. Now the reader will observe that two classes, together with their negatives, yield four and only four combinations. (By the negative of a class is understood everything in the universe of discourse excluded from that class.) For example, in the universe of discourse restricted to human beings there are the things which are both street-cleaners and poor (symbolized as $S\,P$), or which are street-cleaners and not poor ($S\,\bar{P}$), or not street-cleaners and poor ($\bar{S}\,P$) or neither street-cleaners nor poor ($\bar{S}\,\bar{P}$). The universe of discourse is thus divided into four possible compartments. However, in general not all these possible compartments will contain individuals as members. Which ones do and which ones do not depends upon what is *asserted* by propositions referring to that universe of discourse.

Let us therefore draw two overlapping circles within a rectangle, and so obtain automatically four distinct compartments, one for each of the four logical possibilities indicated. Now since the A proposition asserts that all street-cleaners are included in the class of the poor, the class of those who are street-cleaners and not poor cannot contain any members. To show this on the diagram, we shall agree to blot out by shading the corresponding compartment. The diagram for the A proposition will thus show that the compartment $S\,\bar{P}$ is missing. We may also indicate this explicitly by writing under the rectangle $S\,\bar{P} = 0$, where 0 means that the class in question contains no members. Hence the proposition *All street-cleaners are poor* declares that in its universe of discourse there are no individuals who are both street-cleaners and not poor.

In the case of the I proposition the procedure of representing it is somewhat different. If we ask what *Some street-cleaners are poor* asserts, we find that it does *not* say that there *are* individuals who are street-cleaners and not poor (let the reader recall what we said above about the meaning of "some"). Neither does it say that *every* one of the four possible compartments has members. The minimum which the proposition requires for its truth is that the class of indi·

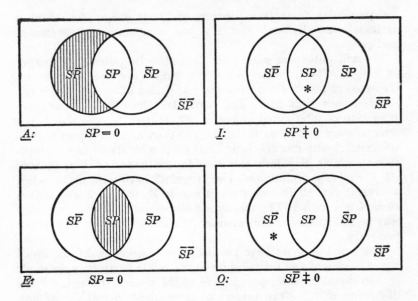

viduals who are street-cleaners and poor be *not* empty. We shall agree to designate this minimum by placing an *asterisk* into the SP compartment, to show that it cannot be empty. We thereby leave indeterminate whether the other compartments have members or not. We may indicate this further by writing $SP \neq 0$ under the rectangle, which signifies that the left-hand member of this inequality is not devoid of members. The reader should study carefully the remaining diagrams. He will find that the analysis of the E and O propositions is similar to that of the A and I propositions respectively.

The Existential Import of Categoricals

If we now compare the diagrams, we discover that there is a remarkable difference between universal and particular propositions. Universals do not affirm the existence of any individuals, but simply *deny* the existence of certain kinds of individuals. Particulars do not deny the existence of anything, but simply *affirm* that certain classes do have members. Consequently, the universal *All street-cleaners are poor* means only this: *If any individual is a street-cleaner, why, then he is poor.* It does not say that there actually are individuals who are street-cleaners. On the other hand, the particular *Some street-cleaners are poor* means that there is at least one individual who is at the same time a street-cleaner and poor.

We will anticipate some later discussion by putting the matter as follows. The universal *All street-cleaners are poor* is to be interpreted to assert: *For all instances or values of* X, *if* X *is a street-cleaner, then* X *is poor.* The particular *Some street-cleaners are poor* is to be interpreted to assert: *There is an* X, *such that* X *is a street-cleaner and* X *is poor.* We are thus becoming prepared to understand why modern logic finds fault with classifying a proposition such as *Napoleon was a soldier* with propositions such as *All Frenchmen are soldiers.* The latter, we have seen, means when analyzed: *For all instances or values of* X, *if* X *is a Frenchman then* X *is a soldier.* The former, on the other hand, cannot in any way be interpreted in this manner. We shall return to this matter presently.

The conclusion we have reached, that universals do not imply the existence of any verifying instances, while particulars do imply it, will doubtless seem paradoxical to the reader. (Indeed, a fuller discussion than we can undertake is required to make clear how much of this conclusion is a matter of convention and how much is forced upon us by logical considerations.) The reader will perhaps cite propositions like *All dogs are faithful* and urge that they do imply the existence of dogs. Now it may well be that when the reader asserts *All dogs are faithful* he also intends to assert *There are dogs.* But he should note that then he makes two separate and distinct assertions. But the proposition *All those who are free from sin may cast stones* clearly does not imply that there actually are any individuals free from sin. The universal proposition may be simply a hypothesis concerning a class which we know cannot have any members.

Thus Newton's first law of motion states: All bodies free of impressed forces persevere in their state of rest or of uniform motion in a straight line forever. Will the reader affirm that this proposition asserts the existence of any body which is not under the influence of an impressed force? We need remind him only of the law of gravitation, according to which *all* bodies attract one another. What Newton's first law does assert is the hypothesis that *if* a body were free from impressed forces, it would persevere in its state of rest or in uniform motion in a straight line forever. In the same way, the principle of the lever states what would be the case if the lever were a perfectly rigid body; it does not assert that there is such a body. Indeed, reflection upon the principles of the sciences makes it quite clear that universal propositions in science always function as *hypotheses*, not as statements of fact asserting the existence of individuals which are instances of it. It is true, of course, that if there were no applications of the universal, it would be useless for the science which deals with matters of fact. It is also true that the *meaning* of universal propositions requires at least *possible* matters of fact. But we cannot identify abstract possibilities denoted by universals with actual existences in which these possibilities are annulled by or are combined with other possibilities. Thus, inertia is a phase of all mechanical action, though no instance of inertia by itself can be found in nature. The principle of the lever holds to the extent that bodies are actually rigid, even though no instances of pure rigidity exist in isolation from other properties of bodies.

We may view this matter from another angle. Hitherto we have been discussing propositions as asserting relations between classes of individuals. But we have seen (page 33) that propositions may be interpreted as asserting connections between attributes. When universal propositions are regarded as not implying the existence of any individuals, it is the interpretation in terms of constant relations between attributes which comes to the fore.

It should be noted, finally, that in raising questions of existential import we do not necessarily confine the reference of terms to the physical universe. When we ask, "Did Jupiter have a daughter?" or, "Was Hamlet really insane?" we are not raising questions of *physical* existence, but of the existence of individuals within a universe of discourse controlled by certain assumptions, such as the statements of Homer or Shakespeare. An individual who may thus be said to "exist" in one universe of discourse may not have an existence in another. The proposition *Samson is a pure myth* denies existence to Samson in the universe of authentic history, but obviously not in the field of biblical mythology.

When, therefore, it is said in formal logic that universal propositions do not imply, while particulars do imply, the existence of instances, the reader may find it helpful to interpret this (in part at least) on the basis of the different function each type of proposition plays in scientific inquiry. Just as we cannot validly infer the truth of a proposition concerning some matter of observation from premises which do not include a proposition obtained through observation, so we cannot infer the truth of a particular proposition from universal premises alone; unless indeed we tacitly take for granted the existence of members of the classes denoted by the terms of the universal proposition.

§ 3. COMPOUND, SIMPLE, AND GENERAL PROPOSITIONS

The analysis of propositions thus far has been restricted to those having the categorical form. But logical relations hold between more complicated forms of propositions. Consider the following:

1. The weight of *B* is equal to *G*.
2. The lines *AB* and *CD* are parallel.
3. If the angles *AFG, CGF,* are greater than two right angles, the remaining angles *BFG, DGF,* are less than two right angles.
4. The sum of the interior angles on the same side is equal to, greater than, or less than two right angles.

A comparison of the first two propositions with the last two shows that the second set contains propositions as components or elements, while the first set does not. Thus *The angles* AFG, CGF, *are greater than two right angles* and *The sum of the angles on the same side is equal to two right angles* are themselves propositions which are components in 3 and 4.

Let us apply the characterization *compound* to all propositions which contain other propositions as components. But the reader must be warned that the form of a sentence is not always indicative of the kind of proposition which it expresses. Let him recall the discussion at the end of the last section, where an analysis of categorical propositions was made.

Compound Propositions

Four types of *compound* propositions may be distinguished. Each type relates the component propositions in a characteristic manner.

1. Consider the proposition *If war is declared, then prices go up.* We have agreed to call the proposition introduced by "if" (*War is declared*) the *antecedent,* and the one introduced by "then" (*Prices go up*) the *consequent.* Sometimes the particle "then" is omitted, but it is tacitly understood in such cases. A compound proposition which connects two propositions by means of the relation expressed by "if . . . then" is called *hypothetical* or *implicative.*

When a hypothetical proposition is asserted as true, what do we mean? We clearly do not mean to assert the truth of the antecedent nor the truth of the consequent, although both may in fact be true. What we mean to affirm is that *if* the antecedent is true, the consequent is also true, or in other words, that the two are so connected that the antecedent cannot be true without the consequent's also being true. A hypothetical proposition is sometimes said to express doubt. But this is a misleading way of characterizing such a proposition. We may indeed doubt whether *War is declared,* but when we affirm the hypothetical proposition we do not doubt that *If war is declared, prices go up.*

The antecedent and consequent of a hypothetical proposition may themselves be compound propositions. The analysis of propositions with respect to their logical form will therefore be facilitated if we employ special symbols expressly devised to exhibit logical form. Let us agree that an accent placed over a parenthesis will signify the *denial* or *negative* of the proposition contained in it; hence *It is false that Charles I died in bed* may be written (Charles I died in bed)'. Also, let us replace the verbal symbols "if . . . then" by the ideographic symbol ⊃. The hypothetical *If Charles I did not die in bed, then he was beheaded* may then be written (Charles I died in bed)' ⊃ (he was beheaded).

2. Consider next the proposition *Either all men are selfish or they are ignorant of their own interests.* The relation connecting the compared propositions is expressed by "either . . . or." We shall call the component propositions *alternants,* and the compound proposition an *alternative* proposition.

What do we mean to affirm in asserting an alternative proposition? We do not intend to assert the truth or falsity of any of the alternants: we do not say that *All men are selfish* nor that *All men are ignorant of their own interests.* All that we do assert is that *at least one* of the alternants is true.

Do we mean to say, however, that *both* alternants *cannot* be true? Usage in everyday conversation in this respect varies. An editorial which sums up the economic situation in the alternative proposition *Either this country will adopt national economic planning, or a revolution cannot be avoided* would generally be taken to mean that one, but not both, of the alternatives must be true. On the other hand, when we say *Either he is a fool or he is a knave* we do not mean to exclude the possibility that both alternatives are true. In the interest of unambiguity, we shall adopt the interpretation according to which the minimum is asserted by such a proposition. Henceforth an alternative proposition will be understood to mean one in which *at least one* of the alternatives is true, and *perhaps both*.

It is convenient to introduce a special symbol for the relation expressed by "either . . . or." We shall use the symbol ∨ between the alternants to express this relation. *Either he is a fool or he is a knave* may then be written (He is a fool) ∨ (he is a knave).

3. Consider next the compound proposition *The moon is full, and Venus is a morning star.* The relation connecting the component propositions is the conjunctive "and." We shall call such compound propositions *conjunctives,* and their components *conjuncts.*

What does a conjunctive proposition assert? Obviously, it asserts not only the truth of *The moon is full* and the truth of *Venus is a morning star* taken *singly;* it asserts the truth of the conjuncts *taken together.* Consequently, if either one of the conjuncts is false, the conjunctive proposition must itself be false. The conjunctive proposition must be regarded as a *single* proposition, and not as an *enumeration* of several propositions.

We shall employ a special symbol for the relation expressed by "and." A dot (.) between propositions will hereafter represent a conjunction. Thus *The moon is full and Venus is a morning star* may be written (The moon is full) . (Venus is a morning star).

4. The reader may wonder of what earthly use a conjunctive proposition can be in inference. A conjunctive proposition, he may claim, would never be adduced as evidence for any of its conjuncts. Thus if we are in doubt concerning the truth of *My watch keeps accurate time* would we offer in evidence the conjunctive *My watch keeps accurate time, and all spring-driven mechanisms are subject to climatic influences?* It is obviously more difficult to establish the truth of a conjunctive than to establish the truth of one of its conjuncts.

We may reply, however, that something may be inferred from a conjunctive which cannot be inferred from either of its conjuncts alone. Moreover, the *denial* of a conjunctive proposition yields a proposition that is extremely useful for inference. Indeed, the denial of a conjunctive proposition yields the fourth type of compound proposition. Thus, the denial of the proposition *My watch keeps accurate time, and all spring-driven mechanisms are subject to climatic influences* is *It is not the case that both my watch keeps accurate time and all spring-driven mechanisms are subject to climatic influences.* This means that at least one of the component propositions *My watch keeps accurate time* and *All spring-driven mechanisms are subject to climatic influence* must be false. We shall call the denial or negative of a conjunctive proposition a *disjunctive* proposition and its components *disjuncts*. Since a conjunctive asserts that *both* its conjuncts are *true*, its denial, which is a disjunctive proposition, asserts that *at least one* of the disjuncts is *false*. Both of two disjuncts cannot be true.

We have seen that in everyday conversation the alternants in an alternative proposition may be taken to be mutually exclusive. Thus in *Either he is single or he is married* the truth of one of the alternants excludes the truth of the other. Such alternative propositions *tacitly* assert a *disjunctive* proposition as well. As the usual meaning of *Either he is single or he is married* includes "He cannot be both," it can be expressed as follows: [(He is single) V (he is married)] . [(He is single) . (he is married)]'.

Let us now employ the foregoing distinctions to exhibit the logical form of some compound propositions. Consider the following argument: If every distinct racial group is characterized by a distinct culture, then either all nations differ from one another culturally, or national distinctions do not coincide, in whole or in part, with racial ones. But neither is it the case that the different nations possess distinct cultures, nor is it true that national distinctions do not coincide at any point with racial distinctions. Hence it is not true that each race has a distinct culture.

Let us use the letters p, q, r, to designate the following component propositions in this argument.

$p \equiv$ Every distinct racial group is characterized by a distinct culture.

$q \equiv$ All nations differ from one another culturally.

$r \equiv$ National distinctions do not coincide, in whole or in part, with racial ones.

The premises and conclusion of the argument may therefore be represented as follows:

a. $p \supset (q \vee r)$
b. $q' . r'$
c. p'

Each of the propositions a, b, and c is of a logical form different from those of the other two, a difference which the symbolism helps to bring out. The validity of the argument depends on the structure or form of the proposition a, b, and c, since the conclusion follows from the premises only if the following is true:

d. $(a . b) \supset c$

The reader should note that an important distinction can be drawn between the relation which the antecedent of a hypothetical proposition has to its consequent (as in proposition *a*), and the relation which the premises of a valid argument have to the conclusion (as in *d*). For the former relation material (or factual) evidence must be offered; while for the relation between premises and conclusion such evidence is both irrelevant and impossible, since this latter relation holds only when one of the terms related is logically or analytically contained in the other. The two relations, however, have a common trait, namely, that neither holds when the antecedent or premise is true and the consequent or conclusion is false. It is this common trait which is denoted by "if . . . then" or ⊃. The reader should be on guard against the fallacy of supposing either that two things in any way alike cannot be unlike in some other way, or that two things in some ways distinct cannot also be alike in other ways.

Simple Propositions

The analysis of compound propositions into propositional elements clearly belongs to logic. But the analysis of a sentence into its verbal elements is an affair of grammar. Logically propositions are prior to words, in the sense that the propositions are not produced by the union of words—but the meaning of the words can be derived only from some propositional context. Ultimately the meaning of words is determined by elementary propositions of the form *This is a truffle, This is the color magenta,* and the like, where the word "this" may be replaced by some gesture of pointing. But while propositions cannot be analyzed into verbal constituents, attention to the latter is often an aid in analyzing or classifying propositions for logical purposes. Consider the following propositions:

1. Archimedes was modest.
2. Archimedes was a mathematician.
3. Archimedes was a greater mathematician than Euclid.

According to the traditional doctrine, each of these is a categorical proposition and its components are a subject, a predicate, and a copula joining them; any proposition such as *Archimedes loved mathematics* or *Archimedes ran naked through the streets crying Eureka* is to be analyzed by transforming it into *Archimedes was one who loved mathematics* or *Archimedes was one who ran naked,* and so on. It may be questioned whether such transformation does not change the meaning somewhat. But in any case it is possible to analyze propositions in other ways than the traditional one. Thus, using proposition 2 given above as a model, we can regard every proposition as asserting that some object is a member of a class. Proposition 1 would then assert that Archimedes was a member of the class of beings called modest, and proposition 3 would assert his membership in the class of mathematicians greater than Euclid. This second mode of analysis is related to the first mode as the point of view of extension is to that of intension.

An entirely different mode of analyzing propositions is to resolve them into the assertion of some relation between at least two objects. Thus our first proposition asserts a relation between Archimedes and modesty (the substance-attribute relation), our second proposition asserts a relation which may be called that of class membership between Archimedes and the class of mathematicians. Such propositions as *Archimedes solved Hiero's problem* may thus be analyzed as *Archimedes stood in the relation of solver to Hiero's problem.*

Now it is quite clear that no one of these modes of analysis can claim to be the only one; nor are they mutually exclusive. Nevertheless, each of these modes of analysis fits some propositions better than others. It seems quite forced to say that in the proposition *The author of* Macbeth *is the author of* Hamlet, "the author of *Hamlet*" is an attribute of "the author of *Macbeth.*" It seems more appropriate to view it as the assertion of a relation of identity in denotation, despite a difference in intension or connotation.

Of more direct logical importance is it to note that if we fail to discriminate between class-membership propositions and those which typify some other relation, we miss something that bears on the nature of implication. Thus, while some relations are transitive, that of class membership is not. *Archimedes was a greater mathematician than Euclid and Euclid was a greater mathematician than Aristotle* implies that *Archimedes was a greater mathematician than Aristotle.* But *Archimedes was a member of the Syracusan city-state and the Syracusan city-state was a member of the Graeco-Carthaginian alliance* does not imply that *Archimedes was a member of the Graeco-Carthaginian alliance.*

In Chapter VI we shall undertake a more systematic study of the relation between classes and of the logical properties of relations in general.

General Propositions

Consider the proposition: *All mathematicians are skilled logicians*. This cannot be fittingly regarded as a proposition of the subject-predicate type, for it does not predicate a character or quality to some individual. Nor does it assert that an individual is a member of a class. Nor would it be accurate to say that it asserts a relation between one individual and one or more others. What it does assert is the specific relation of inclusion between *two classes*. Propositions which deal with the relations between classes, that is, with the total or partial inclusion (or exclusion) of one class in another, are called *general* propositions. We have already indicated what the proper analysis of such propositions should be, in discussing categorical propositions in a previous section. Let us now approach the same conclusion from a slightly different angle.

The series of propositions *Archimedes was a mathematician, Euclid was a mathematician, Ptolemy was a mathematician,* are all of the same form. They differ only in having different terms as subjects. Let us now examine the *expression* "*x* is a mathematician." This is not a proposition, because it is incapable of being true or false. But propositions may be obtained from it by substituting proper values for *x*. All the propositions so obtained will have the same form. An expression which contains one or more variables, and which expresses a proposition when values are given to the variables, is called a *propositional function*.

We may vary not only the subject but other terms of the proposition as well. By varying the relation in *Archimedes was killed by a Roman soldier,* we may obtain *Archimedes was praised by a Roman soldier, Archimedes was spoken to by a Roman soldier, Archimedes was a cousin of a Roman soldier,* and so on. If we represent the relation by a variable *R,* we get the propositional function: Archimedes *R* a Roman soldier. (It is to be read: Archimedes has the relation *R* to a Roman soldier.) In such a manner, by letting the terms and relations in a proposition vary, and by representing them by variables, we are able to exhibit logical form or structure in a precise fashion.

When we state that *All mathematicians are trained logicians* what we mean is that if *any* individual is a mathematician he is also a trained logician. We are really affirming an *implication* between being a mathematician and being a trained logician. This may be expressed as an implication between propositions obtained from propositional functions, as follows:

[For all values of x, (x is a mathematician) $\supset$ (x is a trained logician)], where the sign $\supset$ indicates as usual the "if . . . then" relation between the propositions, obtained from the propositional functions by giving values to x.

Propositions of this type, which assert the inclusion (or exclusion) of one class in (or from) another, are analogous in some ways to compound propositions. They should therefore not be confused with class-membership propositions. For the class-membership relation is not transitive, as we have seen, while the relation of class inclusion is transitive. Thus, if *All mathematicians are trained logicians* and *All trained logicians are college professors,* we may validly infer that *All mathematicians are college professors.*

Let us now express each of the four kinds of categorical propositions in this new notation.

1. *All students are independent thinkers* is equivalent to [For all x's, (x is a student) $\supset$ (x is an independent thinker)].

2. *No students are independent thinkers* is equivalent to [For all x's, (x is a student) $\supset$ (x is an independent thinker)'].

3. *Some students are independent thinkers* is equivalent to [There is an x such that (x is a student) . (x is an independent thinker)].

4. *Some students are not independent thinkers* is equivalent to [There is an x, such that (x is a student) . (x is an independent thinker)'].

The two universal propositions (1 and 2) evidently have a logical form quite distinct from the two particulars (3 and 4), while all four propositions are quite distinct in form from the subject-predicate form of propositions.

CHAPTER III

THE RELATIONS BETWEEN PROPOSITIONS

§ 1. THE POSSIBLE LOGICAL RELATIONS
BETWEEN PROPOSITIONS

The logician's interest in the structure of propositions arises from his desire to exhibit all possible propositional forms in virtue of which propositions imply one another. Propositions may be related in ways other than by implication. Thus *The exchange value of a commodity is proportional to the amount of labor required for its production* and *The supply of a commodity is proportional to the demand* are related propositions, since they are both about economics. And *Continuous eloquence wearies* and *Thought constitutes the greatness of man* are also related in virtue of the fact that Pascal believed both of them. This kind of relatedness, however, is not the logician's concern. The relations between propositions which are logically relevant are those in virtue of which the possible truth or falsity of one or more propositions limits the possible truth or falsity of others. Let us examine them.

The conclusion of Plato's dialogue *Protagoras* finds Socrates summarizing the discussion on the nature of virtue:

"My only object . . . in continuing the discussion, has been the desire to ascertain the nature and relations of virtue; for if this were clear, I am very sure that the other controversy which has been carried on at great length by both of us—you affirming and I denying that virtue can be taught—would also become clear. The result of our discussion appears to me to be singular. For if the argument had a human voice, that voice would be heard laughing at us and saying: 'Protagoras and Socrates, you are strange beings; there are you, Socrates, who were saying that virtue cannot be taught, contradicting yourself now by your attempt to prove that all things are knowledge, including justice, temperance, and cour-age,—which tends to show that virtue can certainly be taught; for if virtue were other than knowledge, as Protagoras attempted to prove, then clearly virtue cannot be taught; but if virtue is entirely knowledge, as you are seeking to show, then I cannot but suppose that virtue is capable of being taught. Protagoras, on the other hand, who started by saying that it might be taught, is now eager to prove it to be anything rather than knowledge; and if this is true, it must be quite incapable of being taught.' Now I, Protagoras, perceiving this terrible confusion of our ideas, have a great desire that they should be cleared up." [1]

Let us examine the following propositions in this excerpt:

a. Virtue cannot be taught.
b. If virtue is not knowledge, then virtue cannot be taught.
c. If virtue is knowledge, then virtue can be taught.
d. Virtue can be taught.
e. Virtue is knowledge.
f. Virtue is not knowledge.

Very little reflection is required to show that propositions *a* and *d* are connected *logically,* and not only because both are about virtue. For there is clearly a limitation upon their possible truth or fal-sity. Both propositions cannot be true, since one affirms what the other denies; and both propositions cannot be false, for the same reason. Precisely the same relation holds between *e* and *f*. Such propositions are *contradictories* of one another.

How about *b* and *c?* The reader may be tempted to regard these as contradictories also. This, however, would be erroneous. Reflec-tion shows that there is no contradiction in saying that virtue can be taught under certain contingencies (if virtue is knowledge) but not under others (if virtue is not knowledge). There is, indeed, no mutual limitation upon the possible truth or falsity of these two propositions. Such propositions, even though they deal with the same subject matter, are logically *independent*. The reader should determine for himself whether there are any other pairs of inde-pendent propositions in the set above.

Let us now consider *b* and *f* asserted *jointly,* thus forming a con-junctive proposition, and ask for the relation between this conjunc-tive and *a*. It is easy to see that if *both b and f* are true, *a* must also be true. But if *a* is true, does anything follow concerning the

[1] Plato, *The Dialogues,* tr. by B. Jowett, 1892. 5 vols., Vol. I, pp. 186-87.

truth of *both b and f*? Evidently not, for *a* may be true on other grounds than those supplied by the conjunctive *b and f*; for instance, human obstinacy, bad habits, or the weakness of the flesh; and the conjunctive may be false even though *a* is true, for it may be true, for example, that virtue is knowledge and yet cannot be taught. Propositions so related that if the first is true the second is also true, but if the second is true the first is *undetermined* or *not thereby limited* in its truth-value, are said to be in the relation of *superaltern to subaltern*. The convenient name of *superimplication* has also been devised for this relation. Can the reader find other combinations of propositions in this set which are in this relation?

We have thus far identified three types of relations between propositions: contradictoriness, independence, relation of superaltern to subaltern. Are these all the possible relations there are? We can obtain an exhaustive enumeration of such relations if we examine all the possible truth-values of a pair of propositions (where the "truth-value" of a proposition is either truth or falsity). Let *p* symbolize any proposition, and *q* any other. The following table contains all their possible truth-values. We must allow for the possibility that the truth-value of one or other of the propositions is not limited or determined by the other, by denoting such lack of determination as "Undetermined."

	p	q		p	q
1	True	True	4	False	True
2	True	False	5	False	False
3	True	Undetermined	6	False	Undetermined

Two propositions may be related to each other in any one of these six ways. But to impose only a *single* one of these six conditions upon a pair of propositions is not sufficient to determine their logical relation to one another *uniquely*. Thus the relation called contradictory, such as between *e* and *f*, needs two conditions to determine its properties, namely, the conditions 2 and 4. The relation of superimplication also requires two conditions, namely, 1 and 6. Reflection shows that the other possible logical relations similarly require two of these six conditions to determine them. By pairing each of the first three conditions with each of the last three, we then get nine possible relations between propositions, not all of which, however, are distinct.

1. If p is true, q is true.
   If p is false, q is true.

[handwritten: whether P is true of false has no bearing ong]

In this case, the truth-value of q is not limited by the truth-value of p. Two propositions so related are said to be *independent*.

2. If p is true, q is true.
   If p is false, q is false.

[handwritten: if the same thing occurs for q as did p they are equivalent]

Two propositions so connected are said to be *equivalent*.

3. If p is true, q is true.
   ·If p is false, q is undetermined.

[handwritten: >]

Propositions so related are said to be in the relation of *super-altern* (or *principal*) *to subaltern*. As noted before, we shall also use the designation *superimplication*.

4. If p is true, q is false.
   If p is false, q is true.

[handwritten: Opposite = contradictory]

The reader will recognize this as the case of *contradictory* relation.

5. If p is true, q is false.
   If p is false, q is false.

Here the falsity of q does not depend on the truth or falsity of p, and the propositions are *independent*.

6. If p is true, q is false.
   If p is false, q is undetermined.

In this case, p and q are said to be *contraries:* both cannot be true, but both may be false.

7. If p is true, q is undetermined.
   If p is false, q is true.

In this case, both propositions cannot be false, but both may be true. Such propositions are called *subcontraries.*

8. If p is true, q is undetermined.
   If p is false, q is false.

In this case, the relation of p to q is the *converse* of the relation in 3, and p is said to stand in the relation of <u>*subimplication*</u> or that <u>of *subaltern to principal*</u> to q.

9. If p is true, q is undetermined.
   If p is false, q is undetermined.

In this case, p and q are also *independent,* since the truth-value of p does not determine the truth-value of q.

There are, therefore, seven distinct types of logical relations between one proposition or set of propositions and another proposition or set. (Note that 1, 5, and 9 are of the same type.) Propositions may be (1) equivalent, (2) related as principal to subaltern, (3) related as subaltern to principal, (4) independent, (5) subcontraries, (6) contraries, or (7) contradictories. These are all the fundamental types of logical relations between propositions, and *every discussion we shall enter into in the present book may be regarded as illustrating one of them.* A full understanding of these seven relations will give the reader an accurate synoptic view of the province of logic.[2]

§ 2. INDEPENDENT PROPOSITIONS

We have agreed to call two propositions independent, if the truth-value of one of them in no way determines or limits the truth-value of the other. Thus, if we were considering whether the proposition *Pericles had two sons* is true or false, we should not regard the truth or falsity of the proposition *Hertz discovered electric waves* as evidence either way. When one proposition is thus no evidence at all for the truth or falsity of the other, we also speak of the former as irrelevant to the latter. One of the duties of a court of law or of any other rational procedure is to rule out irrelevant testimony. This does not deny that propositions which we now do not know to be in any way related may later be discovered to be indirectly connected with each other. No one before the middle of the 18th century could have seen any connection between prop-

---

[2] There will be seemingly more relations if we introduce the question of symmetry or reversibility of the relations between the propositions p and q. Thus the relation between a hypothesis and its logical consequence will then be described by the tetrad: If p is true, q is true; if p is false, q is undetermined; if q is true, p is undetermined; if q is false, p is false. It is an interesting exercise for the student to try to determine how many tetrads of this kind are logically possible.

ositions about thunder and lightning, about the color of mother of pearl and about the attractive power of a lodestone; and yet they are now all part of electromagnetic theory. But formal logic is not concerned with guaranteeing factual omniscience. The logical test of independence is simply whether it is possible for a given proposition to be a) true, or b) false, or c) have its truth undetermined, irrespective of whether another given proposition is true or false. Thus a) if the proposition, *The angle of reflection of a light ray is always equal to the angle of its incidence,* is true whether the hypothesis *Light consists of corpuscles* is true or false, the former proposition is independent of the latter. Similarly, b) any proposition which can be demonstrated to be false, such as *The sum of two sides of a triangle is not greater than the third side,* will be independent of any proposition which may be considered as true or as false, e.g., *Through a point outside of a straight line only one parallel can be drawn.* c) A third instance of one proposition being independent of another can be seen in the pair, *The greatest contribution to physics in the 18th century was made by England* and *Sir Philip Sidney was the author of the Letters of Junius.*

In all these pairs of propositions, the truth-value of the first member of each pair is not limited or determined by whether the second member is true or false.[3]

§ 3. EQUIVALENT PROPOSITIONS

The realization that there are several ways of saying the same thing is very valuable in the search for truth. Futile controversies flourish not only because everyone prefers his own formulation of the beliefs he holds, but also because this preference makes very few of us willing to analyze apparently opposing expressions of belief in order to discover whether the obvious differences are verbal or whether they are material. In any case, the examination of what propositions are equivalent is an essential part of all rational inquiry.

Several forms of equivalent propositions have been studied by traditional logic. In turning to examine these, the reader will do well to employ either the diagrammatic representation of categorical propositions or the algebraic statements which express their import.

---

[3] Further consideration of the tests for, and proof of, the independence of propositions will be taken up in Chapter VII.

Conversion

Consider what the proposition *No agricultural country is tol-erant on religious questions* asserts. Obviously, it contains the same information as *No countries tolerant on religious questions are agricultural,* for if agricultural countries are excluded from being tolerant, the latter must also be excluded from the former. These two propositions are equivalent—if one is true or false, the other is the same. They have the same terms as subject and predicate, but the subject of the first is the predicate of the second, and the predicate of the first is the subject of the second. The second proposition is said to be the *converse* of the first. The process by which we pass from a proposition to another that has the same truth-value and in which the *order* of subject and predicate is interchanged, is called *conversion.* An *E* proposition can therefore be converted.

Can each of the other categoricals be converted? May we validly infer from *All bald men are sensitive* the proposition *All sensi-tive men are bald?* We certainly may not. The reader will see this more clearly if he will note that in the first proposition the term "sensitive" is undistributed while in the converse the same term is distributed. This is not permissible, for it would be tantamount to asserting something of all of a class on the evidence of an assertion concerning only an indefinite part of that class. Indeed, we may state as a general principle: *In inferences from categorical propo-sitions no term may be distributed in the conclusion which is un-distributed in at least one of the premises.* Consequently, from *All bald men are sensitive* we may infer no more than *Some sensitive men are bald.* Thus, an *A* proposition can be converted only by *limitation* or *per accidens,* that is, its quantity must be changed. But as we saw before, no inference *per accidens* is valid without the assumption that the class denoted by the subject has members, in this case bald men.

The converse of the *I* proposition *Some Republicans are con-servatives* is *Some conservatives are Republicans.* Hence the con-verse of an *A* proposition may be regarded as the converse of its subaltern.

What is the converse of *Some Italians are not dark-haired?* Is the reader tempted to say it is *Some dark-haired individuals are not Italians?* But this is clearly a fallacious inference. From the proposition *Some mortals are not men* it does not follow that

Some men are not mortals. Technically, this is expressed by saying that such an inference violates the principle concerning the distribution of terms. Indeed, the *O* proposition has no converse; but, as we shall see later, we can infer that *Some men not having dark hair are Italians.*

Obversion

We may obtain equivalent propositions in another way. If *All employees are welcome,* what may we infer about the relation of employees to those who are unwelcome? Evidently *No employees are unwelcome* is a valid conclusion. These two propositions are equivalent: the first declares that nobody is both an employee and unwelcome, and the second asserts the same thing. The inference is called *obversion* and each proposition is the *obverse* of the other. The subjects of the propositions are the same, but the predicate term of one is the negative or contradictory of the other; and the quality of the propositions is different. Care must be taken that the predicate of the obverse should be the contradictory of the predicate in the premise. Thus the obverse of *All leaves are green* is not *No leaves are blue,* for "green" and "blue" are not contradictory terms—they are merely contrary. Two terms are *contradictory* in a universe of discourse if they are exhaustive as well as exclusive; two terms are *contrary* if they are simply exclusive. The proper obverse of *All leaves are green* is *No leaves are non-green,* or in more colloquial English *No leaves are other in color than green.*

Each of the four types of categoricals may be obverted simply—that is, without limitation. The reader should verify that the obverse of *No Laplanders are educated* is *All Laplanders are uneducated;* of *Some college presidents are intelligent* is *Some college presidents are not unintelligent;* and of *Some gases are not poisonous* is *Some gases are nonpoisonous.*

Conversion and obversion are two forms of inference for passing from one proposition to another which is equivalent to it. Other types studied in traditional logic can be defined in terms of successive applications of these two.

Contraposition

If *All reasonable petitions are investigated,* what may be inferred concerning the relation of the uninvestigated things either to the reasonable petitions, or to the non-reasonable petitions? The reader may admit that one permissible conclusion is *No uninvestigated things are reasonable petitions* and that another is *All uninvesti-gated things are non-reasonable petitions.* But if the reader should not see that these conclusions necessarily follow, he will be able to do so if he performs the following series of obversions and conversions. We shall consider all four categorical propositions together.

1. All reasonable petitions are investigated.	No reasonable petitions are investigated.	Some reasonable petitions are investigated.	Some reasonable petitions are not investigated.
2. No reasonable petitions are uninvestigated.	All reasonable petitions are uninvestigated.	Some reasonable petitions are not uninvestigated.	Some reasonable petitions are uninvestigated.
3. No uninvestigated things are reasonable petitions.	Some uninvestigated things are reasonable petitions.		Some uninvestigated things are reasonable petitions.
4. All uninvestigated things are non-reasonable petitions.	Some uninvestigated things are not non-reasonable petitions.		Some uninvestigated things are not non-reasonable petitions.

The first row contains the four categorical propositions. The second row contains the corresponding *obverses* of the propositions in the first row. The third row contains the *converses* of the propositions in the second row. And the fourth row contains the *obverses* of the propositions in the third row.

The propositions in the third row are called the *partial contra-positives* of the corresponding propositions in the first row. The partial contrapositive of a proposition is one in which the subject is the contradictory of the original predicate, while the predicate is the original subject; it also differs in quality from the original proposition. The *I* proposition has no partial contrapositive, and the *E* has one by limitation. The partial contrapositives of the *A* and *O* are equivalent to the original proposition.

The propositions in the fourth row are the *full contrapositives* of the corresponding propositions in the first row. The full contra-positive is a proposition in which the subject is the contradictory of the original predicate, and the predicate is the contradictory of the original subject. It has the same quality as the original propo-sition. As before, the *I* proposition has no full contrapositive, and the *E* has one only by limitation.

Obverted Converse

We have obtained equivalent propositions by performing a series of obversions and conversions, *in this order,* upon each of the four types of categoricals. A different set of equivalent propositions are obtained, however, if instead we first convert a given proposition, then obvert the result. The following table summarizes the outcome:

1. All reasonable petitions are investigated.	No reasonable petitions are investigated.	Some reasonable petitions are investigated.	Some reasonable petitions are not investigated.
2. Some investigated things are reasonable petitions.	No investigated things are reasonable petitions.	Some investigated things are reasonable petitions.	
3. Some investigated things are not non-reasonable petitions.	All investigated things are non-reasonable petitions.	Some investigated things are not non-reasonable petitions.	

It will be noted that the *E* and *I* have an obverted converse without limitation, the *A* has a limited obverted converse, while the *O* has none at all.

Inversion

If *All physicists are mathematicians,* what may be inferred about the relation of the non-physicists to the mathematicians, or to the non-mathematicians? Let us discover what may be validly inferred by a successive application of conversions and obversions.

We may begin by first converting the proposition, then obverting, and so on, until we obtain a proposition which satisfies the problem; or we may begin by first obverting, then converting and so on. Let us develop the alternative methods in parallel columns, the first method in the left-hand column, the second in the right-hand one.

All physicists are mathematicians.	All physicists are mathematicians.
Some mathematicians are physicists.	No physicists are non-mathematicians.
Some mathematicians are not non-physicists.	No non-mathematicians are physicists.
	All non-mathematicians are non-physicists.
	Some non-physicists are non-mathematicians.
	Some non-physicists are not mathematicians.

Hence, if we first convert an *A* proposition we are soon brought to a halt, because an *O* proposition cannot be converted. If we first obvert, we get two propositions which are satisfactory. *Some non-physicists are not mathematicians* is called the *partial inverse* of the original proposition. Its subject is the contradictory of the original subject, its predicate is the original predicate. *Some non-physicists are non-mathematicians* is called the *full inverse*. Both its subject and its predicate are the contradictories of the original subject and predicate respectively.

Has each form of categorical proposition an inverse? If the reader will use the method we have indicated, he will discover that from *No professor is unkind* he can infer *Some non-professors are unkind* (the *partial inverse*) and *Some non-professors are not kind* (the *full inverse*). But no inverses can be obtained from either an *I* or an *O* proposition. Hence, only universals have inverses, and in each case inversion is by limitation.

The process of inversion may lead to absurd results as when, from *All honest men are mortal* we seem to get *Some dishonest men are immortal*. Where has the error crept in? The answer is: In our careless use of negatives. The true inverse of our proposition is *Some non-honest-men are non-mortal,* which is not at all an absurd result. For the class of all beings that are not *honest men* is wider than the class *dishonest men* and includes triangles and the like which are certainly non-mortal.

"But look here!" the reader may object. "The partial inverse of *All physicists are mathematicians* is *Some non-physicists are not mathematicians.* In the first proposition the predicate is undistributed, although the same term is distributed in the second. How then can you maintain that the second is a valid consequence of the first? Does it not violate the principle concerning distribution of terms?"

If the reader has understood the discussion of the existential import of propositions, he will have a ready reply. A universal proposition, he will say, asserts *nothing* about the existence or non-existence of instances; particulars, on the other hand, do have existential import. Consequently, a particular can never be validly inferred from a universal or combination of universals, *unless* the premises include a proposition asserting that the classes denoted by the terms of the universal contain at least one member. And specifically, the conversion of *A* is valid only if the predicate denotes such a class.

The source of the trouble in inversion is now apparent. To get the inverse of *All physicists are mathematicians* we are required to convert *All non-mathematicians are non-physicists*. This can be done only if we add the further premise *Some men are non-physicists* or what is the same thing *Some men are not physicists*. If this premise is supplied, the partial inverse does not violate the principle concerning distribution of terms.

If universals always did have an existential import, then not only would the terms of such propositions denote classes with members, but the contradictory terms would do so as well. Thus if *All men are mortal* required that there should be men and mortals, since we may validly infer *All immortals are non-men,* we would be compelled to affirm that there are immortals as well as non-men. That universals do not always have existential import, even in everyday conversation, can be seen from the following. Students of mathematics know that the ancient Greek problem, to construct a square equal in area to a circle with compass and ruler, is demonstrably impossible. We may therefore assert confidently that *No mathematicians are circle-squarers*. Its partial inverse is *Some non-mathematicians are circle-squarers*. But we assuredly did not intend to assert anything whose consequence is that there are some people who can in fact square the circle—for there is a proof that this cannot be done. Hence the original proposition could not have been intended to assert the existence of circle-squarers.

Inference by Converse Relation

If *Chicago is west of New York* we may validly infer that *New York is east of Chicago;* if *Socrates was a teacher of Plato* we may infer that *Plato was a pupil of Socrates;* if *Seven is greater than five* we may infer that *Five is less than seven*. In each of these pairs of propositions the two are equivalent. Such inferences are of the form: If *a* stands to *b* in a certain relation, *b* stands to *a* in the *converse relation*.

Equivalence of Compound Propositions

We must now examine what are the *equivalent* forms of compound propositions.

Consider the hypothetical *If a triangle is isosceles, its base angles are equal*. To assert it means, as we have seen, to assert that the truth of the antecedent involves the truth of the consequent, or that the antecedent could not be true and the consequent false. Hence the hypothetical simply asserts that the conjunctive proposi-

tion *A triangle is isosceles, and its base angles are unequal* is false;
or, what is the same thing, that the disjunctive proposition *It is
not the case that both a triangle is isosceles and its base angles are
unequal* is true. It follows that from a hypothetical we may infer
a disjunctive proposition.

Moreover, we may infer the hypothetical from the disjunctive as
well. For if *It is not the case that both a triangle is isosceles and
its base angles are unequal,* then the truth of one of the disjuncts
is incompatible with the truth of the other: if one disjunct is true,
the other must be false. From this disjunctive proposition we may
therefore infer *If a triangle is isosceles, its base angles are equal.*
Hence a disjunctive proposition can be found which is *equivalent*
to a hypothetical.

If we employ our previous symbols, we may write this as follows:

[(A triangle is isosceles) $\supset$ (its base angles are equal)] $\equiv$
[(A triangle is isosceles) . (its base angles are equal)$'$]$'$.

But this discussion also shows how we can infer an equivalent
hypothetical from any hypothetical proposition. For if in the
equivalent disjunctive the second disjunct is supposed true, the
other disjunct must be false. We may therefore infer *If the base
angles of a triangle are unequal, it is not isosceles.* Hence we may
write:

[(A triangle is isosceles) $\supset$ (its base angles are equal)] $\equiv$
[(The base angles of a triangle are equal)$'$ $\supset$ (the triangle is isosceles)$'$].

These equivalent hypotheticals are said to be the *contrapositives*
of each other.

Consider next the alternative proposition *Either a triangle is
not isosceles or its base angles are equal.* To assert it means to assert
that *at least one* of the alternants is true. If, therefore, one of the
alternants were false, the other would have to be true. Hence we
may infer from the alternative above the following hypothetical *If
a triangle is isosceles, its base angles are equal.* Moreover, the alternative may be inferred from this hypothetical. For the latter is
equivalent to *It is not the case that both a triangle is isosceles and
its base angles are unequal,* which asserts that *at least one* of the
disjuncts must be false. From the disjunctive we may therefore
infer *Either a triangle is not isosceles, or its base angles are equal.*
We therefore may write the equivalence:

[(A triangle is isosceles)′ ∨ (its base angles are equal)] ≡
[(A triangle is isosceles) ⊃ (its base angles are equal)]

It follows that for every hypothetical there is an equivalent alternative, an equivalent disjunctive, and an equivalent hypothetical. A similar statement holds for every alternative and every disjunctive proposition. On the other hand, a conjunctive proposition is not equivalent to any one of the other three forms of compound propositions.

Let us now state the equivalents of *If he is happily married, he does not beat his wife.* They are *If he beats his wife, he is not happily married, Either he is not happily married or he does not beat his wife,* and *It is not the case that both he is happily married and he beats his wife.* In symbols they will read:

[(He is happily married) ⊃ (He does not beat his wife)] ≡
[(He does not beat his wife)′ ⊃ (He is happily married)′] ≡
[(He is happily married)′ ∨ (He does not beat his wife)] ≡
[(He is happily married) . (He does not beat his wife)′]′

These equivalents may be stated more compactly, and the forms of the equivalent propositions exhibited more clearly, if we adopt further symbolic conventions. Let *p* represent the antecedent of a hypothetical proposition, and *q* its consequent. Any hypothetical may then be symbolized by ($p ⊃ q$). The equivalences will then be written as follows:

$$(p ⊃ q) ≡ (q' ⊃ p') ≡ (p' ∨ q) ≡ (p . q')'$$

We shall discuss in Chapter VII equivalences between *systems* of propositions. We may, however, offer at this point an example of two propositions which are equivalent in virtue of their place in a system. Let *p* ≡ *In Newtonian physics, light is reflected from a surface so that the angle of incidence is equal to the angle of reflection* and let *q* ≡ *In Newtonian physics light is reflected from a surface so that its path is a minimum:* *p* and *q* are equivalent.

§ 4. THE TRADITIONAL SQUARE OF OPPOSITION

Traditionally, the *opposition* between propositions has not been conceived in a manner as general as we have indicated. Since on the traditional view all propositions were analyzable into subject and predicate, only propositions in that form could be opposed. The opposition of compound propositions was not discussed, and the discussion of the opposition of singular propositions was most un-satisfactory.

In this section we shall examine the traditional account of oppo-sition. According to it, two propositions are said to be opposed when they have the same subject and predicate, but differ in quan-tity or quality or both.

Consider, therefore, the four propositions:

A. All republics are ungrateful.
E. No republics are ungrateful.
I. Some republics are ungrateful.
O. Some republics are not ungrateful.

In discussing the existential import of propositions, we have seen that the universals do not require the existence of republics, while the particulars do. We cannot, therefore, without further assump-tions, infer the truth of the *I* proposition from the truth of the *A* proposition. To do so, we require the assumption that there are republics. We shall make that assumption in the present section once for all, and explore the consequences of this hypothesis.

No two of the four propositions above are independent of one another, and no two are equivalent. We may, however, identify the other five relations of the possible nine as follows. The reader will find it helpful to make use of the diagrammatic representation of propositions.

1. *All republics are ungrateful* and *Some republics are not un-grateful* cannot both be true, and they cannot both be false. If one is true, we may validly infer the falsity of the other; and if one is false we may infer the truth of the other. Hence the *A* and *O* propo-sitions are *contradictories;* and the same holds for the *E* and *I* propositions.

2. *All republics are ungrateful* and *No republics are ungrateful* cannot both be true, so that if one were true, we could infer the falsity of the other. But if one were false, the truth-value of the other would be undetermined. Hence the *A* and *E* propositions are *contraries.*

3. Examining *All republics are ungrateful* and *Some republics are ungrateful,* we find that the truth of the second may be inferred from the truth of the first. But if the first is false, we can infer noth-ing about the truth-value of the second. Hence the *A* proposition is the principal or superaltern to the *I* proposition, which is the subaltern. The same relation holds for the *E* and *O* propositions.

4. On the other hand, from the falsity of the *I* proposition we

may infer the falsity of the *A* proposition. But from the truth of the *I* proposition we cannot infer the truth-value of the *A* proposition. Hence the *I* proposition stands to the *A* proposition as the subaltern to the principal. Similarly for the *O* and *E* propositions.

5. Finally, the truth of *Some republics are ungrateful* is compatible with the truth of *Some republics are not ungrateful,* although when we remember our convention that the word "some" is not to exclude "all" we see that we cannot infer the truth of one from the truth of the other. But if either of them is false, the other must be true. Hence the *I* and *O* propositions are subcontraries. This result also follows from the fact that the *A* and *E* propositions are contraries. For since the *O* and *I* propositions are the contradictories of the *A* and *E* propositions respectively, and since contraries cannot both be true, the *O* and *I* propositions cannot both be false; while since the *A* and *E* propositions may both be false, the *O* and *I* propositions may both be true.

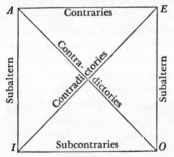

These relations between the categorical propositions have been represented in the ancient square of opposition. We may also construct the following table of valid inferences from each of the four categoricals.

	A	*E*	*I*	*O*
If *A* is true		False	True	False
If *A* is false		Undetermined	Undetermined	True
If *E* is true	False		False	True
If *E* is false	Undetermined		True	Undetermined
If *I* is true	Undetermined	False		Undetermined
If *I* is false	False	True		True
If *O* is true	False	Undetermined	Undetermined	
If *O* is false	True	False	True	

In conclusion, we may point out that without the assumption concerning existence we have made at the beginning of this section, the *I* and *O* propositions cannot be inferred from the *A* and *E* proposition respectively. Moreover, without this assumption, the *A* and *E* propositions would not be contraries, since both might then be true. Thus *All immortal men are in this room* and *No immortal men are in this room* would be both true if there were no immortal men. For if it is false that there are immortal men, then (on the interpretation we have given to particular propositions) both the propositions *Some immortal men are in this room* and *Some immortal men are not in this room* are false. Hence the contradictories of these propositions must be true.

§ 5. THE OPPOSITION OF PROPOSITIONS IN GENERAL

One of the most fruitful sources of intellectual confusion is the too facile assumption that any two propositions which are not equivalent are mutually exclusive. Thus men have debated about the relation of mind to body, of heredity to environment, of selfishness to altruism, of art to nature, frequently without realizing that while the alternatives are not equivalent, it does not follow that they are mutually exclusive. It is well to note that two things related as part to whole are not identical, and yet surely are not contraries. The proposition *All Orthodox Greeks are true believers* is not the same as *All Christians are true believers* but the two are surely not incompatible.

The Contradictory Opposition of Compound Propositions

We have seen this relation illustrated in the traditional square of opposition by such simple cases as *All Mohammedans are true believers* and *Some Mohammedans are not true believers*. But it is a mistake to suppose that it is always easy to tell which propositions do have that relation to one another.

Suppose the reader in studying Rousseau's *Social Contract* found himself in violent disagreement with the opening sentence of the first chapter: "Man is born free; and everywhere he is in chains." How would he contradict this assertion? Or suppose he wished to deny a statement appearing later on: "The strongest is never strong enough to be always the master, unless he transforms strength into right, and obedience into duty." With what proposition would he contradict this? Or, finally, what would he say is the contradictory of this: "Sovereignty, being the exercise of the general will, is the will either of the body of the people or of only a part of it"?

Let us begin with the conjunctive proposition *p: Man is born free; and everywhere he is in chains.* Since to assert this means to assert that both conjuncts are true, to deny it must mean that not both conjuncts are true, or what is the same thing, that at least one of them is false. Hence the alternative *q: Either some men are not born free or man is not in chains everywhere* is the proper contradictory of the original proposition. The reader should convince himself that these two propositions, *p* and *q*, cannot both be true and cannot both be false. Other forms of the contradictory can be obtained, since the alternative is equivalent to *If all men are born free, they are not in chains* as well as to *If man is in chains everywhere, some men are not born free.*

Consider next *The strongest is never strong enough to be always the master, unless he transforms strength into right, and obedience into duty.* This is really a hypothetical proposition, and may be expressed as *If the strongest does not transform strength into right and obedience into duty, he is never strong enough to be always master.* It is therefore equivalent to the disjunctive *It is not the case that both the strongest does not transform strength into right and obedience into duty, and he is sometimes strong enough to be always the master.* Hence its contradictory is *The strongest does not transform strength into right and obedience into duty, and he is sometimes strong enough to be always master.*

Finally, *Sovereignty, being the exercise of the general will, is the will either of the body of the people or of only a part of it* is an alternative proposition, which may be stated explicitly as *Either sovereignty, being the exercise of the general will, is the will of the body of the people, or it is the will of only a part of it.* Since this proposition is equivalent to a disjunctive one, its contradictory is the following conjunctive: *Sovereignty is not the will of the body of the people, and it is not the will of only a part of it.*

It follows that the contradictory of a hypothetical, disjunctive, or alternative proposition can always be stated in the form of a conjunctive proposition. On the other hand, the contradictory of a conjunctive is either a hypothetical, an alternative, or a disjunctive proposition. The precise relations between compound propositions and their contradictories may be compactly stated symbolically. Since

$$(p \supset q) \equiv (q' \supset p') \equiv (p' \lor q) \equiv (p \cdot q')',$$

the contradictory of any one of them will contradict any other. Hence

$$(p \supset q)' \equiv (q' \supset p')' \equiv (p' \lor q)' \equiv (p \cdot q').$$

Or in words, the contradictory of "if p then q" is "p and q'"; the contradictory of "either p or q" is "p' and q'"; the contradictory of "not both p and q" is "p and q."

The reader should note the equivalence $(p' \lor q)' \equiv (p \cdot q')$. This relation is perfectly general, and it does not matter what propositions we substitute for the symbols. Let us therefore replace p' by r; then p will be replaced by r'. We then get

$$(r \lor q)' \equiv (r' \cdot q'),$$

a relation known as De Morgan's theorem. It asserts that the negative (or contradictory) of an alternative proposition is a conjunctive in which the conjuncts are the contradictories of the corresponding alternants. Another form of this theorem is given by

$$(p \cdot r)' \equiv (p' \lor r'),$$

which states that the negative of a conjunctive is an alternative proposition in which the alternants are the contradictories of the corresponding conjuncts.

We have found that specially devised symbols are a great help in exhibiting with great clarity the logical structure of propositions—a structure which is obscured by the unwieldiness of ordinary language. The reader will therefore doubtless agree that symbols are not an obstacle to understanding, but rather an aid. The generalizing power of modern logic, as of modern mathematics, is due in large measure to the adequacy of the symbolism it has adapted for the task.

As a test of his comprehension, we may ask the reader to give the contradictory of *Some men are poor but honest*. It must be understood that the force of the word "but" in this proposition is that the poor are generally dishonest although some also happen to be honest. Hence its explicit meaning is *Some men are poor and honest, and some men are poor and dishonest*. It follows that *Some men are not poor and honest* is not the contradictory of the original statement, and neither is *All men are not both poor and honest*. Application of the previously discussed principles shows that the contradictory is *Either all men are not both poor and honest or all men are not both poor and dishonest*. Similar considerations show that the contradictory of *John came home yesterday on a bicycle* is not *John did not come home yesterday on a bicycle* but rather *Either John did not come home or John did not come home yesterday or John did not come home on a bicycle.*

Contrary Opposition

This relation has also been illustrated in the traditional square of opposition. But clearly other examples of contrary propositions can be found. *I am seven feet tall* and *I am six feet tall. Socrates was the wisest of the Greeks* and *Plato was the wisest of the Greeks. Columbus was the first European to discover America* and *Leif Ericson was the first European to discover America.* These are examples of pairs of contraries which do not fall into the framework of the traditional scheme. It is evident that general propositions may have more than one contrary.

What is the contrary of *Either the book was stolen or I mislaid it?* One contrary is *The book was not stolen and I did not mislay it, and my brother did not borrow it;* these two compound propositions may be both false, for example, when *My brother borrowed it* is true. Symbolically, and in general, the following pair of compound propositions are contraries:

$$(p \lor q) \qquad \text{and} \qquad (p' \cdot q' \cdot r)$$

where *p, q,* and *r* are any propositions.

It should be clear from these examples that two propositions may be incompatible with each other even though neither may in fact be true. This elementary point seems to have been often overlooked in some of the great intellectual controversies in the history of human thought. The bitter fights between idealists and realists, between revolutionists and conservatives, between evolutionists and fundamentalists, between theists and deists, have been waged not only on the assumption that the respective points of view are exclusive of one another, but also on the supposition that if one of the parties were proved in the wrong, the other would be proved right. But such is the irony of history that these famous historical oppositions are not today generally acknowledged as dividing the truth between them.

Subcontrary Opposition

In addition to the propositions falling into the traditional schedule, the following pairs illustrate the relation of subcontrary opposition: *There is a page in this book containing misprints* and *There is a page in this book containing no misprints. Hydrogen is*

not the lightest element and *Helium is not the lightest element.*
San Marino is not the smallest country of Europe and *Andorra
is not the smallest country of Europe.* The two propositions in each
pair cannot both be false, but both may be true.

Other examples of this important relation are: Under the pre-
vailing organization of governments, the propositions: *Some European countries are monarchies* and *Some European countries are
republics* are subcontraries. In a country which is planning to raise
taxes, but where the budget must be balanced by increasing either
the tariff or the income tax: *The income tax will be raised* and
The tariff will be increased are again subcontraries. The relation
of subcontrariness is thus a very simple one, and it may seem strange
that serious errors should ever be made by failing to understand its
nature or to recognize it in other examples. Yet the history of
human thought shows a powerful tendency to conceive rival hypotheses as contrary or even contradictory when they are in fact
subcontraries. Are we to obey the law or be free to change it? Are
we to follow our elders or are we to try to improve on their ways?
Libraries have been written on these and similar themes on the
assumption that the alternatives were mutually exclusive. But it
is only to an untutored mind that they appear so. Wisdom consists
in seeing ways in which both may be true. Consider, for example,
the controversy with respect to free trade and policies of protection.
The issues are sometimes stated as if it were incompatible with the
best interests of a country to adopt one policy at one time and the
other at another time. But under certain conditions tariffs may be
necessary for the economic development of a country, while under
other conditions they may be detrimental. Hence, while the propositions *Tariffs are detrimental to a country* and *Tariffs are beneficial to a country* are in fact contraries when regarded as formulations of *universal* policies, the actual state of affairs makes it impossible to adopt such universal policies. Hence both propositions
may be true if they are regarded as asserting that under *certain
qualifying conditions* tariffs may be detrimental, and under others,
beneficial. Meat can be both a food and a poison.

Superimplication

Every theory stands to its logical consequences in the relation of
principal to subaltern—in the relation of superimplication. For
this reason we shall study this and the converse relation in some
detail in the sequel. Here we may note a single illustration of this
type of opposition that is a little more complicated than the tra-

ditional schedule allows. Let p represent the conjunction of postulates and axioms of Euclid, and q represent *The sum of the angles of a triangle is equal to two right angles:* then p is the principal or superimplicant to q.

In this connection, it will be useful to refer to a distinction, canonized by traditional logic, between immediate and mediate inference. An inference is said to be *immediate* when a proposition is inferred from a *single* other proposition; and inference is *mediate* when *at least two* propositions are required in the premises. But this distinction is not significant if any two propositions can be combined into one. We must also remember that some forms of so-called immediate inferences require special assumptions in order to be valid.

Logicians have sometimes been led into drawing a very sharp distinction between equivalent propositions, while on the other hand they have sometimes questioned whether the "immediate inferences" from one to another of an equivalent pair of propositions was a "genuine" case of inference at all. Reflection shows, however, that a part at least of this controversy arises because it is forgotten how arbitrary is the distinction between a proposition and what it implies. Two propositions so related that if the first is true the second is also true, and if the first is false the second is false also, are identical for certain purely logical purposes. For this reason it is not very significant whether we call the contrapositive of a proposition an immediate inference from the latter or whether we regard it as being its equivalent. None the less, although two equivalent propositions are identical with regard to their truth-value, the conventional meaning of the inferred proposition is often an elaboration of the meaning of the premise. It is true, however, that the dividing-line between equivalent propositions which have the same meaning and equivalent propositions which are not precisely alike in meaning is not a sharp one.

Two special cases of immediate inference which fall under the relation of subalternation should also be mentioned. These illustrate the logic of relations, which has been systematically studied only within recent times.

(a) Inference by Added Determinants

We may infer one proposition from another, if we *limit* the subject and predicate of the premise by the *same determinant*. Thus, from *Users of snuff are consumers of tobacco* we may infer *American users of snuff are American consumers of tobacco*. From *All popes are Italians* we may infer *All tall popes are tall Italians.* These propositions, however, are not equivalent. We cannot infer from *All American professors are American scholars* that *All professors are scholars.*

Care must be taken to qualify the subject and predicate with a determinant having the same meaning. Thus, if we argue that because *All husbands are wage-earners* therefore *All unsuccessful husbands are unsuccessful wage-earners* the determinant "unsuccessful" does not have the same meaning when applied to the subject as when it is applied to the predicate, although the same word is used. A husband is unsuccessful relative to his functions as husband; a wage-earner is unsuccessful relative to his wage-earning functions. Hence determinants whose meaning involves a reference to different standards cannot be employed for inference by added determinants.

(b) Inference by Complex Conception

We may infer one proposition from another if we employ the subject and predicate as parts of a more complex conception Thus if *New York is the world's largest city* then *The center of New York is the center of the world's largest city.* If *A horse is an animal* then *The head of a horse is the head of an animal.* The inference consists in inferring that if one term stands to another in a certain relation, then whatever is related to the first term in some specific way stands to whatever is related to the second term in the same specific way in that same certain relation. Such inferences, however, do not yield equivalent propositions. We cannot infer from *The color of his nose is the color of a beet* that *His nose is a beet.*

We must observe the same caution as in the preceding type of inference. Thus it is fallacious to argue that because *All radicals are citizens* therefore *The wealthiest of radicals is the wealthiest of citizens.* For the person standing in the relation of "being the wealthiest of radicals" is measured by different standards of wealth than the person who stands in the relation of "being the wealthiest of citizens."

The Relation of Subimplication or Converse Subaltern

If *p* stands for *The angle sum of an isosceles triangle is equal to two right angles* and *q* for *The angle sum of any triangle is equal to two right angles*, *p* is the subimplicant or subaltern to *q*. For if *p* is true, nothing follows as to the truth of *q*, while if *p* is false, *q* must be false. As we shall see, the relation of a verifying instance of a theory to the theory is the relation of subaltern to principal.

It will become apparent later that no number of verifying propositions relating to a theory can demonstrate the theory, although strictly speaking only one contrary instance of a theory is needed to refute it. But great care must be exercised in making sure that what appear to be contrary instances are really so in fact.

CHAPTER IV

THE CATEGORICAL SYLLOGISM

§ 1. THE DEFINITION OF CATEGORICAL SYLLOGISM

Consider the proposition *Tom Mooney is a danger to society.*
What would constitute adequate evidence for this proposition? One
may perhaps argue as follows: *All social radicals are a danger to
society; and Tom Mooney is a social radical; it follows that Tom
Mooney is a danger to society.* The reader would then have to admit that the first two propositions do imply the third, and *if* the first
two were true, the third would be true necessarily. The conclusion is
therefore a subaltern to the premises, since if the conclusion were
true it would not follow that the premises are. It is also clear, however, that although the premises *if true* would be adequate evidence
for the truth of the conclusion, the question *whether* the premises
are true in fact is not determined by the logical relation in which
they stand to the conclusion.

Arguments of this type are frequently employed. Some of them
appear to be perfectly sound, although on reflection they are discovered to be faulty. An inference such as *All Parisians are Frenchmen, no Bostonians are Parisians, therefore no Bostonians are
Frenchmen* or *All radicals are foreign-born, no patriotic citizen
is a radical, therefore no patriotic citizen is foreign-born* is often
regarded as sound by those who do not reflect. That neither argument is valid can be shown easily if we employ precisely the same
type of inference, but about a different subject matter. Thus *All
triangles are plane figures, no squares are triangles, therefore no
squares are plane figures* is an argument of the same type as either
of the preceding ones, but it will deceive practically no one.

Can we not discover some general rules, easy to apply, to which
arguments of this type must conform to be valid? The matter was
investigated by Aristotle, who laid the foundation for all subse-

quent logical inquiry, and his results have constituted the substance of logical doctrines for two thousand years. It is only in comparatively recent times that Aristotle's researches have received extension. The following discussion, however, makes little use of more modern logical techniques, although our procedure will follow the traditional analysis of the syllogism and not Aristotle's own. By departing in some ways from Aristotle's discussion of the categorical syllogism we shall at the same time exhibit the nature of a logical or mathematical system.

A *categorical syllogism* is defined as a form of argument consisting of three categorical propositions which contain between them three and only three terms. Two of the propositions are premises, the third is the conclusion. The premises *All football coaches are well paid* and *All baseball players are popular* cannot yield a syllogistic conclusion, since the premises alone contain four terms. The two propositions have no common term, while the premises of every syllogism have a common term. We may, in fact, interpret a syllogistic inference as a comparison of the relations between each of two terms and a third, in order to discover the relations of the two terms to each other. In the illustration with which we began this chapter, the common term is "social radical"; by examining the relations of the other two terms, "Tom Mooney" and "a danger to society," to this common term, the relation between "Tom Mooney" and "a danger to society" was found. For this reason, the syllogism is classified as a *mediate inference*. From the point of view of a generalized logic, however, the syllogism is a particular instance of an inference by *elimination* of one or more terms contained in the premises.

Is the following argument a categorical syllogism? A *is older than* B; B *is older than* C; *therefore* A *is older than* C. It certainly *looks* like one. But since every categorical proposition is to be analyzed into a subject term, a predicate term, and a copula which is some part of the verb "to be," it follows that this argument, although valid, is not a syllogism, since it contains *four* terms. The following argument, due to C. L. Dodgson (Lewis Carroll), is also not a syllogism as it stands, although it may be transformed into one: "A prudent man shuns hyaenas; no banker is imprudent; therefore no banker fails to shun hyaenas."

The term which is contained in both premises is the *middle term;* the predicate of the conclusion is the *major term;* and the subject of the conclusion is the *minor term.* The premise which

contains the major term is the _major premise,_ and the premise containing the minor term is the _minor premise._ The order in which
the premises are stated does not, therefore, determine which is the
major premise. In the syllogism _All mystery tales are a danger to
health, for all mystery tales cause mental agitation, and whatever
is a cause of mental agitation is a danger to health_ the conclusion
is stated first, and the major premise last. It is usual, however, to
state the major premise first.

§ 2. THE ENTHYMEME

Although syllogistic reasoning occurs frequently in daily discourse, often its presence is not noticed because the reasoning is
incompletely stated. A syllogism that is incompletely stated, in
which one of the premises or the conclusion is tacitly present but
not expressed, is called an _enthymeme._

The following are familiar illustrations of enthymemes: _This
medicine cured my daughter's cough; therefore this medicine will
cure mine._ The inference is valid on the tacit admission of the
major premise: _Whatever is a cure for my daughter's cough is a
cure for mine._ An enthymeme in which the major premise is unexpressed is of the _first order._

All drunkards are short-lived; therefore John won't live long.
Here the missing premise is the minor: _John is a drunkard._
Enthymemes suppressing the minor premise are of the _second
order._

Usury is immoral, and this is usury. The conclusion _This is im-
moral_ is here left unexpressed. Such an enthymeme is of the _third
order._ The value of such enthymemes for purposes of innuendo is
doubtless well known to the reader.

Although enthymemes do not introduce any new form of inference, their recognition is of very great importance practically. As we
shall see, so-called inductive inferences are often believed to constitute a special mode of reasoning, when in fact they are simply
enthymemes of the first order.

§ 3. THE RULES OR AXIOMS OF VALIDITY

We have, so far, merely defined what we shall understand by a
categorical syllogism. We have not yet stated the conditions under
which such an argument is valid. We shall do this by enumerating

five propositions which jointly express the determining factors of any valid categorical syllogism. They are referred to as the *rules* or *axioms*. We shall state them without any attempt to prove them, since they will be our "first principles," in terms of which we shall demonstrate other propositions. Nevertheless, although we make no attempt to prove the axioms, we assert them as expressing the conditions of valid syllogistic inference. Reflection on the syllogism as a form of inference in which a connection between two terms may be asserted because of their relations to a common third term, may enable us to "see" that these axioms do in fact express the conditions of validity. But such "seeing" must not be mistaken for *proof*. Since the axioms are principles of logic, we touch upon a fundamental characteristic of logical principles: not all logical principles can be demonstrated logically, since the demonstration must itself employ some principles of logic; and in particular, no proof of the principle of identity (If anything is A it is A) is possible, without assuming that the "anything that is A," which occurs in one part of such an alleged proof is identical with the "anything that is A" occurring in another part.

The axioms of the categorical syllogism fall into two sets, those which deal with the quantity or distribution of terms, and those which deal with the quality of the propositions.

Axioms of Quantity
1. The middle term must be distributed at least once.
2. No term may be distributed in the conclusion which is not distributed in the premises.

Axioms of Quality
3. If both premises are negative, there is no conclusion.
4. If one premise is negative, the conclusion must be negative.
5. If neither premise is negative, the conclusion must be affirmative.

These axioms, together with the principles of hypothetical inference, are sufficient to develop the entire theory of the categorical syllogism. The axioms are not independent of each other, since we can derive some of them from the others. However, we shall take all of them as the axiomatic basis for our analysis.

§ 4. THE GENERAL THEOREMS OF THE SYLLOGISM

We shall now demonstrate four theorems.

Theorem I. The number of distributed terms in the conclusion must be *at least one less* than the total number of distributed terms in the premises.

Proof: The number of terms distributed in the conclusion cannot be greater than the total number distributed in the premises (Axiom 2).

The middle term, which must be distributed at least once in the premises (Axiom 1), does not appear in the conclusion (*definition of middle term*).

Therefore the conclusion must contain at least one distributed term less than the premises.

Theorem II. If both premises are particular, there is no conclusion.

Proof: The two particular premises may be either (a) both negative, (b) both affirmative, or (c) one affirmative and one negative.

a. If both premises are negative, there is no conclusion (Axiom 3).

b. A particular affirmative proposition distributes no terms. If both premises are particular affirmative, the premises contain no distributed terms. Hence, there is no conclusion (Axiom 1).

c. An affirmative particular has no distributed terms, and a negative particular has only one. Hence the premises contain one and only one distributed term. Therefore, *if* there is a conclusion, it cannot contain *any* distributed terms (Theorem I). But since one premise is negative, the conclusion must be negative (Axiom 4). Therefore at least *one* term of the conclusion must be distributed. The assumption that there is a conclusion requires us to maintain that it contains at the same time *no* distributed terms and *at least one*. This is absurd. Hence there is no conclusion.

Theorem III. If one premise is particular, the conclusion must be particular.

Proof: The premises cannot both be particular (Theorem II). They must therefore differ in quantity, and may be either (a) both negative, (b) both affirmative, or (c) one affirmative and one negative.

a. If both premises are negative, there is no conclusion (Axiom 3).

b. One premise is an affirmative universal, the other an affirmative particular. The universal distributes only one term, the particular none. Hence the premises contain no more than one distributed term. Therefore the conclusion, if there is any, contains no distributed term (Theorem I). But a universal proposition contains at least one distributed term. Hence the conclusion, if there is any, is particular.

c. We may distinguish two cases: (a) the universal is negative, the particular is affirmative; (β) the universal is affirmative, the particular is negative.

a. The universal distributes two terms, the particular none. Hence the premises distribute two terms.

β. The universal distributes one terms, the particular also one. Hence the premises distribute two terms. In either case, therefore, the premises contain two and only two distributed terms. The conclusion, if there is any, cannot contain more than one distributed term (Theorem I). But the conclusion must be negative (Axiom 4), and its predicate must therefore be distributed. Hence its subject cannot be distributed, and it must be particular.

Theorem IV. If the major premise is an affirmative particular and the minor is a negative universal, there is no conclusion.

Proof: Since, by hypothesis, the minor is negative, the conclusion, if there is any, must be negative (Axiom 4), and its predicate, which is the major term, must be distributed. Hence the major term must be distributed in the major premise (Axiom 2). But the particular affirmative distributes none of its terms. There is therefore no conclusion.

The five axioms and these four theorems which we have demonstrated rigorously by their aid enable us to enumerate all possible valid syllogisms. The reader will do well to notice the nature of the demonstration: it has been shown that the theorems are necessary consequences of the axioms, so that if the axioms are accepted, the theorems must be accepted also, on pain of contradiction.

§ 5. THE FIGURES AND MOODS OF THE SYLLOGISM

But before we enumerate all the valid syllogistic forms, let us consider some syllogisms:

1. No musicians are Italians.
   All barbers are musicians.
   ∴ No barbers are Italians.

2. All gentlemen are polite.
   No gamblers are polite.
   ∴ No gamblers are gentlemen.

3. Some books are not edifying.
   All books are interesting.
   ∴ Some interesting things are not edifying.

4. All business men are self-confident.
   No self-confident men are religious.
   ∴ No religious men are business men.

Although these are all valid syllogisms, they differ from one another in two ways: (1) in the position of the middle term; and (2) in the quality and the quantity of the premises and the conclusion. In the first example, the middle term is the subject of the major and the predicate of the minor: in the second example, the middle term is the predicate of both premises; in the third, the middle term is the subject of both premises; and in the fourth, the middle term is the predicate of the major and the subject of the minor. The position of the middle term determines the *figure* of the syllogism, and on the basis of this distinction there are four possible figures. Letting $S, P, M,$ denote the minor term, major term, and middle term respectively, we may symbolize the four figures as follows:

$M - P$	$P - M$	$M - P$	$P - M$
$S - M$	$S - M$	$M - S$	$M - S$
∴ $S - P$	∴ $S - P$	∴ $S - P$	∴ $S - P$
First Figure	*Second Figure*	*Third Figure*	*Fourth Figure*

Aristotle recognized only the first three figures. The introduction of the fourth is generally attributed to Galen, and is therefore called the Galenian figure. Logicians have disputed whether the fourth figure represents a type of reasoning distinct from the first three, and whether Aristotle was or was not mistaken in not recognizing it. If the distinction between figures is made on the basis of the *position* of the middle term, there can be no dispute that there are four distinct figures. But Aristotle did not distinguish the figures in this way. His principle of distinction was the *width* or extent of the middle term as compared with the other two. On this basis there are just three figures: the middle may be wider than one and narrower than the other, wider than either, and narrower than either.

The second way in which syllogisms may differ is with respect to the quantity and quality of the premises and the conclusion.

This determines the *mood* of the syllogism. The first of the four syllogisms above is in the first figure, in mood *EAE*. The syllogism

5. All wholesome foods are cleanly made.
   All doughnuts are wholesome food.
   ∴ All doughnuts are cleanly made.

is a syllogism in the first figure, in mood *AAA*. Syllogisms may therefore differ in both figure and mood (for example, 1 and 3 above) or in figure alone (2 and 4) or in mood alone (1 and 5). However, not all moods are valid in every figure.

Let us count the total number of syllogistic forms, whether valid or not, taking account of differences in mood and figure. Since there are four types of categorical propositions, the major premise may be any one of the four types, and similarly for the minor premise and the conclusion. There are therefore $4 \times 4 \times 4$ or 64 syllogistic moods in each figure, and 64×4 or 256 syllogistic forms in all four figures. Most of these, however, are invalid. But how shall we discover the valid forms? It would be an appalling task to examine each of 256 forms. Such a procedure is not necessary, however, since the invalid forms may be eliminated by applying the axioms and theorems.

Let us write down every possible combination of premises, where the first letter indicates the major premise, and the second letter the minor:

AA	*EA*	*IA*	*OA*
AE	*EE*	*IE*	*OE*
AI	*EI*	*IO*	*OI*
AO	*EO*	*II*	*OO*

But Axiom 3 shows that the combinations *EE, EO, OE,* and *OO* are impossible; Theorem II eliminates *II, IO, OI;* and Theorem IV eliminates *IE*. We are therefore left with the following eight combinations of premises, each of which will yield a valid syllogism in some or all figures: *AA, AE, AI, AO, EA, EI, IA, OA*. The eight combinations which have been eliminated yield no conclusion in *any* figure.

There now remains the task of discovering the valid moods in each figure. This may be done in either of the following ways:

1. Write premises in each of the figures having the quantity and quality indicated by each of the permissible combinations, and by inspection find those which yield a valid conclusion. This method has the disadvantage of being long.

2. Establish special theorems for each figure, and eliminate by their aid the invalid combinations of premises. This method is very elegant, and we shall employ it.

In what follows we shall assume once for all that the classes denoted by the terms of the propositions are not empty, and explore the consequences of this assumption. It will permit us to perform immediate inferences by limitation.

§ 6. THE SPECIAL THEOREMS AND VALID MOODS OF THE FIRST FIGURE

Since the form of the first figure is symbolized by

$$
\begin{array}{c}
M - P \\
S - M \\
\hline
\therefore S - P
\end{array}
$$

we prove:

Theorem I. The minor premise must be affirmative.

Suppose the minor is negative: then the conclusion must be negative (Axiom 4), and P must be distributed. Hence P must be distributed in the major premise (Axiom 2), so that the major must be negative. However, both premises cannot be negative (Axiom 3), and the minor must therefore be affirmative.

Theorem II. The major premise must be universal.

Since the minor premise must be affirmative, its predicate M cannot be distributed. Hence M must be distributed in the major (Axiom 1), making the latter universal.

By means of the special Theorem I, we may therefore eliminate the combinations AE, AO, and by means of the second theorem, the combinations IA and OA. Only the following four yield valid conclusions in the first figure: AA, AI, EA and EI. The six valid moods are therefore AAA, $\widehat{(AAI)}$, AII, EAE, $\widehat{(EAO)}$, EIO.

The moods we have encircled are called *subaltern* or *weakened moods,* because although the premises warrant a universal conclusion, the actual conclusion is only particular, and therefore "weaker" than it could be. Four of these six valid moods have been given special names, the vowels of which correspond to the quantity and quality of the premises and conclusion. Thus, AAA is *Barbara,* AII is *Darii,* EAE is *Celarent,* and EIO is *Ferio.* The names have been devised to form mnemonic verses by which the different moods in each of the figures may be recalled, and the moods in figures other than the first reduced to the first. We shall return to the problem of reduction.

§ 7. THE SPECIAL THEOREMS AND VALID MOODS OF THE SECOND FIGURE

The form of the second figure is symbolized by

$$
\begin{array}{c}
P - M \\
S - M \\
\hline
\therefore S - P
\end{array}
$$

We prove:

Theorem I. The premises must differ in quality.

If both premises are affirmative, the middle term M is undistributed in each. Hence one of the premises must be negative (Axiom 1). But both premises cannot be negative (Axiom 3). Hence they differ in quality.

Theorem II. The major premise must be universal.

Since one of the premises is negative, the conclusion is negative (Axiom 4), and P, the major term, must be distributed. Hence P must be distributed in the major premise (Axiom 2), so that the latter is universal.

Theorem I eliminates the combinations AA, AI, and Theorem II eliminates IA and OA. We are left with four combinations in this figure: AE, AO, EA, and EI, from which we obtain six valid moods. *AEE* (*Camestres*), *AEO*, *AOO* (*Baroco*), *EAE* (*Cesare*), *EAO*, and *EIO* (*Festino*). The moods encircled are weakened syllogisms.

§ 8. THE SPECIAL THEOREMS AND VALID MOODS OF THE THIRD FIGURE

Employing the symbolic form of the third figure

$$
\begin{array}{c}
M - P \\
M - S \\
\hline
\therefore S - P
\end{array}
$$

we can prove:

Theorem I. The minor must be affirmative.

Suppose the minor negative: the conclusion would then be negative (Axiom 4) and *P,* its predicate, would be distributed. Hence *P* would be distributed in the major premise (Axiom 2), so that the latter would be negative. But this is impossible (Axiom 3), so that the minor cannot be negative.

Theorem II. The conclusion must be particular.

Since the minor must be affirmative, *S* cannot be distributed in the premises. Hence *S* cannot be distributed in the conclusion (Axiom 2), and the latter must be particular.

The first theorem eliminates the combinations *AE* and *AO,* and we are left with the six: *AA, AI, EA, EI, IA, OA.* Keeping in mind the second theorem, we obtain six valid moods: *(AAI)* *(Darapti),* *AII* *(Datisi),* *(EAO)* *(Felapton), EIO (Ferison), IAI (Disamis)* and *OAO (Bocardo).* In this figure there are no weakened moods. The two moods which we have encircled are called *strengthened syllogisms* because the same conclusion may be obtained even if we substitute for one of the premises its subaltern.

§ 9. THE SPECIAL THEOREMS AND VALID MOODS OF THE FOURTH FIGURE

With the aid of the symbolic representation of the fourth figure

$$
\begin{array}{c}
P - M \\
M - S \\
\hline
\therefore S - P
\end{array}
$$

we can prove:

Theorem I. If the major premise is affirmative, the minor is universal.

If the major is affirmative, its predicate *M* is not distributed. *M* must therefore be distributed in the minor premise (Axiom 1) and the latter is universal.

Theorem II. If either premise is negative, the major must be universal.

If either premise is negative, the conclusion is negative (Axiom 4) and its predicate *P* will be distributed. Hence *P* must be distributed in the major premise (Axiom 2), which must, therefore, be universal.

Theorem III. If the minor is affirmative, the conclusion is particular.

If the minor is affirmative, its predicate S is not distributed. Hence S cannot be distributed in the conclusion (Axiom 2) and the latter must be particular.

The first theorem eliminates the combinations *AI, AO,* the second eliminates *OA.* We are left with the five combinations: *AA, AE, EA, IA* and *EI.* Remembering the third theorem, we obtain six valid moods: *AAI* (*Bramantip*), *AEE* (*Camenes*), *AEO*, *IAI* (*Dimaris*), *EAO* (*Fesapo*), and *EIO* (*Fresison*). *AEO* is a weakened syllogism, while *AAI* and *EAO* are strengthened ones.

We thus find that there are just twenty-four valid syllogistic forms in the four figures, each figure containing six moods. The weakened and strengthened forms, however, are legitimate only on the assumption of existential import which we have explicitly made. Where such an assumption is not made, only fifteen valid moods can be obtained.

§ 10. THE REDUCTION OF SYLLOGISMS

We have discovered the valid moods by eliminating all forms incompatible with the axioms of validity and with the theorems derived from them. The only justification of the validity of the remaining forms we have given is that they are in conformity with the axioms. But a different approach to the justification of valid moods was taken by Aristotle, the original writer on the syllogism. According to him, the moods of the first figure were to be tested by applying to them directly a principle known since as the *dictum de omni et nullo.* This principle was, and frequently still is, believed to be "self-evident." It has been stated variously, one form of the *dictum* being: "Whatever is predicated, whether affirmatively or negatively, of a term distributed, may be predicated in like manner of everything contained under it." (Keynes) It is not difficult to show that the *dictum* is equivalent to the axioms and theorems relevant to the first figure. *It cannot, however, be applied directly to syllogisms in other figures.* The first figure was accordingly called the *perfect* figure, the others being *imperfect.*

Let us see how the *dictum* may test the validity of a syllogism in

Barbara: All Russians are Europeans; all communists are Russians; *therefore all communists are Europeans.* "Europeans" is predicated affirmatively of the distributed term "Russians"; hence, according to the *dictum,* it may be predicated affirmatively of "communists," which is contained under "Russians." But the syllogism *All Parisians are Frenchmen; no Bostonians are Parisians; therefore no Bostonians are Frenchmen* does not conform to the *dictum.* "Frenchmen" is predicated affirmatively of the distributed term "Parisians"; it cannot, however, be predicated in any manner of "Bostonians," since the latter term is not contained under "Parisians."

Now if, with Aristotle, we regard the *dictum* as a "self-evident" principle, and if we believe with him that it is the *sole* "self-evident" principle which can test the validity of syllogistic forms, the only way in which moods in figures other than the first can be justified will be by showing that these imply valid moods in the *first* figure.

This process of exhibiting the connection of moods in other figures with moods in the first is called *reduction.* There are two varieties: (1) *direct reduction,* which is performed by conversion of propositions or transposition of premises; and (2) *indirect reduction,* which requires either obversion and contraposition of propositions, or a form of hypothetical inference known as *reductio ad absurdum.*

Although many logicians have regarded the process of reduction as unnecessary and even as invalid, there is no doubt that, given the basis upon which Aristotle develops the theory of the syllogism, reduction is an essential part of the theory. However, if the doctrine of the syllogism is developed on other bases, which do not assume that the first figure has any intrinsic superiority over the others, reduction cannot have the importance with which it has been regarded traditionally. Our own discussion has shown that the first figure need not be taken as central, and as we shall see later, the syllogism may be developed from a point of view even more general than the one we have taken. Moreover, it is possible to state *dicta* for each of the figures, all of which possess the same degree of "self-evidence" as the *dictum de omni.* Nevertheless, in spite of the diminution in the theoretical importance of reduction, it still serves as a valuable logical exercise. We shall now show how the process may be carried out by reducing to the first figure several moods in figures other than the first.

Direct Reduction

Consider the *AEE* syllogism in the second figure:

All almsgiving is socially dangerous.

No educational institution is socially dangerous.

∴ No educational institution in-
dulges in almsgiving.

No socially dangerous institution is
an educational institution.

All almsgiving is socially dangerous.

∴ No almsgiving is undertaken by
an educational institution.

∴ No educational institution in-
dulges in almsgiving.

We have stated its equivalent syllogism on the right, which may be tested directly by means of the *dictum*. The reduction was effected by transposing the premises, converting the minor premise, and finally converting the conclusion. Therefore if we are not in doubt about the validity of the second syllogism, there can be no doubt concerning the validity of the original.

Consider next the *AII* mood in the third figure. It may be reduced to the valid syllogism in the first figure, stated at the right, as indicated:

All brokers are wealthy. ⟶ All brokers are wealthy.

Some brokers are intelligent. —converse→ Some intelligent men are brokers.

∴ Some intelligent men are wealthy.

∴ Some intelligent men are wealthy.

Finally, the *IAI* in the fourth figure may be reduced as follows:

Some horses are spirited animals.

All spirited animals are difficult
to manage.

∴ Some creatures difficult to manage are horses.

All spirited animals are difficult
to manage.

Some horses are spirited animals.

∴ Some horses are difficult to
manage.

∴ Some creatures difficult to manage are horses.

Indirect Reduction

The reader will discover that the two syllogisms which contain a particular negative premise, *AOO* in the second figure and *OAO* in the third, cannot be reduced to the first by conversion and transposition of premises alone. If obversion is also permitted, however, the reader will have no difficulty in effecting the reduction.

But obversion was not included by Aristotle in the permissible means of effecting reduction. He discovered, however, a very important logical principle, which is in fact a generalization of the idea of contraposition of hypothetical propositions. Let us illustrate it before we state it.

Suppose that the premises in the following syllogism are true. We wish to demonstrate that the conclusion is necessarily true.

> Some steel is not magnetic.
> All steels are metals.
> ∴ Some metals are not magnetic.

Now the conclusion is either true or false. If it is false, its contradictory: All metals are magnetic: is true. Combining this proposition with the minor of the syllogism, we get:

> All metals are magnetic.
> All steels are metals.
> ∴ All steels are magnetic.

This, however, is a valid mood in the first figure. But since, by hypothesis, both premises of the original syllogism are true, the conclusion of this second syllogism cannot be true. For it contradicts the original major premise. Consequently, the major of this second syllogism cannot be true, or—what is the same thing—the conclusion of the first syllogism cannot be false. It must, therefore, be true.

The validity of the *OAO* syllogism in the third figure is thus demonstrated by means of a valid syllogism in the first figure and the principle known as the *reductio ad absurdum*. The validity of the *AOO* mood in the second figure may be shown in the same way. This method may be used for other moods as well.

Let us now exhibit the principle of the *reductio ad absurdum* in more abstract form. Let p represent *Some steel is not magnetic,* q represent *All steels are metals,* and r represent *Some metals are not magnetic.* And let p', q', r' symbolize the *contradictories* of each of these propositions respectively. Then the original syllogism asserts that p and q together imply r. Or symbolically, $(p . q) \supset r$. Now what we have shown was that the contradictory of r, together with q, implies the contradictory of p. Symbolically this may be stated: $(q . r') \supset p'$. And the reduction of the first syllogism depends on the *equivalence* between these two implications. This equivalence is an easy extension of the equivalence between a hypothetical proposition and its contrapositive, for we have shown that if *a* and *b* are any two propositions $(a \supset b) \equiv (b' \supset a')$. We now have:

$$[(p \cdot q) \supset r] \equiv [(q \cdot r') \supset p'] \equiv [(p \cdot r') \supset q']$$

The principle of indirect reduction may therefore be analyzed as follows: *The syllogism is a form of inference in which two propositions* p *and* q *jointly imply a third* r, *where the three propositions contain three and only three terms.* If, however, we deny the implication $[(p \cdot q) \supset r]$, we must also deny a second implication which is equivalent to it: $[(q \cdot r') \supset p']$. But this second implication in our illustration above was a valid syllogism in *Barbara,* which cannot be denied. Therefore the first implication, which represents an *OAO* syllogism in the third figure (*Bocardo*) cannot be doubted either. For the denial of the validity of *Bocardo* commits us to the denial of the validity of *Barbara,* which is absurd.

If weakened and strengthened forms are not permitted (that is, if we do not assume existential import for universal propositions), reduction enables us to see that all syllogistic arguments can be reduced to two forms: one in which both premises are universal, and the other in which one premise is particular. The former is an argument in which both propositions may be pure hypotheses; the latter involves statements of fact ultimately dependent on observation.

§ 11. THE ANTILOGISM OR INCONSISTENT TRIAD

The principle involved in indirect reduction has been extended by Mrs. Christine Ladd Franklin in such a way as to provide a new and very powerful method for testing the validity of any syllogism. We shall, however, in discussing this method drop the assumption we have made concerning the existence of the classes denoted by the terms of the syllogism. As a consequence, the weakened and strengthened moods must be eliminated as invalid.

Consider the valid syllogism:

> All musicians are proud.
> All Scotchmen are musicians.
> ∴ All Scotchmen are proud.

If we let *S, M,* and *P* symbolize the terms "Scotchmen," "musicians," and "proud individuals," and if we make use of the analysis we have given of what asserted is by categorical proposition in

Chapter IV, this syllogism must be interpreted to assert the following:

$$M\bar{P} = 0$$
$$S\bar{M} = 0$$
$$\therefore \; S\bar{P} = 0$$

Now if the premises *All musicians are proud* and *All Scotchmen are musicians* necessarily imply *All Scotchmen are proud,* it follows that these premises are incompatible with the *contradictory* of this conclusion. Hence the three propositions:

1. All musicians are proud.
2. All Scotchmen are musicians.
3. Some Scotchmen are not proud:

are *inconsistent* with one another. They cannot all three be true together. Symbolically stated,

$$M\bar{P} = 0$$
$$S\bar{M} = 0$$
$$S\bar{P} \neq 0$$

are inconsistent. A triad of propositions two of which are the premises of a valid syllogism while the third is the contradictory of its conclusion, is called an *antilogism* or *inconsistent triad.*

An examination of the antilogism above reveals, however, that any two propositions of the triad necessarily imply the *contradictory* of the third. (This can be shown to be true in general, and is a further extension of the equivalence between a hypothetical proposition and its contrapositive.) Thus, if we take the first two of the triad as premises, we get:

All musicians are proud.
All Scotchmen are musicians.
∴ All Scotchmen are proud:

$$M\bar{P} = 0$$
$$S\bar{M} = 0$$
$$\therefore \; S\bar{P} = 0$$

which is the original syllogism from which the triad was obtained. If we take the first and third of the triad as premises, we get:

All musicians are proud.
Some Scotchmen are not proud.
∴ Some Scotchmen are not musicians:

$$M\bar{P} = 0$$
$$S\bar{P} \neq 0$$
$$\therefore \; S\bar{M} \neq 0$$

which is a valid mood in the second figure. Finally, if we take the second and third of the triad as premises, we get:

All Scotchmen are musicians.	$S\bar{M} = 0$
Some Scotchmen are not proud.	$S\bar{P} \neq 0$
∴ Some musicians are not proud:	$\therefore M\bar{P} \neq 0$

which is a valid mood in the third figure.

The reader is advised to take a different valid mood of the syllogism, and obtain from it the inconsistent triad and the other two valid syllogisms to which it is equivalent.

The Structure of the Antilogism

Let us now examine the structure of the antilogism. The reader will note, in the first place, that it contains two universal propositions and one particular proposition. This is the same as saying that in the symbolic representation of the members of the triad, there are two *equations,* and one *inequation,* because a universal proposition is interpreted as denying existence, while a particular proposition asserts it. Confining his attention to the symbolic representation, the reader will find, in the second place, that the two universals have a common term, which is once positive and once negative. Finally, the particular proposition contains the other two terms. It can be shown without difficulty that these three conditions are present in every antilogism, and the reader should not hesitate to prove that this is so.

Now since every valid syllogism corresponds to an antilogism, we can employ the conditions we have discovered in every antilogism as a test for the validity of any syllogism. Hence it is possible to develop the theory of the categorical syllogism on the basis of the conditions for the antilogism. The single principle required is: *A syllogism is valid if it corresponds to an antilogism whose structure conforms to the three conditions above.*

The theory of the antilogism represents an attempt to discover a more general basis for the syllogism and other inferences studied in traditional logic. The reader will note the elegance and the power which result from the introduction of specially designed symbols. We shall indicate in the following chapter the close connection between advances in logical theory and improvement in symbolism. We will conclude this discussion, however, by indicating how the antilogism may be used to test syllogisms for their validity.

Is the following valid?

> Some Orientals are polite.
> All Orientals are shrewd.
> $\therefore$ Some shrewd people are polite.

Letting S, P, O stand for the minor, major, and middle terms respectively, the symbolic equivalent of this inference is: $OP \neq 0$, $O\bar{S} = 0$, $\therefore SP \neq 0$. The equivalent antilogism is: $OP \neq 0$, $O\bar{S} = 0$, $SP = 0$. This contains two universals and one particular; the universals have a common term which is once positive and once negative; and the particular contains the other two terms. The syllogism is therefore valid.

Is the following valid?

> Some professors are not married.
> All saints are married.
> $\therefore$ Some saints are not professors.

Letting S, P, M stand for the minor, major, and middle terms, this may be stated symbolically as: $P\bar{M} \neq 0$, $S\bar{M} = 0$, $S\bar{P} \neq 0$. The equivalent antilogism is: $P\bar{M} \neq 0$, $S\bar{M} = 0$, $S\bar{P} = 0$. This contains two universals and one particular, but the common term in the former is not positive once and negative once. Hence the syllogism is invalid.

§ 12. THE SORITES

It sometimes happens that the evidence for a conclusion consists of more than two propositions. The inference is not a syllogism in such cases, and the examination of all possible ways in which more than two propositions may be combined to yield a conclusion requires a more general approach to logic than the traditional discussions make possible—or an elementary treatise permits. In certain special cases, however, the principles of the syllogism enable us to evaluate such more complex inferences. Thus, from the premises:

> All dictatorships are undemocratic.
> All undemocratic governments are unstable.
> All unstable governments are cruel.
> All cruel governments are objects of hate:

we may infer the conclusion:

> All dictatorships are objects of hate.

The inference may be tested by means of the syllogistic rules, for the argument is a *chain* of syllogisms in which the conclusion of one becomes a premise of another. In this illustration, however, the conclusions of all the syllogisms except the last remain unexpressed. A chain of syllogisms in which the conclusion of one is a premise in another, in which all the conclusions except the last one are unexpressed, and in which the premises are so arranged that any two successive ones contain a common term, is called a *sorites*.

The above illustration is an *Aristotelian sorites*. In it, the first premise contains the subject of the conclusion, and the common term of two successive propositions appears first as a predicate and next as a subject. A second form of sorites is the *Goclenian sorites*. The following illustrates it:

> All sacred things are protected by the state.
> All property is sacred.
> All trade monopolies are property.
> All steel industries are trade monopolies.
> ∴ All steel industries are protected by the state.

Here the first premise contains the predicate of the conclusion, and the common term of two successive propositions appears first as subject and next as predicate.

Special rules for the sorites may be given. We shall state them and leave their proof as an exercise for the reader.

Special Rules for the Aristotelian Sorites.

1. No more than one premise may be negative; if a premise is negative, it must be the last.
2. No more than one premise may be particular; if a premise is particular, it must be the first.

Special Rules for the Goclenian Sorites.

1. No more than one premise may be negative; if a premise is negative, it must be the first.
2. No more than one premise may be particular; if a premise is particular, it must be the last.

CHAPTER V

HYPOTHETICAL, ALTERNATIVE, AND
DISJUNCTIVE SYLLOGISMS

§ 1. THE HYPOTHETICAL SYLLOGISM

In the introductory chapter we saw that the province of logical study is the classification and examination of the evidential value of propositions. Subsequently we discovered that a set of propositions may stand to another set in *six* relations of *dependence,* in virtue of which the first set may be taken as adequate evidence for the other set. In the third chapter we examined with some care some of these relations of dependence. We must now study in greater detail the oppositional relation of superimplication. The various forms of this relation occupy a central rôle in the demonstrative sciences as well as in daily discourse.

In George Moore's historical romance *Héloïse and Abélard* the following discussion is reported between a medieval realist and a nominalistic disciple of Abélard:

"It was plain to all that the Nominalist was not fighting fairly by thrusting theology into Dialectics, but since he had chosen to do so he must take the consequences, and everybody knew that the consequences were that the Realist would do likewise. 'Ah, you are quick, pupil and disciple of Pierre du Pallet . . . you are quick to turn what I offered as an analogy into an argument of heresy against my person. I will meet you on the same ground and with the same weapon. Will you tell us if this concept, this image in the mind of man, of God, of matter, for I know not where to seek it, be a reality?' 'I hold it as, in a manner, real.' 'I want a categorical answer.' 'I must qualify—' 'I will have no qualifications, a substance is or is not.' 'Well, then, my concept is a sign.' 'A sign of what?' 'A sound, a word, a symbol, an echo of my ignorance.' 'Nothing then! So truth and virtue of humanity do not exist at all. You suppose

yourself to exist, but you have no means of knowing God; therefore to you God does not exist except as an echo of your ignorance!
And what concerns you most, the Church does not exist except as
your concept of certain individuals whom you cannot regard as a
unity, and who suppose themselves to believe in a Trinity which
exists only as a sound or symbol. I will not repeat your words, pupil,
disciple, whatever you are pleased to call yourself, of Le Sieur Pierre
du Pallet, outside of this house, for the consequences to you would
be deadly; but it is only too clear that you are a materialist, and
as such your fate must be settled by a Church Council, unless you
prefer the stake by judgment of a secular court.' " [1]

Let us distinguish the steps of this argument, supplying the propositions which are taken for granted:

1. If a concept in the mind of man is a sign, it is a sign of a sound,
   and an echo of ignorance.
   If a concept is a sign of a sound, it is a sign of nothing real.
   ∴ If a concept in the mind of man is a sign, it is a sign of
   nothing real.

2. If a concept in the mind of man is a sign, it is a sign of nothing
   real.
   But truth, virtue, God, the Church, the Trinity, are concepts
   in the mind of man.
   ∴ These things are signs of nothing real.

3. If anyone believes that these things represent nothing real,
   such a one is a materialist.
   The Nominalist is such a one.
   ∴ The Nominalist is a materialist.

The substance of the discussion is thus analyzable into three distinct steps. Inferences 2 and 3 are of the same logical form, as we
shall point out in a moment; inference 1 is of different form. Inferences of the type of 2 and 3 are said to be *mixed hypothetical syllogisms*. They contain three propositions: the first, or *major*, premise
is a hypothetical, the second, or *minor*, premise is a categorical, and
the conclusion also is a categorical proposition. Inferences of the
type of 1 are called *pure hypothetical syllogisms*. They contain two
hypotheticals as premises, and a hypothetical as conclusion.

Why is the conclusion in either of the mixed syllogisms above
validly inferable from the premises? The reader is prepared by now
to give an answer. The correct answer is that if we assert a hypo-

[1] Vol. I, p. 70.

thetical proposition and also assert the truth of its antecedent, we necessarily commit ourselves to assert the consequent.

We may state this differently. The conjunctive proposition *If war is declared prices go up, and war is declared* implies the proposition *Prices go up*. In fact, the conjunctive proposition is the principal or superalternant to *Prices go up*. If then we assert the truth of the conjunctive, we must also assert the truth of its subaltern.

The value of this type of reasoning is very evident. For we may often be able to establish the truth of a hypothetical proposition and also the truth of its antecedent more easily than we can the truth of the consequent. The consequent may then be established *indirectly,* as the conclusion of such an inference. Thus, all attempts to trisect any angle with compass and ruler must be regarded today as useless, because the following two propositions are known to be true: If a geometric construction is expressible as an irreducible algebraic equation of degree greater than two, it cannot be constructed by compass and straight edge alone: and: The trisection of an angle is expressible by an irreducible cubic equation. The trisection of an angle by elementary methods is therefore impossible; this is a result which could have been established in no way other than as the conclusion of a mixed hypothetical syllogism.

The schematic form of the argument is: If A is B, then C is D; A is B; therefore C is D. If we employ the symbols previously explained this takes the form: $p \supset q$; p; $\therefore q$. The inference is said to be in the *mood,* or *modus, ponendo ponens.* This expression signifies that by affirming (in the minor premise) we affirm (in the conclusion). It is derived from the Latin *ponere,* which means to take a stand or to affirm.

Suppose we know that *If there is a total eclipse of the sun, the streets are dark* is true. May we then offer as conclusive evidence for *There is a total eclipse of the sun* the proposition *The streets are dark*? If we did, the inference would be fallacious. For the hypothetical simply asserts that if the antecedent is true, the consequent must also be true; it does not assert that the consequent is true *only on the condition* that the antecedent is true. Thus the streets may be dark at night or on cloudy days, as well as during a total eclipse. It is therefore a fallacy to affirm the consequent and infer the truth of the antecedent. We shall have frequent occasions to call the reader's attention to this fallacy. It is sometimes committed by eminent men of science who fail to distinguish between necessary and probable inferences, or who disregard the distinction between demonstrating a proposition and verifying it. For example, if the theory of organic evolution is true, we should find fossil remains of extinct animal forms; but the discovery of such remains is not a proof, is not conclusive evidence, for the theory.

But while it is fallacious to affirm the consequent of a hypothetical, we can obtain a valid conclusion by denying it. Suppose we wished to know whether Tom Mooney is guilty of placing the bomb in the Preparedness Day Parade of 1916 in San Francisco. We may discover, after studying the nature of the bomb, that *If Mooney is guilty, he was on the street corner within ten minutes of the time when the explosion occurred.* But suppose now Mooney has an alibi, and that he can show he was a mile away on an impassable street fifteen minutes before the explosion. We would then have to deny the consequent of the hypothetical, and this denial commits all students of logic, if not all politicians, to the denial of the antecedent. For the hypothetical asserts that it is not the case that the antecedent is true and the consequent false.

The contradictory of the antecedent is, in fact, a subaltern to the conjunctive proposition *If Mooney is guilty, he was on the scene of the explosion within ten minutes of the event* and *He was not on the scene of the explosion within ten minutes of the event.* If we assert the truth of this superaltern, we must assert the truth of the subaltern, because the former implies the latter.

Inferences of this type are the chief methods used to *disprove* suggested theories. Is every point of the earth's surface equidistant from a point internal to it? When we take certain physical principles for granted, it can be demonstrated that *If the earth is a sphere, then a pendulum of specified length will make two swings per second at every point on the earth's surface.* But it can be shown experimentally that there is a variation in the number of swings per second such a pendulum makes as it is moved along a meridian circle. It follows that the earth is not spherical in shape.

This type of argument may be represented schematically as follows: If *A* is *B*, then *C* is *D*; *C* is not *D*; therefore *A* is not *B*. Also as $p \supset q$; q'; $\therefore p'$. The inference is in the *modus tollendo tollens*, for by denying (in the minor) we deny (in the conclusion). The expression is derived from the Latin *tollere*, meaning to lift up or to deny.

Can the consequent of a hypothetical proposition be disproved by offering as evidence the falsity of the antecedent? Suppose we inquire whether two rectangular plots of ground have equal areas. We may perhaps know that *If two rectangular plots have their corresponding sides equal, then their areas are equal.* But suppose we discover by actual measurement that the corresponding sides are unequal. Can we validly infer that the areas are unequal also?

Assuredly we cannot. For example, the sides of one of the plots may be four and five units long respectively, and the sides of the other two and ten units long; nevertheless, the areas of the plots are the same. It is a fallacy, therefore, to deny the antecedent and infer the falsity of the consequent. This fallacy is committed not infrequently by men in public affairs and other hard-headed individuals. Thus it may be claimed that *If Congress interferes with the plans of the President, the industrial depression will not be conquered.* And it is frequently believed, as if it were a logical consequence from this, that if only Congress would adjourn or not meet, the depression would be overcome.

§ 2. THE ALTERNATIVE SYLLOGISM

We next consider the valid inferences which can be drawn from an alternative proposition as major premise and a categorical as minor premise. Such arguments are called *mixed alternative syllogisms.* Thomas Paine discussed the nature of the British Constitution in his *Rights of Man* in the form of such an inference:

". . . Governments arise either *out* of the people or *over* the people. The English Government is one of those which arose out of conquest, and not out of society, and consequently it arose over the people. . . ."

Under what conditions may a conclusion be validly drawn from an alternative proposition as the major premise of a syllogism? Suppose the reader thinks he has been overcharged by the telephone company for services rendered during some month, and he decides to take action. He may decide *Either I will write the company or I will call at its offices.* If this proposition is true, *at least one* of the alternants must be true, but the possibility of both being true is not excluded. Hence if the reader should write his letter of protest, we cannot infer validly that he will not also visit the company's offices; or if he should make his intended visit, we cannot infer validly that he will not also write the letter. We reason fallaciously from an alternative major premise when we conclude that one of the alternants is false because the other is true.

On the other hand, if the reader should suddenly be called out of town, so that he cannot make a personal call on the company, it follows that he will write the letter. Or if he finally decides that letter-writing is of no use, it follows that he will visit the offices. Hence an alternative syllogism is valid when the minor denies one of the alternants, and the conclusion affirms the truth of the other.

THE DISJUNCTIVE SYLLOGISM

We shall restate this result in order to exhibit the oppositional relation of the premises to the conclusion. The conjunctive *Either I will write the company, or I will call at its offices, and I will not write* implies the proposition *I will call at its offices.* The conjunctive is thus the superaltern to the conclusion.

The alternative syllogism, we shall see in detail later, is frequently employed to *eliminate* suggested explanations or solutions of problems. Which factor in the total environment explains the variations in the local weather? We may suppose tentatively that the possible factors are the distance from the sun, the duration of exposure to the sun's rays, the variations in air currents. If we can eliminate one of these possibilities, it will follow, *on the supposition that the alternative proposition is true,* that the cause of local weather is to be found among the remaining suggested explanations. But the reader should note that we do *not* eliminate any of the other factors if we can show, for example, that local weather varies with the behavior of the air currents. For it may be that each of the other factors contributes something to the character of the local weather.

The schematic form of this type of inference is: Either *A is B* or *C is D; A is not B;* therefore *C is D.* Or: $p \lor q; p'; \therefore q$. The inference is said to be in the *modus tollendo ponens,* because by denying (in the minor) we affirm (in the conclusion).

§ 3. THE DISJUNCTIVE SYLLOGISM

"But," the reader may protest, "an inference you have classified as invalid is often admitted as quite correct. For suppose you did not know the exact month of Shakespeare's birth, although you could assert that *Either he was born in April or in May.* And suppose that you subsequently discovered that he was born in April. Would you not infer that Shakespeare was not born in May? And in that case, would you not go counter to the rule you had set up that in alternative syllogisms the minor must *deny* one of the alternants?"

The reader is quite right. But does his illustration really violate the rule we have stated? Examination shows that it does not. For the inference is valid only if we assume an *unexpressed* premise—namely, that one of the alternants *excludes* the other. The major premise in the reader's example when stated in full is as follows: *Either Shakespeare was born in April or in May, and he was not born both in April and in May.* This is a conjunctive proposition, and the part of it which is the real premise for the reader's argu ment is the conjunct stating a *disjunction*. Such disjunctive propo-sitions are often taken for granted and therefore not expressed ex-plicitly. Nevertheless, they should be made explicit to make clear all the premises involved.

It is advisable, therefore, to consider separately *disjunctive syl-logisms*. In such arguments the major is a disjunctive proposition and the minor a categorical. Let us find the conditions under which they are valid.

Suppose we know that *It is not the case that both my watch is an accurate timekeeper* and *the behavior of all mechanisms is in-fluenced by climatic changes*. To assert a disjunctive proposition means to assert that at least one of the disjuncts is false. Conse-quently, if we assert *The behavior of all mechanisms is influenced by climatic changes* we must also assert as an inference that *My watch is not an accurate timepiece*. But it would be fallacious to conclude that because one of the disjuncts is false the other is true. A disjunctive syllogism is valid if the minor asserts one of the dis-juncts and the conclusion denies the other.

The schematic form of the argument is: *Not both A is B and C is D; A is B;* therefore *C is not D*. Or $(p \cdot q)'$; p; $\therefore q'$. The infer-ence is said to be in the *modus ponendo tollens,* since by affirming (in the minor) we deny (in the conclusion).

We may now summarize the valid and invalid inferences we have been examining so far in the present chapter.

	Valid	*Invalid*
Ponendo ponens	If p then q p $\therefore q$	If p then q q $\therefore p$
Tollendo tollens	If p then q q' $\therefore p'$	If p then q p' $\therefore q'$
Tollendo ponens	Either p or q p' $\therefore q$	Not both p and q p' $\therefore q$
Ponendo tollens	Not both p and q p $\therefore q'$	Either p or q p $\therefore q'$

§ 4. THE REDUCTION OF MIXED SYLLOGISMS

Some of these principles are doubtless very familiar to the reader, and all of them may have been employed by him all his life, without his having explicitly formulated the principles according to which he had been drawing his inferences. Neither their familiarity nor their simplicity takes away from their importance. These principles are fundamental to all logical theory. They emerge repeatedly in every inquiry into the evidential value of propositions advanced to support other propositions.

These principles, however, are not independent of one another. If the reader bears in mind the equivalences which have been established between compound propositions, he will have no difficulty in reducing an argument in one modus to an argument in any other. We shall therefore simply state the equivalences between the four modi in the following table without further comment:

	Equivalent Syllogisms	*Symbolic Form*
Ponendo ponens	If a man is civilized, he has questioned his first principles. This man is civilized. ∴ This man has questioned his first principles.	$p \supset q$ p $\therefore q$
Tollendo tollens	If a man has not questioned his first principles, he is not civilized. This man is civilized. ∴ This man has questioned his first principles.	$q' \supset p'$ p $\therefore q$
Tollendo ponens	Either a man is not civilized, or he has questioned his first principles. This man is civilized. ∴ This man has questioned his first principles.	$p' \, v \, q$ p $\therefore q$
Ponendo tollens	It is not the case that both a man is civilized and he has not questioned his first principles. This man is civilized. ∴ This man has questioned his first principles.	$(p \cdot q')'$ p $\therefore q$

§ 5. PURE HYPOTHETICAL AND ALTERNATIVE SYLLOGISMS

We must now turn to the pure hypothetical syllogisms to which we were introduced at the beginning of this chapter.

Consider the following argument:

If the production cost of a commodity is reduced, a greater economic demand sets in for it.

If a commodity is produced in large quantities, the production cost per unit is reduced.

∴ If a commodity is produced in large quantities, a greater economic demand sets in for it.

The first two premises conjoined imply the conclusion, so that the latter is a subaltern to the premises. The premise which contains as component the consequent of the conclusion is called the *major* premise; the premise which contains the antecedent of the conclusion is called the *minor*. The validity of the syllogism clearly depends on the *transitivity* of the "if . . . then" or implication relation. It may be schematized as follows: If C is D, then E is F; if A is B, then C is D; therefore, if A is B, then E is F. Or more abstractly, $q \supset r; p \supset q; \therefore p \supset r$.

Let us now examine:

If a man is healthy, his body is not undernourished.
If a man is poor, his body is undernourished.
∴ If a man is healthy, he is not poor.

In this syllogism the minor is written first. It is valid argument, although it is not quite of the same form as the first illustration. It may be schematized as follows: If A is B, C is not D; if E is F, C is D; therefore if A is B, E is not F. Or as: $r \supset q'; p \supset q; \therefore r \supset p'$. The dependence of the validity of the argument upon the transitivity of the "if . . . then" relation is not as evident now as before. Nevertheless, this condition is still the basis for the valid inference. We can show this by reducing it to a syllogism having the same form as the first one. We need only substitute the equivalent contrapositive of the major premise, as follows:

If a man's body is not undernourished, he is not poor.
If a man is healthy, his body is not undernourished.
∴ If a man is healthy, he is not poor.

Not all pure hypothetical syllogisms are valid. The following is not:

If workmen unite, they enjoy satisfactory conditions of labor.
If workmen are not conscious of their common interests, they do not unite.
∴ If workmen are not conscious of their common interests, they do not enjoy satisfactory conditions of labor.

The reader should discover for himself by actual trial that the form of this invalid syllogism is different from either of the valid forms above, and that it cannot be reduced to either one of the valid forms.

Inferences in which the premises are two alternative propositions are called *pure alternative syllogisms*. They occur rather rarely. Consider the following:

Either men are cowards, or they protest against unjust treatment.
Either men are not cowards, or they do not protect their own economic interests.
∴ Either men do not protect their own economic interests, or they protest against unjust treatment.

This syllogism is valid. But we need not examine, in this place, the conditions of validity, since the reader may *test* the validity of any pure alternative syllogism by reducing it to a pure hypothetical form. The one above may be reduced as follows:

If men are not cowards, they protest against unjust treatment.
If men protect their own economic interests, they are not cowards.
∴ If men protect their economic interests, they protest against unjust treatment.

The conclusion of this pure hypothetical is obviously equivalent to the conclusion of the pure alternative syllogism above.

§ 6. THE DILEMMA

Hypothetical and alternative propositions may be combined in various ways to yield arguments more complex than any considered so far. We cannot study them all, and shall confine ourselves to the argument known as the dilemma. But the reader should note that the dilemma introduces no new logical principle, and that except for the dictates of tradition and the interesting uses to which it may be put, there is no good reason why we should discuss it rather than other complex forms of reasoning.

The *dilemma* is an argument in which one premise, the major, is the conjunctive assertion of two hypothetical propositions, and in which a second premise, the minor, is an alternative proposition. The minor either affirms alternatively the antecedents of the major, or denies alternatively its consequents.

Dilemmas in which the minor alternatively affirms the antecedents of the major are said to be *constructive*. Those in which the minor alternatively denies the consequents of the major are *destructive*. In constructive dilemmas, the antecedents of the major must be different propositions, while its consequents may be either different or identical. In the former case, the dilemma is *complex constructive*, in the latter, *simple constructive*. When the dilemma is destructive, the consequents of the major must be different, while the antecedents may be either different or identical. In the former case, the dilemma is *complex destructive*, in the latter, *simple destructive*. There are, therefore, four distinct kinds of dilemmas. Let us illustrate each.

1. Complex Constructive Dilemma

If women adorn themselves for ostentation, they are vain; and if women adorn themselves in order to attract men, they are immoral.

Either women adorn themselves for ostentation or in order to attract men.

∴ Either women are vain, or they are immoral.

2. Simple Constructive Dilemma

If it is assumed that the angle sum of a triangle is two right angles, Euclid's Postulate 5 can be demonstrated; and if it is assumed that these are two similar triangles with unequal areas Postulate 5 can be demonstrated.

It is assumed that either the angle sum of a triangle is two right angles, or that there are two similar triangles with unequal areas.

∴ Euclid's Postulate 5 can be demonstrated.

3. Complex Destructive Dilemma

If the country goes to war, the unemployment problem can be solved; and if the country does not change its industrial structure, a revolution will take place.

Either the unemployment problem cannot be solved, or a revolution will not take place.

∴ Either the country will abstain from war, or it alters its industrial structure.

4. Simple Destructive Dilemma

If you have a habit of whistling, you are a moron; if you have a habit of whistling, you are not musical.

Either you are not a moron or you are musical.
∴ You have not a habit of whistling.[2]

The Value of Dilemmas

Dilemmatic reasoning is of special value in those cases where we are unable to assert the truth of *any one* of the antecedents or the falsity of *any one* of the consequents in a set of hypothetical propositions, but where we can assert *alternatively* their respective truth or falsity. Thus, although we may not know for what purposes some particular woman adorns herself, on the basis of the premises in the first example above we can conclude that at any rate she is either vain or immoral. And for certain purposes, that may be all the information we need.

The dilemma has become associated in the minds of many with sharp intellectual practices common in debates and polemical literature. This has led to the view that the dilemma is a fallacious form of reasoning. But such an opinion has as little foundation as a similar opinion would have concerning any other valid form of inference, which may none the less be fallaciously used. It is worth while, therefore, because of this persistent misunderstanding, to examine the possible ways of avoiding the admission of the conclusion of a dilemma. But it should be clear that this can be done only by taking exception to the *material truth* of one or other of its premises.

Escaping Between the Horns

The opponent against whom a dilemma is directed may destroy the force of the argument by pointing out that the alternatives enumerated in the minor premise are not exhaustive. Since the alternatives are said to be the "horns of the dilemma" upon which the adversary is to be impaled, he is said "to escape between the horns" by this method.

How may this be done for the first dilemma stated above? St. Thomas Aquinas, who has discussed the question "Whether the Adornment of Women is Devoid of Mortal Sin?" in his *Summa Theologica,* points out that women may adorn themselves not only

---

[2] It might properly be urged that the common meaning "dilemma" is an argument in which there are two alternative hypotheses, and that what we have called the simple destructive dilemma contains no such alternative, but is only a hypothetical syllogism with a disjunctive consequent in the major premise, for example *If you have a habit of whistling you are a moron or you are not musical.* But this objection is only verbal, since we have defined the dilemma to include the last form.

for the reasons given, but also to hide their physical defects, in which case he believes their action is meritorious. Furthermore, one of the alternatives in the minor may be broken into several alternatives which do not all have the same consequences. Thus St. Thomas distinguishes between the women who adorn themselves to attract men who are not their husbands, and those who adorn themselves to attract their husbands. In the latter case, according to the saint, a woman's action is meritorious.

Taking the Dilemma by the Horns

The opponent may challenge the truth of the major premise. He can do this by flatly contradicting the major, or by showing that some one or other of the antecedents leads to different consequents from those stated. He is then said to "take the dilemma by the horns," that is, by the alternatives offered. Thus, in the first of the above dilemmas we may accept the alternatives offered but deny the major by maintaining that if women adorn themselves to attract men, they do so only in order to save men from worse follies; in that case they should be regarded as kindly.

Rebutting a Dilemma

Finally, the adversary may answer a dilemma with another argument whose conclusion *contradicts* the original conclusion. A rebutting dilemma, however, often only *appears* to contradict the first conclusion. It may then convince an untrained audience, but its logical value is meretricious.

An Athenian mother is said to have cautioned her son from entering public life:

> If you tell the truth, men will hate you; if you tell lies, the gods will hate you.
> But you must either tell the truth or tell lies.
> ∴ Either men or the gods will hate you.

The son is reported to have replied with a rebutting dilemma:

> If I tell the truth, the gods will love me; if I tell lies, men will love me.
> But I must either tell the truth or tell lies.
> ∴ Either men or the gods will love me.

The reader is now equipped to see that the conclusion of the second dilemma does not contradict the conclusion of the first. It only *appears* to do so, although in fact the two conclusions are perfectly compatible. For the genuine contradictory of the first conclusion is *Men will love me and the gods will love me.*

We may symbolize a dilemma and its specious rebuttal as follows: The first dilemma is:

$$(p \supset q) \cdot (r \supset s)$$
$$p \lor r$$
$$\therefore q \lor s$$

The rebutting dilemma is: $(p \supset s') \cdot (r \supset q')$
$$p \lor r$$
$$\therefore s' \lor q'$$

It is clear that $(q \lor s)$ and $(s' \lor q')$ are not contradictories.

CHAPTER VI

GENERALIZED OR MATHEMATICAL LOGIC

§ 1. LOGIC AS THE SCIENCE OF TYPES OF ORDER

In the previous chapters we have seen that the validity of a demonstration depends not on the truth or falsity of the premises, but upon their form or structure. We have therefore been compelled to recognize that the fundamental task of logic is the study of those objective relations between propositions which condition the validity of the inference by which we pass from premises to conclusions.

Logic has sometimes been defined as the normative science which studies the norms distinguishing sound thinking from unsound thinking. The reader is prepared now to appraise such a definition, and consequently to regard such a characterization of logic as inadequate. For since the study of logic aims to discover the structure of propositions and their objective relations to one another, the capacity of such structures to serve as norms of thought is not their exclusive function, however important it may be. Too great an emphasis on the normative capacity of the structures may incline the student to neglect many of their essential properties in favor of those which may seem to have direct bearing upon normative considerations. Because traditional logic has stressed this side of logical forms, it has failed to consider such forms with sufficient generality and has neglected to undertake a study of all possible formal structures.

Until very recently it was commonly held that Aristotle had explored once for all the entire subject matter of logic. Thus, Kant declared of logic: ". . . Since Aristotle it has not had to retrace a single step, unless we choose to consider as improvements the removal of some unnecessary subtleties, or the clearer definition of its matter, both of which refer to the elegance rather than to the solidity of the science. It is remarkable also, that to the present day, it has not been able to make one step in advance, so that, to all appearance, it may be considered as completed and perfect." [1]

If, however, the reader will turn to some of the illustrations of mathematical reasoning we have cited, he will soon discover that traditional logic has fallen short of its self-appointed task. For types of inference are employed in them which cannot, except with high artificiality or inconsistency of analysis, be reduced to any of the traditional forms. Thus, implications like the following: *If A is taller than B, and B is taller than C, then A is taller than C* do not fall into any of the types traditionally discussed. From the point of view of logic as an organon which is to guide and test inferences, traditional logic has been remiss in not studying systematically those logical relations which are the basis for the complicated inferences in the mathematical and natural sciences.

In one sense, however, Kant's evaluation of traditional logic is sound. For it has successfully analyzed certain kinds of inferences, and has made clear the formal factors upon which their validity depends. Much of what it has done is of permanent value. Its chief drawbacks are less with what it has done and more with what it has failed to do. Thus it discovered the subject-predicate form of propositions, but failed to note that an identical grammatical construction may cloak propositions of very different types. It stressed the necessity of a copula, but overlooked the logical properties of the copula upon which the validity of an inference rests. It was therefore hindered from developing a more general theory of inference and a more satisfactory calculus of reasoning than the syllogism. The theory of compound propositions was neglected by it, and the important topic of the existential import of propositions was not explicitly considered. Finally, it did not explore logical principles systematically, and so lacked a method for obtaining all the propositions which may be asserted on logical grounds alone.

These limitations may serve to indicate what a program of logical study should include when logic is conceived more adequately. Dissatisfaction with the limited contents of ancient logic is not entirely modern. Thus the Port Royal logicians discussed certain non-syllogistic inferences, such as *The sun is a thing insensible; the Persians worship the sun; therefore the Persians worship a thing insensible*. But they did not make a systematic study of them.

The scope of a more general logic was clearly indicated by

1 *Critique of Pure Reason*, tr. by Max Müller, p. 688.

Leibniz. In his *New Essays concerning the Human Understanding* (1704) he discussed various kinds of asyllogistic inferences, and pointed the way to a "universal mathematics" which would provide the intellectual instruments for exploring any realm of order whatsoever. Elsewhere he indicated more clearly its main features. On the one hand, there should be constructed a "universal language" or "universal characteristics," in order to express by means of specially devised symbols the fundamental, unanalyzable concepts (the "alphabet of human thought") of all the sciences.[2] The modes of combining these symbols must be clearly determined, and all the sciences may then be restated by their means in order to exhibit clearly the logical structure of their subject matter. On the other hand, there should be invented a "universal calculus," as an instrument for operating on the system of ideas expressed symbolically in the universal characteristics. The relations between propositions would then be systematically discovered, and labor and thought would be economized in investigating rationally any subject matter. Leibniz's ideas have been realized in some measure in recent years, through the work of mathematicians and philosophers. But his own contributions were fragmentary, and had little influence on the history of logical studies until his ideas were discovered independently by others.

A renaissance of logical studies began in the first half of the nineteenth century, due almost entirely to the writings of two English mathematicians, Augustus De Morgan and George Boole. Reflection on the processes of mathematics convinced them that an indefinitely larger number of valid inferences were possible than had been hitherto recognized. De Morgan's most notable contribution was to lay the foundation for the theory of relations. Boole discovered that logical processes might be both generalized and expedited if proper symbolic conventions were made. His book *An Investigation of the Laws of Thought* (1854; the title is a misnomer) marked an epoch in the history of logic. It showed, with undeniable power and success, that the methods of mathematics are applicable not only to the study of quantities, but to *any ordered realm whatsoever,* and in particular to the relations between classes and between propositions. The view that the study of logic was the study of *types of order* gradually forced itself upon men. Since Boole's

[2] The idea of a universal mathematical language had already been envisioned by Raymond Lully in the thirteenth century.

time, mathematicians like Weierstrass, Dedekind, Cantor and Peano, and philosophers like Peirce, Frege, Russell, and Whitehead, have made clear the close connection between logic and mathematics.

§ 2. THE FORMAL PROPERTIES OF RELATIONS

An analysis of the general ideas employed in mathematics shows that one of the most pervasive is that of *relation*. A clear understanding of its nature is, moreover, indispensable in the study of propositional structure.

Relations can be illustrated easily, although difficult to define. "Being greater than," "being colder than," "being as old as," "being the father of," are examples of some relations in which objects of various kinds may stand to one another. An object is said to be in a relation if in our statement about it explicit reference must be made to another object. The term *from* which the relation goes is called the *referent*, the term *to* which it goes is the *relatum*. In *Napoleon was the husband of Josephine* the relation is "being the husband of," which connects "Napoleon" and "Josephine." "Napoleon" is the *referent*, "Josephine" the *relatum*. Such a relation is *dyadic*. In *Borgia gave poison to his guest* the relation is "giving," which connects "Borgia," "poison," and "guest." Such a relation is *triadic*.[3] A *tetradic* relation is illustrated in *The United States bought Alaska from Russia for seven million dollars*. Examples of other polyadic relations may be given, although relations with more than four terms are not common.

Further examples of dyadic relations are: *Mussolini is an Italian:* here the relation is "being a member of a class." In *Italians are Europeans* the relation is "being included in the class." The concept of relation replaces the concept of the copula: the copula of traditional logic is a special type of dyadic relation. We shall discuss some of the properties of dyadic relations upon which valid inference depends. But all polyadic relations may also be classified on the basis of the distinctions we shall make.

[3] We have said that the proposition *Borgia gave poison to his guest* illustrates a *triadic* relation. What it asserts is of course also expressible by *Borgia poisoned his guest*, which seems to illustrate a *dyadic* relation. It would be a mistake, however, to regard the distinction between dyadic and triadic relations as merely a verbal matter. Our example only shows that the same situation may be analyzed from *different* though related aspects. The relation of "giving" is triadic, the relation of "poisoning" is dyadic. The two relations are not identical.

Symmetry

In *Napoleon is the husband of Josephine* the relation is "being the husband of"; in *Josephine is the wife of Napoleon* the relation is "being the wife of." This latter relation is said to be the *converse* of the former. If Napoleon stands to Josephine in the relation of "husband of," Josephine does not stand to Napoleon in that same relation. Consequently, the relation "being the husband of" is said to be *asymmetrical*.

In *John is as old as Tom* the relation "being as old as" is symmetrical, for if John has that relation to Tom, Tom has the same relation to John. A symmetrical relation is one which is the same as its converse; an asymmetrical relation is incompatible with its converse. But if *Gentlemen prefer blondes* it may be that *Blondes prefer gentlemen,* or it may also not be. Relations like "loving," which are sometimes symmetrical and sometimes not, are said to be *nonsymmetrical*.

Transitivity

If A *is the father of* B and B *is the father of* C, *then* A *is* not *the father of* C. A relation like "being the father of" is said to be *intransitive*. But if *John is older than Tom* and *Tom is older than Harry,* then *John is older than Harry.* The relation of "being older than" is *transitive*. Some relations are sometimes transitive, sometimes intransitive. If *Caesar is a friend of Brutus* and *Brutus is a friend of Cassius,* Caesar may be a friend of Cassius or he may not. Such relations are said to be *nontransitive*.

The distinctions based on symmetry and transitivity are independent of one another, and we may therefore obtain any one of the following nine types of relations. a. Transitive symmetrical, for example, "being as old as." b. Transitive asymmetrical, for example, "ancestor of." c. Transitive nonsymmetrical, for example, "not older than." d. Intransitive symmetrical, for example, "spouse of." e. Intransitive asymmetrical, for example, "father of." f. Intransitive nonsymmetrical, for example, "nearest blood-relative of." g. Nontransitive symmetrical, for example, "cousin of." h. Nontransitive asymmetrical, for example, "employer of." i. Nontransitive nonsymmetrical, for example, "lover of."

Correlation

A third principle of classification pays attention to the number of objects to which the referent or relatum may be connected by the given relation.

If *Mr. A is a creditor of Mr. B,* other men besides Mr. A may stand in such a relation to Mr. B, and other men besides Mr. B may stand in that relation to Mr. A. Such a relation is said to be *many-many.*

If *Johann Christian Bach is a son of Johann Sebastian Bach,* other individuals besides Johann Christian may stand in this relation to Johann Sebastian, but there is only one individual to whom Johann Christian may stand in this relation. The relation "son of" is called a *many-one* relation.

The converse of a many-one relation is a *one-many* relation. Thus, in *J. S. Bach is the father of J. C. Bach,* J. S. Bach may stand in this relation to other individuals besides J. C. Bach, but only one individual can stand in this relation to J. C. Bach.

Finally, in *Ten is greater by one than nine,* there is only one number to which "ten" may have this relation, and only one number which has this relation to "nine." Relations like "greater by one than" are called *one-one,* and they play a fundamental rôle in the theory of correlations.

Connexity

A fourth principle of classification depends on whether a relation holds between *every pair* of a collection or not. Consider the integers and the relation "greater than." Any two integers either stand to each other in the relation "greater than" or in the converse relation "less than." A relation with this property is said to have *connexity,* otherwise not. The relation "greater than by two" does not possess connexity.

§ 3. THE LOGICAL PROPERTIES OF RELATIONS IN SOME FAMILIAR INFERENCES

Many of the inferences we have studied in previous chapters can be interpreted to depend on the nature of the relations of class inclusion or exclusion. We must indicate briefly in what way the logical properties of these relations, as well as of others, is significant for the study of valid inferences.

1. The conversion of categorical propositions depends on the *symmetry* or *nonsymmetry* of the class inclusion (or exclusion) relation. *All firemen are muscular* may be interpreted to assert that the class "firemen" is included in the class "muscular men." This proposition cannot be converted simply, because total inclusion of one class in another is a nonsymmetrical relation. But *Some firemen are muscular* may be converted, because partial inclusion of

classes is a symmetrical relation. Also *No firemen are muscular* may be converted simply, because total exclusion of one class from another is symmetrical.

2. The validity of categorical syllogisms depends on the *transitivity* of the relation of class inclusion. Consider the syllogism *All men are cowards; all professors are men; all professors are cowards.* It may be interpreted to assert that if the class "men" is included in the class "cowards," and the class "professors" included in the class "men," then the class "professors" is included in the class "cowards." The relation is obviously transitive. Valid syllogisms in other moods and figures may be shown to depend on the same logical property of the copula.

But in those syllogisms where one of the premises is singular, a different analysis is required. Consider the syllogism: *All men are cowards; Mussolini is a man; Mussolini is a coward.* It asserts that if the class "men" is included in the class "cowards," and if "Mussolini" is *a member of* the class "men," then he is *a member of* the class "cowards." In the minor a different type of relation is asserted from that asserted in the major; for the relation "is a member of" is nontransitive (see p. 49), while the relation "is included in" is transitive. The validity of the inference illustrates a modified form of the *dictum de omni*.

3. All the so-called relational (or *a fortiori*) syllogisms depend on the transitivity of the relations. Thus in *John is older than Tom, Tom is older than Henry, John is older than Henry,* the relation "is older than" is transitive.

4. Consider next the sorites:

> All professors are handsome.
> All handsome men are married.
> All married men are well fed.
> ∴ All professors are well fed.

It is clear that the transitivity of the relation of class inclusion is the basis for the inference.

5. Let us finally examine the pure hypothetical syllogism:

> If it rains, I will take my umbrella.
> If I take my umbrella, I am sure to lose it.
> ∴ If it rains, I am sure to lose my umbrella.

Each of the three propositions asserts an implication. The conclusion is a valid consequence because the implication relation is transitive.

§ 4. SYMBOLS: THEIR FUNCTION AND VALUE

If the value of distinguishing various kinds of relations were confined to laying bare the basis of inferences already familiar, the reader might regard such investigations as without much profit. In fact, however, the study of the logical properties of relations is the gateway to the systematic study of more complex inferences. But the more complex forms of inference cannot be studied with any care until a specially devised symbolism is introduced. Because of the prominence of such special symbols in the generalized study of logic, the latter has also been called *symbolic* or *mathematical* logic.

The importance of symbols in the development of modern logic cannot be overestimated. According to Peirce: "The woof and warp of all thought and research is symbols, and the life of thought and science is the life inherent in symbols; so that it is wrong to say that a good language is *important* to good thought, merely, for it is the essence of it." [4] We must therefore inquire into the function and value of symbols.

1. *The Generic Traits of Language.* It will be best to begin with the generic traits of all languages. Languages differ from one another in two ways: different phonetic or ideographic elements are employed in them; and different groups of ideas are expressed by fixed phonetic and graphic elements. But the experiences which a language intends to express and communicate vary in an unlimited manner, while the language employs only a finite number of fundamental linguistic elements, which may be called word stems. It follows that every language, as we know it, must be based upon a far-reaching classification or categorization of experience. Sense impressions and emotional states are grouped on the basis of broad similarities, although no two of them are identical in every respect. Such groupings indicate, therefore, the presence of a large number of characteristics common to each group. Furthermore, various kinds of relations between these several groupings also come to be noted, and require to be expressed in language.

What groupings of experiences are made depends upon the interests of those using the language, as well as upon the subject matter which comes to be expressed. Consequently, the categorizations of experience which are satisfactory for one purpose may be inept for another; and the language which functions as a satisfactory symbolic scheme on one occasion may be too clumsy or too subtle for

[4] Collected Papers, Vol. II, p. 129.

another. In any case, the reader must note that *all* language, and
not merely symbolic logic, is symbolic. All communication and inquiry must take place by means of words, sounds, graphic marks,
gestures, and so on. Words *refer* to something, whether it be to the
emotions, to ideas, or to that which ideas are about. When we say,
"There is a fire next door," the sounds we utter *are* not what they
signify. The sounds, for example, do not burn, they are not a definite number of feet distant, and so on. They do signify something
to someone.

Since the groupings of experiences upon which languages are
based are generally not sharply demarcated from one another, all
languages suffer in some degree from vagueness. Thus, although
the number of distinguishable shades of color is very large, only a
few colors receive special names. In different languages different
colors receive special names, and the limits of what constitutes
one color are also frequently different. Even in scientific languages
there is a fringe of uncertainty as to the limits of the denotation
or application of names.

In virtue of the fact that on the one hand the number of word
stems in any language is small, while on the other hand the number of varieties of experience is unlimited, it is necessary to represent many of the latter by combining the word stems in some manner. These modes of combination are the *formal elements* in the
language, and are the theoretical basis for grammar. But it is clear
that the formal aspects of a language are not altogether arbitrary.
For the combination of word stems must represent experiences so
made up that they are analyzable into relations between what is
denoted by the word stems taken in isolation. Although grammar
cannot be a substitute for logical analysis, there is a kinship between logic and grammar. For grammatical structure also represents certain abstract relations which a subject matter possesses
when expressed in language.

Ordinary languages have been devised to meet practical needs,
for which fine distinctions may be useless or even a hindrance. Most
language is emotive or ceremonial in character, aiming to convey
or provoke some emotion. These facts, coupled with the foregoing
considerations, make it clear that such languages cannot be used
to represent adequately, and without serious modification, those
distinctions which are the outcome of subtle analyses, or which arise
from a classification of experience made for different purposes.
Therefore, if we wish to avoid the distortion which the emotional
and intellectual overtones of ordinary words introduce when we

are making careful analyses; if we wish to restrict as much as possible the vagueness of common symbols; if we desire to prevent the often subtle transformations which the meaning of verbal symbols undergoes—then it is essential to devise a specially constructed symbolism.

Linguistic Changes

How words change their meanings is a fascinating study. We shall have occasion to point out in the next chapter some of the confusions which have taken place in the philosophy of mathematics because this fact of change has been overlooked. We shall restrict ourselves here to noting two ways in which the original meaning of words may become totally lost and other meanings substituted for it.

One such way has been called *generalization*. The same symbol may come to denote a *more extended class* of objects, so that it no longer denotes with accuracy the more specific things it may once have symbolized. Thus "paper" once denoted papyrus; it was next employed to denote writing material made of old rags; today it symbolizes not only the product of rags, but also the product of chemically treated wood pulp. The history of the word "number" also illustrates such a process of progressive generalization. It once denoted only integers, then gradually included fractions, irrationals, transcendentals like π, and even determinants. Other such words are "force," "energy," "geometry," and "equality."

A second way in which meanings become altered is by *specialization*. The same symbol may become restricted in its application to a smaller range of objects, so that it comes to denote more specific characters than it once did. Thus the word "surgeon" once meant anyone who worked with his hands; today it is restricted to those with special medical training. Other words whose history illustrates the process of specialization are "minister," "physician," and "artist."

A fertile and interesting source of change in the meaning of words arises when their application is broadened because of a *metaphorical extension* of their meaning. Thus "governor" originally meant a steersman on a boat, "spirit" meant breath; a bend in a pipe is called an "elbow," the corresponding parts of a pipe-fitting are called "male" and "female," and so on.

The Value of Special Symbols

Let us now state summarily the advantages which we can expect from a specially devised symbolism. In the first place, such symbols enable us to distinguish and keep distinct different meanings. We need only agree to employ a different symbol for each distinct notion and to have no symbol represent more than one notion. The ambiguity with which ordinary language is infected is then at a minimum.

In the second place, a convenient symbol enables us to concentrate upon what is essential in a given context. When in mathematics we substitute a single letter like R for a complex expression like $(a + b + c + d)$; or when we use letters like S, P, M for the terms "Socrates," "mortal," "man," in a syllogism, we make clear that the results of our reasoning depend not on the *special* meaning of these expressions, but on the abstract relations which connect them with others.

A third important function of symbols is to exhibit clearly and concisely the *form* of propositions. This has long been recognized in mathematics. Thus, to take an elementary illustration, the difference in form between $4x^2 = 5x - 1$ and $4x^3 = 5x^2 - 1$, and the identity in form of $x + y = 1$ and $4x = 3y$, can be perceived at a glance. In the first pair of equations one is quadratic, the other cubic; both equations of the second pair are linear. It would be well-nigh humanly impossible to carry out a long series of inferences if such equations were stated in words. Thus the verbal statement of what is represented by Maxwell's equations would easily fill several pages and the essential relations between the various factors involved would thus be hidden. An adequate symbolism makes clear just what it is that is constant or invariable in a proposition, and what is variable. The invariable features are its form or structure.

A fourth and no mean advantage of such symbols is their labor-saving and thought-saving function. When once a symbolism has been perfected, much that hitherto required concentrated attention can be performed mechanically. Very often a good symbolism may suggest conclusions which otherwise would have escaped the thinker completely. The discovery of negative and imaginary numbers, Maxwell's introduction of the dielectric displacement and the subsequent discovery of ether waves, are directly due to the suggestiveness of symbols. For this reason, it has been said that "in calculation the pen sometimes seems to be more intelligent than the user." It is the ability of a properly constructed symbolism to function as a *calculus* which makes evident their importance in a striking manner.

§ 5. THE CALCULUS OF CLASSES

The development of an adequate symbolism, together with the discovery of the formal properties of relations, made it possible both to generalize traditional logic and to establish a powerful calculus.

For example, the operations of addition, multiplication, and so on of the mathematical sciences may be viewed in terms of the theory of relations. Thus the operation of addition is based upon a triadic relation. The relation $a + b = c$ connects the two summands a and b with c. It is a many-one relation, for to every pair of summands there corresponds one and only one sum, while to one sum there corresponds an indefinite number of pairs of summands. But if the sum and one of the summands is fixed, the other summand is uniquely determined. Such triadic relations, which are exemplified in various kinds of operations, can be studied in great detail.

It is not necessary, however, that the operations should be those of ordinary algebra. Operations, of an altogether *nonquantitative* type have been found for combining classes, when these are taken in extension.

We shall sketch briefly the general theory of classes and of propositions. We may, however, preface what follows with this advice taken from C. L. Dodgson: "When you come to any passage you don't understand, *read it again:* if you *still* don't understand it, *read it again:* if you fail, even after *three* readings, very likely your brain is getting a little tired. In that case, just put the book away, and take to other occupations, and next day, when you come to it fresh, you will very likely find that it is *quite* easy."

In the history of symbolic logic, the theory of classes was developed first, because it was first noted that the Aristotelian logic may be interpreted as dealing with the mutual relations of classes. In a *systematic* exposition of logical principles, however, the logic of classes is not prior to other logical principles. For to assert that two classes are related in any way is to assert a *proposition.* Every investigation of the theory of classes employs principles that belong to the theory of propositions. The theory of propositions is, therefore, required for every other logical inquiry, and should be developed first. But in an elementary discussion, such as ours, where the intent is to suggest the direction in which traditional logic may be extended rather than to provide a systematic analysis of such a generalized logic, we may neglect this point. No great harm will be done if we reverse the logical order, and follow the temporal order of development.

Operations and Relations

We shall understand by a "class" a group of individuals each having certain properties, in virtue of which they are said to be members of the class. Thus the class "man" is the set of individual men, the class "even numbers" is the set of even integers, and so on. In other words we shall treat classes in extension. The domain of possible classes is called the *universe of discourse*, or simply the *universe*. It will be symbolized by 1. It may happen that a class has no members. Thus the class of twenty-foot men has no members, although it does have a defining characteristic, namely, "twenty-foot men." Such a class will be called the *null* or *zero* class, and will be symbolized by *0*. The notion of a null class, although puzzling to beginners, has many technical advantages.

Classes may be operated upon in three ways, each operation or combination receiving a special notation. Consider the class "males" in the universe of human beings. Exclude from the universe this class, and we get the class "females." The individuals who are members of the universe but are not members of the class "males," will be said to belong to the *negative* of the class "males." Hence "females" is the negative of "males" in this universe of discourse. A class and its negative are mutually exclusive, and they exhaust the universe. If a represents a class, $\bar{a}$ (to be read *"not-a"*) represents its negative.

Consider next the two classes "English books" and "French books." The class which contains *either French or English books* will be said to be the *logical sum* of these classes. The operation of combining them in this way will be called *logical addition*. If a and b are classes, their logical sum is represented by $a + b$. This may be read as "a plus b," or as "either a or b." The alternation is, as usual in logic, *not* disjunctive. The symbol $+$ is employed because logical addition has certain formal analogies to the addition of ordinary arithmetic.

Consider next the classes "professors" and "bad-tempered individuals." Suppose we wish to pick out all the individuals who are members of *both* classes, and so obtain the class "bad-tempered professors." Such an operation is called *logical multiplication,* and the result is called the *logical product* of the classes. If a and b are classes, their product is symbolized by $a \times b$, or (more conveniently) by ab.

How the idea of a null class arises may now be evident. We assume that the results of multiplying classes are classes. The logical product of "women" and "locomotive engineers" is "female locomotive engineers." Hence this is a class even though it may have no members.

We have been considering operations upon classes. But we cannot establish a calculus unless *relations* between classes are also symbolized. The difference between operations upon classes and relations between classes is this: operations upon classes yield *classes;* the assertions of relations between classes are *propositions,* not classes. The relation we shall regard as fundamental is that of class inclusion. One class will be said to be included in another if every member of the first is also a member of the second. If a and b are classes, we symbolize the proposition a *is included in* b by $a < b$.

The relation $<$ is transitive and nonsymmetrical, for if $a < b$, and $b < c$, then $a < c$; but if $a < b$, it does not follow that $b < a$. We may define the *equality* of two classes in terms of mutual inclusion. Class a is equal to b if a is included in b and b is included in a—in other words, if they have the same members. In symbols, $(a = b) \equiv (a < b) \ . \ (b < a)$, where the sign $=$ indicates *equality between classes,* the sign $\equiv$ indicates *equivalence* between propositions, and the dot (.) indicates the *joint assertion* of two propositions.

Principles of the Calculus of Classes

In order to get the calculus started, we must state a number of fundamental principles which define very explicitly the nature of the operations and relations we have just been discussing. The following set of principles are those which are usually assumed.

1. *Principle of identity:* for every class, $a < a$.
This principle asserts that every class is included in itself. From the definition of equality and this principle, it follows that $a = a$.
2. *Principle of contradition: $a\bar{a} = 0$*
Nothing is a member of both a and *not-a*.
3. *Principle of excluded middle: $a + \bar{a} = 1$*
Every individual in the universe is either a member of a or of *not-a*.
4. *Principle of commutation: $ab = ba$*
$$a + b = b + a$$
We may illustrate this as follows: The class of individuals who

are both German and musical is the same as the class of those who are both musical and German; the class of individuals who are either German or musical is the same as the class of those who are either musical or German.

5. *Principle of association:* $(ab)\ c = a\ (bc)$
$$(a + b) + c = a + (b + c)$$
6. *Principle of distribution:* $(a + b)\ c = ac + bc$
$$ab + c = (a + c)\ (b + c)$$

The first expresses what is analogous to the well-known properties of ordinary numbers. The second, however, introduces a significant difference between the present algebra and the ordinary (quantitative) kind.

7. *Principle of 'autology:* $aa = a$
$$a + a = a$$

Both of these principles mark a radical difference between ordinary (quantitative) algebra and the present one.

8. *Principle of absorption:* $a + ab = a$
$$a\ (a + b) = a$$
9. *Principle of simplification:* $ab < a$
$$a < a + b$$

In virtue of these two principles it follows that the zero class is included in every class $(0 < a)$ and that every class is included in the universe $(a < 1)$. To see this, all that needs to be done is to let $b = 0$ in the first, and $b = 1$ in the second expression.

10. *Principle of composition:* $[(a < b)\ .\ (c < d)] \supset (ac < bd)$
$$[(a < b)\ .\ (c < d)] \supset [(a + c) < (b + d)]$$

Here we are employing, as usual, the symbol $\supset$ for the relation of implication, and the dot (.) for the joint assertion of two propositions. The first expression reads: If a is included in b, and c is included in d, then the logical product of a and c is included in the logical product of b and d.

11. *Principle of syllogism:* $[(a < b)\ .\ (b < c)] \supset (a < c)$

If a is included in b, and b in c, then a is included in c. The relation "included in" is herewith declared to be transitive.

The Representation of the Traditional Categorical Propositions

Let us now represent symbolically each of the four categorical propositions.

All a's *are* b's may be represented as $(a < b)$. It can be shown, moreover, that this is equivalent to $(a\bar{b} = 0)$, so that we have $(a < b) \equiv (a\bar{b} = 0)$.

No a's *are* b's is equivalent to *All* a's *are* non-b's. Hence, it may be symbolized as $(a < \bar{b})$. But this expression is equivalent to $(ab = 0)$, so that $(a < \bar{b}) \equiv (ab = 0)$.

Since the particular propositions are the contradictories of the universals, they deny what the latter affirm. Hence *Some* a's *are* b's must deny *No* a's *are* b's (symbolically, $a < \bar{b}$). It may be represented as $(a < \bar{b})'$ or as $(ab \neq 0)$.

Some a's *are not* b's must contradict $(a < b)$. Hence, it may be represented as $(a < b)'$ or as $(a\bar{b} \neq 0)$.

Each of these four symbolic forms should be familiar to the reader from our previous analysis of the categorical propositions.

Proof of De Morgan's Theorem

In the space at our disposal we cannot develop the calculus of classes to show its great power. But we wish to illustrate the nature of proofs in this calculus by offering a demonstration of De Morgan's theorem as applied to classes.

We wish to find the negative of the class $(a + b)$.

In virtue of the principle of excluded middle, $a + \bar{a} = 1$, and $b + \bar{b} = 1$. Also, by the principle of simplification, $1 \times 1 = 1$, and hence $(a + \bar{a})(b + \bar{b}) = 1$. Applying the distributive and associative principles this may be written: $(ab + a\bar{b} + \bar{a}b) + \bar{a}\bar{b} = 1$.

Consider now the two classes $(ab + a\bar{b} + \bar{a}b)$ and $\bar{a}\bar{b}$. They exhaust the universe, since their sum is 1; and they are mutually exclusive, since their product is 0. Hence either one is the negative of the other.

But $ab + a\bar{b} + \bar{a}b = ab + a\bar{b} + \bar{a}b + ab$, by applying the principle of tautology. The right-hand member by the distributive principle is equal to $a(b + \bar{b}) + b(a + \bar{a}) = a + b$. Therefore, since $\bar{a}\bar{b}$ is the negative of $(ab + a\bar{b} + \bar{a}b)$, which is equal to $(a + b)$, it is also the negative of this latter.

Hence we get $\overline{(a + b)} = \bar{a}\,\bar{b}$, one form of the De Morgan's theorem.

Let us now obtain the negative of ab.

By an argument identical with the above, (ab) and $(a\bar{b} + \bar{a}b + \bar{a}\bar{b})$ are negatives of one another. But we also have:

$$a\bar{b} + \bar{a}b + \bar{a}\bar{b} = a\bar{b} + \bar{a}b + \bar{a}\bar{b} + \bar{a}\bar{b}$$
$$= (a\bar{b} + \bar{a}\bar{b}) + (\bar{a}b + \bar{a}\bar{b})$$
$$= \bar{b}(a + \bar{a}) + \bar{a}(b + \bar{b})$$
$$= \bar{b} + \bar{a} = \bar{a} + \bar{b}$$

Hence $\overline{(a \times b)} = \bar{a} + \bar{b}$, a second form of De Morgan's theorem. These results may be generalized for any finite number of classes

thus: $\overline{(a+b+c+d+\cdots)} = \bar{a}\,\bar{b}\,\bar{c}\,\bar{d}\,\ldots$ and $\overline{(abcd\cdots)} =$
$\bar{a}+\bar{b}+\bar{c}+\bar{d}+\cdots$

§ 6. THE CALCULUS OF PROPOSITIONS

The calculus of propositions was first developed as another in-terpretation of the symbolism elaborated in the theory of classes. The two calculi have, up to a certain point, an identical formal structure, and every proposition in the theory of classes has a cor-responding proposition, obtainable by a suitable interpretation, in the theory of propositions. The following table can serve as a dic-tionary for translating the theorems of the calculus of classes into theorems in the calculus of propositions:

$a, b, c, \ldots$ any classes	$p, q, r, \ldots$ any propositions
$\bar{a}$, the negative of class a	p', the contradictory of proposition p
$a + b$, the logical sum of two classes	$p \vee q$, the logical sum of two proposi-tions, or their alternative assertion
$a\,b$, the logical product of two classes	$p \cdot q$, the logical product of two prop-ositions, or their joint assertion
$a < b$, a is included in b	$p \supset q$, p implies q.
0, the class having no members	The proposition which is false
1, the class containing all classes	The proposition which is true

By means of this dictionary all the principles which are true for classes may be restated, in different symbolism, for propositions.

Nevertheless, such an approach to the theory of propositions has several drawbacks, although it does help to bring out the formal analogies between the two calculi. In the first place, as already men-tioned, there are several theorems which are true when the terms are propositions, but false when they are classes. Thus *If* p *implies* q *or* r, *then* p *implies* q *or* p *implies* r *is a true theorem for propo-sitions.* (Symbolically, it is $[p \supset (q \vee r)] \supset [(p \supset q) \vee (p \supset r)]$. It is false when interpreted for classes. For example, it is false that *If all English people are either men or women, then all English people are men or all English people are women.*

A more serious objection arises from the fact that in developing the calculus of propositions, we wish to enumerate *all* the princi-ples of inference we are employing. If we develop the theory of propositions systematically and deductively, thus beginning with a number of undemonstrated principles for propositions, we can dem-onstrate every other principle. With enough care we can guard our selves against the danger of employing a principle of inference not yet assumed or demonstrated. Consequently, with such a process we can arrive at a satisfactory systematization of logical principles. If, however, we use the class calculus as the basis for developing the theory of propositions, we can no longer use such a method of obtaining all the principles of inference.

Just as in the calculus of classes where all classes are interpreted in extension, so in the calculus of propositions all propositions are considered only with respect to their *truth-values* and not for the *specific meaning* of what they assert. The reader must be clear about this if he does not want to commit bad blunders.

Let us illustrate this point by analyzing the definition of *implication* which is often given in discussions of symbolic logic. $(p \supset q)$ is defined as equivalent to $(p' \lor q)$ or to $(p \cdot q')'$. In words: p implies q is true if *"not-p or q"* is true.

But *"not-p or q"* is true in any one of the following cases: (1) p is true and q is true; (2) p is false and q is true; (3) p is false and q is false. The only case which would make it false is when p is true and q is false. It follows that *"p implies q"* is true in any one of the first three cases. But if we examine these cases, we must say that so long as p is false, no matter what q is, *"p implies q"* is true; and so long as q is true, no matter what p is, *"q is implied by p"* is true. This may be stated in the paradoxical fashion that a false proposition implies any proposition, and that any proposition implies a true one. Each of the following propositions must therefore be true: $2 + 2 = 5$ *implies that Sacco and Vanzetti were executed for murder* and *Alfred Smith was defeated for President in 1928 implies that the base angles of an isosceles triangle are equal.*

The paradox disappears, however, if the reader dismisses from his mind the prejudice in favor of the usual meaning of the word "implication" and recognizes that, by definition, we have made it denote something else in the propositional calculus. The distinction is recognized by calling the first *formal* and the latter *material* implication.[5] (Sometimes the former is called *entailment, tautologous implication,* or *strict implication.*) The assertion of formal implication, as we saw in our first chapter, involves no assumption as to the factual truth or falsehood of either of two propositions, but only that they are so connected by virtue of their structure (which they share with all other propositions of the same form) that it is *impossible* for the implicating proposition to be true and the implied

[5] This use of the word "formal" must not be confounded with the use in the *Principia Mathematica* of Whitehead and Russell.

one to be false. *Material implication* is the name we give to the fact that one of a pair of propositions happens to be false or else the other happens to be true.

The two kinds of implications are, however, not unrelated. The formal implication of the syllogism means that in every specific instance of the syllogism there is a material implication between the premises and the conclusion. But this account leaves out the fact that in every syllogism there is a necessity, based on an element of identity not directly present in all other cases of material implication. When we say that *Whales are mammals and all mammals have lungs* implies *Whales have lungs* there is a connection not present when we say that *Dante was born in 1250* implies that *Lithium is a metal* (because the first happens to be false and the second true). This, however, also involves a question of metaphysics, to wit, whether all truths are necessarily connected in the ultimate nature of things.

CHAPTER VII

THE NATURE OF A LOGICAL OR
MATHEMATICAL SYSTEM

§ 1. THE FUNCTION OF AXIOMS

Although the Babylonians and Egyptians had much information about the eclipses of the sun and the moon, the measurement of land and the construction of buildings, the disposition of geometric figures in order to form symmetrical designs, and computation with integers and fractions, it is generally recognized that they had no *science* of these matters. The idea of a science was a contribution of the Greeks.

Information, no matter how reliable or extensive, which consists of a set of isolated propositions is not science. A telephone book, a dictionary, a cookbook, or a well-ordered catalogue of goods sold in a general store may contain accurate knowledge, organized in some convenient order, but we do not regard these as works of science. Science requires that our propositions form a logical *system*, that is, that they stand to each other in some one or other of the relations of equivalence and opposition already discussed. Therefore in the present chapter we continue our study of the nature of proof, in order to make clearer some of the generic characteristics of deductive systems. Such a study, we shall find, is identical with the study of the nature of mathematics.

Let us remember that no proposition can be *demonstrated* by any experimental method. The reader is doubtless familiar with the Pythagorean theorem that in a right triangle the square on the hypotenuse is equal to the sum of the squares on the arms. He has, no doubt, "proved" or "demonstrated" it in his school days. Nevertheless every gathering of college-trained men is likely to contain at least one member who, when asked how the theorem may be proved, will suggest protractors, carefully drawn triangles, and finely graduated rulers. In this respect, such an individual has made no essential advance upon the methods of the ancient Egyptian surveyors.

Suppose, for instance, we were to attempt to prove the Pythagorean theorem by actually drawing the squares on the three sides of a right triangle on some uniformly dense tinfoil, then cutting them out and by weighing them seeing whether the square on the hypotenuse does actually balance the other two squares. Would this constitute a proof? Obviously not, for we can never know that the tinfoil is in fact absolutely uniform in density, or that the pieces cut out are perfect squares. Hence, if in a number of experiments we should fail to find a perfect balance in the weights, we should not consider that as evidence against the view that there *would* be a perfect equilibrium *if* our lines were perfectly straight, the angles of the square were perfect right angles, and the mass of the tinfoil were absolutely uniform. A logical proof or demonstration consists, as we have seen, in exhibiting a proposition as the necessary consequence of other propositions. The demonstration asserts nothing about the factual truth of either the premises or their logical consequences.

"But look here!" the reader may protest. "Don't we prove that the theorems in geometry are *really* true? Isn't mathematics supposed to be the most certain of the sciences, in which some property is shown to hold for all objects of a definite type, once and for all? If you examine any statement of a theorem, for example the Pythagorean, you find something asserted about 'all' triangles. Now if you admit that something is in fact proved true of all triangles, why do you refuse to admit that we are establishing the 'material' truth of such a theorem? Doesn't 'all' really mean 'all'?"

This protest, however, simply ignores that fact already noted that a logical proof is a "pointing-out" or "showing" of the implications between a set of propositions called axioms and a set called theorems, and that the axioms themselves are not demonstrated.

The reader may reply: "The axioms are not proved, because they need no proof. *Their truth is self-evident.* Everybody can recognize that propositions like *The whole is greater than any one of its parts* or *Through two points only one straight line may be drawn* are obviously true. They are therefore a satisfactory basis for geometry, because by their means we can establish the truth of propositions not so obvious or self-evident."

Such a reply represents a traditional view. Up to the end of the nineteenth century it was generally believed that the axioms are materially true of the physical world, and that the cogency of the demonstrations depends upon their being thus materially true. Nevertheless, this view of the axioms confuses three different issues:

1. How is the material truth of the axioms established?
2. Are the axioms materially true?
3. Are the theorems the logical consequences of the explicitly stated axioms?

We must consider these separately.

1. The answer generally given to the first question is that the axioms are self-evident truths. But this view is a rather complacent way of ignoring real difficulties. In the first place, if by "self-evidence" is meant psychological obviousness, or an irresistible impulse to assert, or the psychological unconceivability of any contrary propositions, the history of human thought has shown how unreliable it is as a criterion of truth. Many propositions formerly regarded as self-evident, for example: *Nature abhors a vacuum; At the antipodes men walk with their heads beneath their feet; Every surface has two sides,* are now known to be false. Indeed, contradictory propositions about every variety of subject matter, thus including most debatable propositions, have each, at different times, been declared to be fundamental intuitions and therefore self-evidently true. But whether a proposition is obvious or not depends on cultural conditions and individual training, so that a proposition which is "self-evidently true" to one person or group is not so to another.

This view assumes a capacity on the part of human beings to establish universal or general propositions dealing with matter of fact simply by examining the *meaning* of a proposition. But, once more, the history of human thought, as well as the analysis of the nature of meaning, has shown that there is an enormous difference between *understanding the meaning* of a proposition and *knowing its truth.* The truth of general propositions about an indefinite number of empirical facts can never be absolutely established. The fundamental reason, therefore, for denying that the axioms of geometry or of any other branch of mathematics, are self-evidently true is that each of the axioms has at least one significant contrary.

"But doesn't the mathematician discover his axioms by observation on the behavior of matter in space and time?" the reader may ask. "And aren't they in fact more certain than the theorems?"

In order to reply, we must resort to the ancient Aristotelian distinction between the *temporal order* in which the logical dependence of propositions is discovered and the *logical order* of implications between propositions. There is no doubt that many of the axioms of mathematics are an expression of what we believe to be the truth concerning selected parts of nature, and that many advances in mathematics have been made because of the suggestions of the natural sciences. But there is also no doubt that mathematics as an *inquiry* did not historically begin with a number of axioms from which subsequently the theorems were derived. We know that many of the propositions of Euclid were known hundreds of years before he lived; they were doubtless believed to be materially true. Euclid's chief contribution did not consist in discovering additional theorems, but in exhibiting them as part of a system of connected truths. The kind of question Euclid must have asked himself was: Given the theorems about the angle sum of a triangle, about similar triangles, the Pythagorean theorem, and the rest, what are the minimum number of assumptions or axioms from which these can be inferred? As a result of his work, instead of having what were believed to be independent propositions, geometry became the first known example of a deductive system. The axioms were thus in fact *discovered later* than the theorems, although the former are *logically prior* to the latter.

It is a common prejudice to assume that the logically prior propositions are "better known" or "more certain" than the theorems, and that in general the logical priority of some propositions to others is connected in some way with their being true. Axioms are simply assumptions or hypotheses, used for the purpose of systematizing and sometimes discovering the theorems they imply. It follows that axioms *need not* be known to be true before the theorems are known, and in general the axioms of a science are much less evident psychologically than the theorems. In most sciences, as we shall see, the material truth of the theorems is not established by means of first showing the material truth of the axioms. On the contrary, the material truth of axioms is made *probable* by establishing empirically the truth or the probability of the theorems.

2. We must acknowledge, therefore, that an answer to the question, "Are the axioms materially true?" cannot be given on grounds of logic alone, and that it must be determined by the special natural science which empirically investigates the subject matter of such axioms. But it must also be admitted that the material truth

or falsity of the axioms is of no concern to the logician or mathe-matician, who is interested only in the fact that theorems are or are not implied by the axioms. It is essential, therefore, to distin-guish between *pure mathematics,* which is interested only in the facts of implication, and *applied mathematics,* or natural science, which is interested also in questions of material truth.

3. Whether the theorems are logical consequences of the axioms must, therefore, be determined by logical methods alone. This is not, however, always as easy as it appears. For many centuries Euclid's proofs were accepted as valid, although they made use of other assumptions than those he explicitly stated. There has been a steady growth in the logical rigor demanded of mathematical demonstrations, and today considerable logical maturity, as well as special technical competence, is a prerequisite for deciding ques-tions of validity. Indeed, in certain branches of mathematics the cogency of some demonstrations has not yet been established.

We may now state summarily our first results concerning the nature of a logical system. Propositions can be demonstrated by exhibiting the relations of implication between them and other propositions. But not all propositions in the system can be dem-onstrated, for otherwise we would be arguing in a circle. It should, however, be noted that propositions which are axiomatic in one sys-tem may be demonstrated in another system. Also, terms that are undefined in one system may be definable in another. What we have called pure mathematics is, therefore, a *hypothetico-deductive system.* Its axioms serve as hypotheses or assumptions, which are entertained or considered for the propositions they imply. In gen-eral, the logical relation of axioms and theorems is that of a prin-cipal to its subaltern. If the whole of geometry is condensed into one proposition, the axioms are the antecedents in the hypothetical proposition so obtained. But they also characterize, as we shall see presently, the formal structure of the system in which the theorems are the elements.

§ 2. PURE MATHEMATICS—AN ILLUSTRATION

The reader is probably familiar with some examples of logical systems from his study of mathematics, and we have already con-sidered one example of such a system in our discussion of the syllo-gism. It will be valuable, however, to start anew. Consider the following propositions, which are the axioms for a special kind of geometry.

Axiom 1. If A and B are distinct points on a plane, there is at least one line containing both A and B.

Axiom 2. If A and B are distinct points on a plane, there is not more than one line containing both A and B.

Axiom 3. Any two lines on a plane have at least one point of the plane in common.

Axiom 4. There is at least one line on a plane.

Axiom 5. Every line contains at least three points of the plane.

Axiom 6. All the points of a plane do not belong to the same line.

Axiom 7. No line contains more than three points of the plane.

These axioms seem clearly to be about points and lines on a plane. In fact, if we omit the seventh one, they are the assumptions made by Veblen and Young for "projective geometry" on a plane in their standard treatise on that subject. It is unnecessary for the reader to know anything about projective geometry in order to understand the discussion that follows. But what are points, lines, and planes? The reader may think he "knows" what they are. He may "draw" points and lines with pencil and ruler, and perhaps convince himself that the axioms state truly the properties and relations of these geometric things. This is extremely doubtful, for the properties of marks on paper may diverge noticeably from those postulated. But in any case the question whether these actual marks do or do not conform is one of *applied* and not of *pure* mathematics. The axioms themselves, it should be noted, do not indicate what points, lines, and so on "really" are. For the purpose of discovering the implications of these axioms, it is unessential to know what we shall understand by points, lines, and planes. These axioms imply several theorems, not in virtue of the visual representation which the reader may give them, but in virtue of their logical form. Points, lines, and planes may be any entities whatsoever, undetermined in every way except by the relations stated in the axioms.

Let us, therefore, suppress every explicit reference to points, lines, and planes, and thereby eliminate all appeal to spatial intuition in deriving several theorems from the axioms. Suppose, then, that instead of the word "plane," we employ the letter S; and instead of the word "point," we use the phrase "element of S." Obviously, if the plane (S) is viewed as a collection of points (elements of S), a line may be viewed as a class of points (elements) which is a subclass of the points of the plane (S). We shall therefore substitute for the word "line" the expression "l-class." Our original set of axioms then reads as follows:

Axiom 1′. If A and B are distinct elements of S, there is at least one l-class containing both A and B.

Axiom 2′. If A and B are distinct elements of S, there is not more than one l-class containing both A and B.

Axiom 3′. Any two l-classes have at least one element of S in common.

Axiom 4′. There exists at least one l-class in S.

Axiom 5′. Every l-class contains at least three elements of S.

Axiom 6′. All the elements of S do not belong to the same l-class.

Axiom 7′. No l-class contains more than three elements of S.

In this set of assumptions no explicit reference is made to any specific subject matter. The only notions we require to state them are of a completely general character. The ideas of a "class," "sub-class," "elements of a class," the relation of "belonging to a class" and the converse relation of a "class containing elements," the notion of "number," are part of the fundamental equipment of logic. If, therefore, we succeed in discovering the implications of these axioms, it cannot be because of the properties of space as such. As a matter of fact, none of these axioms can be regarded as propositions; none of them is in itself either true or false. For the symbols, S, l-class, A, B, and so on are *variables*. Each of the variables denotes any one of a class of possible entities, the only restriction placed upon it being that it must "satisfy," or conform to, the formal relations stated in the axioms. But until the symbols are assigned specific values the axioms are *propositional functions*, and not propositions.[1]

Our "assumptions," therefore, consist in relations considered to hold between undefined terms. But the reader will note that although no terms are *explicitly* defined, an *implicit* definition of them is made. They may denote anything whatsoever, provided that what they denote conforms to the stated relations between themselves. This procedure characterizes modern mathematical

---

[1] The statement in the text is concerned with forms such as "X is a man," which does not assert anything until some definite value is assigned to the variable X. In this case, the truth of the proposition asserted by the sentence (obtained by substituting a determinate value of X) depends upon the value assigned to X. Propositions, however, of the form X *is a man implies X is mortal, for all values of* X do assert something which is true no matter what value is assigned to X. In this case, X is said to be an apparent variable, since the truth of the proposition does not depend upon the value given to X.

technique. In Euclid, for example, *explicit* definitions are given of points, lines, angles, and so on. In a modern treatment of geometry, these elements are defined *implicitly* through the axioms. As we shall see, this latter procedure makes it possible to give a variety of interpretations to the undefined elements, and so to exhibit an identity of structure in different concrete settings.

We shall now demonstrate six theorems, some of which may be regarded as trite consequences of our assumptions.

Theorem I. If A and B are distinct elements of S, there is one and only one *l-class* containing both A and B. It will be called the *l-class AB*.

This follows at once from Axioms 1' and 2'.

Theorem II. Any two distinct *l-classes* have one and only one element of S in common.

This follows from Axioms 2' and 3'.

Theorem III. There exist three elements of S which are not all in the same *l-class*.

This is an immediate consequence of Axioms 4', 5', and 6'.

Theorem IV. Every *l-class* in S contains just three elements of S.

This follows from Axioms 5' and 7'.

Theorem V. Any class S which is subject to Axioms 1' to 6' inclusively contains at least seven elements.

Proof. For let A, B, C be three elements of S not in the same *l-class*. This is possible by Theorem III. Then there must be three distinct *l-classes*, containing AB, BC, and CA, by Theorem I. Furthermore, each of these *l-classes* must have an additional element, by Axiom 5'. And these additional elements must be distinct from each other, and from A, B, C, by Axiom 2'.

Let these additional elements be designated by D, E, and G, so that ABD, BCE, and CAG form the three distinct *l-classes* mentioned. Now AE and BG also determine *l-classes*, which must be distinct from any *l-classes* yet mentioned, by Axiom 1'. And they must have an element of S in common, by Axiom 4', which is distinct from any element so far enumerated, by Axiom 2'. Let us call it F, so that AEF and BFG are *l-classes*.

Consequently, there are at least seven elements in S.

Theorem VI. The class S, subject to all seven assumptions, contains no more than seven elements.

Proof. Suppose there were an eighth element T. Then the *l-class* determined by AT and BFG would have to have an element in common, by Axiom 3'. But this element cannot be B, for the elements AB determine the *l-class* whose elements are ABD, so that $ABTD$ would need to belong to this very same *l-class;* which is impossible by Axiom 7'. Nor can this element be F, for then $AFTE$ would have to belong to the *l-class* AEF; nor G, for then $AGTC$ would need to belong to the *l-class* AGC; these results are impossible for the same reason (Axiom 7').

Consequently, since the existence of an eighth element would contradict Axiom 7', such an element cannot exist.

We have now exhibited a miniature mathematical system as a hypothetico-deductive science. The deduction makes no appeal whatsoever to experiment or observation, to any sensory elements. The reader has had a taste of pure mathematics. Whether anything in the world of existence conforms to this system requires empirical knowledge. If this be the case, that portion of the actual world must have the systematic character indicated formally in our symbolic representation. That the world does exemplify such a structure can be verified only within the limits of the errors of our experimental procedure.

§ 3. STRUCTURAL IDENTITY OR ISOMORPHISM

We want to show now that an abstract set such as the one discussed in the previous section may have more than one concrete representation, and that these different representations, though extremely unlike in material content, will be identical in logical structure.

Let us suppose there is a banking firm with seven partners. In order to assure themselves of expert information concerning various securities, they decide to form seven committees, each of which will study a special field. They agree, moreover, that each partner will act as chairman of one committee, and that every partner will serve on three and only three committees. The following is the schedule of committees and their members, the first member being chairman:

Domestic railroads	Adams,	Brown,	Smith
Municipal bonds	Brown,	Murphy,	Ellis
Federal bonds	Murphy,	Smith,	Jones
South American securities	Smith,	Ellis,	Gordon

Domestic steel industry	Ellis,	Jones,	Adams
Continental securities	Jones,	Gordon,	Brown
Public utilities	Gordon,	Adams,	Murphy

An examination of this schedule shows that it "satisfies" the seven axioms if the class S is interpreted as the banking firm, its elements as the partners, and the *l-classes* as the various committees.

We exhibit one further interpretation, which at first sight may seem to have nothing in common with those already given. In the following figure there are seven points lying by threes on seven lines, one of which is "bent." Let each point represent an element of S, and each set of three points lying on a line an *l-class*. Then all the

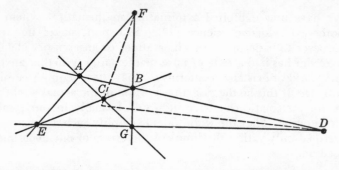

seven assumptions are satisfied. This geometric pattern exemplifies the *same formal relations* as does the array of numbers and the schedule of the banker's committees we have already given. A third representation will be found on page 146.

Let us examine these three representations. We find, in the first place, that we can make correspond in a one-one manner every element of one interpretation with elements of the other two. And in the second place, every relation between the elements in one representation corresponds to a relation with the same logical properties between the *corresponding* elements in the other two. Thus, as an illustration, the element 0 in the numerical interpretation given below, can be placed in one-one correspondence with the point A in the geometrical interpretation, and also with Mr. Adams in the banking firm; the element 1 corresponds to point B, and also to Mr. Brown, and so on. And the three termed relation between the numbers 0, 1, 3 (page 146) in virtue of which they belong to the same group, corresponds to the relation between the points ABD in virtue of which they lie on the same line, and also corresponds to the relation between Messrs. Adams, Brown, and Smith in virtue of which they are on the same committee; and so on.

Two or more systems which are related in this manner are said to be *isomorphic* or to have an *identical structure* or *form*. We may now give a general definition of *isomorphism*. Given two classes S, with elements a, b, c, . . . and S', with elements a', b', c', . . . ; suppose the elements of S can be placed in one-one correspondence with those of S', so that, say, a corresponds to a', b to b', and so on. Then, if for every relation R between elements of S (so that, for example, $a\ R\ b$) there is a relation R' between the corresponding elements of S' ($a'\ R'\ b'$), the two classes are *isomorphic*.

We are now prepared to understand the great importance of the mathematical method as a tool in the natural sciences. In the first place, a hypothesis or set of assumptions may be studied for its implications without raising questions of material truth or falsity. This is essential if we are to understand *to what* a given hypothesis commits us. In the second place, a hypothesis when abstractly stated is capable of more than one concrete representation. Consequently, when we are studying pure mathematics we are studying the possible structures of many concrete situations. In this way we discover the constant or invariable factor in situations sensibly different and undergoing change. Science has been characterized as a search for system (order, constancy) amidst diversity and change. The idea of isomorphism is the clearest expression of what such a system means.

Some examples of isomorphism are well known. An ordinary map is a useful device because the relations between the points on it have a structure identical with the relations between the places in the countryside to which the map points correspond. In physics, we can see how the formula of inverse squares applies to electrical attraction and repulsion as well as to the force of gravitation. This is possible because these different subject matters have an identical formal structure with respect to the properties studied. Physics also discovers that the same set of principles is applicable to the motion of planets, the dropping of a tear, and the swinging of a pendulum. It is the isomorphism found in diverse subject matter which makes possible theoretical science as we know it today. An elementary exposition of a "dictionary" which translates theorems of Euclidean into non-Euclidean geometry the reader will find in Henri Poincaré's *The Foundations of Science*, page 59. From an abstract point of view these different geometries have an identical structure.

It should be noted that two systems may not be identical in structure *throughout* and yet share many common properties. Euclidean and non-Euclidean geometries have many theorems in common, while at the same time some theorems in one system are formally incompatible with some theorems in the other. This suggests the possibility that two systems may be incompatible with each other in their totality and yet possess a common subsystem. We may illustrate this as follows. Consider the system determined by Axioms 1′ to 7′. Consider also the system obtained by replacing 7′ with the assumption 7′′: *No* 1-class *contains more than four elements of S.* These two systems are not isomorphic, as comparison of the representation of the first system (page 146) with that of the second system (page 147) will show. Nevertheless, all the theorems in both systems which follow from the first six axioms will be the same. The system determined by Axioms 1′ to 6′ is therefore a common subsystem of the incompatible systems determined by 1′ to 7′ on the one hand and by 1′′ to 7′′ on the other.

This is a very important observation. Research in the natural sciences often tempts us to believe that a theory is true because some consequence of the theory has been verified. Nevertheless, an identical consequence may be drawn from an alternative and incompatible theory. We cannot, therefore, validly affirm either theory. With care, however, we may discover those common assumptions of both theories upon which the identical consequence depends. It may then be possible to ascertain *which* of the assumptions in virtue of which the theories are *different* theories are in disagreement with experimental findings.

One further remark needs to be made about deductive systems. Every system is of necessity *abstract:* it is the structure of certain *selected* relations, and must consequently omit the structure of other relations. Thus the systems studied in physics do not include the systems explored in biology. Furthermore, as we have seen, a system is deductive not in virtue of the special meanings of its term, but in virtue of the universal relations between them. The specific quality of the things which the terms donate do not, as such, play any part in the system. Thus the theory of heat takes no account of the unique sensory qualities which heat phenomena display. A deductive system is therefore doubly abstract: it abstracts from the specific qualities of a subject matter, and it selects some relations and neglects others. It follows that there is a *plurality* of systems, each of which may be explored in isolation from the others. Such a plurality of systems may, indeed, constitute a set of subsystems of a single, comprehensive system, but we have no evidence for such a state of affairs. In any case, it is not necessary to know this comprehensive system in order to explore adequately any one of the many less inclusive systems. It appears that human knowledge of the natural world is possible only because it is capable of being studied as a set of relatively autonomous systems.

§ 4. THE EQUIVALENCE OF AXIOM SETS

It has been pointed out that in every deductive system some propositions are indemonstrable *in that system* and some terms indefinable. We have also suggested, however, that a proposition which is an axiom in one system may be a theorem in another. We wish now to illustrate this.

Consider the following assumptions concerning a class S; its elements A, B, C, and so on; and its *l-* (or sub-) *classes a, b, c,* and so on:

Axiom 1'. If a and b are distinct *l-classes* of S there is at least one element of S in both a and b.

Axiom 2'. If a and b are distinct *l-classes* of S there is not more than one element of S in both a and b.

Axiom 3'. Any two elements of S are elements of some one *l-class* of S.

Axiom 4'. There exists at least one element in S.

Axiom 5'. Every element of S belongs to at least three *l-classes* of S.

Axiom 6'. There is no element of S belonging to all the *l-classes* of S.

Axiom 7'. There is no element of S which belongs to more than three *l-classes* of S.

None of these axioms are identical with any axioms of the previous set, although some of the new axioms are identical (except for verbal form) with several of the theorems we had previously demonstrated. Thus, Axiom 3' is identical with Theorem I, Axiom 4' with part of Theorem III. None the less, the previous set of axioms and the present set characterize the same system of relations. These two sets are *equivalent*. Two postulate sets are equivalent if, and only if, every postulate of the first is either a postulate or a theorem in the second, and every postulate of the second is either a postulate or a theorem in the first. The equivalence for the two sets above may be shown by deducing from the first set those postulates in the second set which have not already been demonstrated, and then by deducing from the second set all the postulates of the first. Thus Axiom 1′ follows at once from Axiom 3′, Axiom 5′ follows from Axioms 1′ to 5′, and so on.

It is quite important that the reader become convinced that there are no *intrinsically undemonstrable propositions*. Failure to realize this fact has been one source for the belief in "self-evidently true" propositions. It is quite easy to fall into the mistaken prejudice that because a proposition cannot be demonstrated on one set of premises, it is altogether undemonstrable. Moreover, the fact that two systems may be equivalent without being identical, axiom for axiom, throws fresh light on the question of logical priority. In a given system, one proposition is logically prior to another if the first is required as a premise, or part of the premise, for the second. In another system, however, the relation of logical priority between two propositions may be reversed.

What has been said about undemonstrated propositions is equally true for undefined terms. In the geometry the reader has studied in his youth, points were taken as fundamental and undefined, and lines, circles, defined in terms of them. That there must be undefined terms is clear from any attempt to define a term. We may try to define "equal distances" as follows: The distance between points A and B on a straight line is equal to the distance between C and D, if the segment AB can be moved *by a rigid motion of this segment* so that it coincides with the segment CD. But obviously, the phrase "a rigid motion" cannot itself be defined in terms of "equal distances," on pain of a circular definition. Nevertheless, it is a mistake to suppose that there are *intrinsically* undefinable terms. *Undemonstrability and undefinability are both relative to a system.* It is not necessary to regard points as undefinable provided we select other undefinables, such as lines, in terms of which points may themselves be defined. Thus different axiomatic foundations have been given for Euclidean geometry. Hilbert has found a set of twenty-one assumptions, requiring five primitive or undefined ideas, from which all the theorems of geometry can be deduced. Veblen, on the other hand, discovered twelve assumptions, requiring only two undefined terms, which perform the same task. We cannot pursue this topic any further, except to point out that the number of undefined terms is closely connected with the number and character of the undemonstrated propositions.

§ 5. THE INDEPENDENCE AND CONSISTENCY OF AXIOMS

We must now consider some fundamental questions connected with a set of axioms. What are some of the essential and desirable properties which a set of axioms must possess?

1. Axioms are studied for the propositions they imply. Consequently, *fertility* is one property which axioms should possess; this means that they should imply many theorems. But there is no criterion as to whether a set of assumptions may give rise to a comprehensive set of theorems. It is very likely that fertility is not an intrinsic character of an axiom set, but reflects the ability of the human reasoner to discover their implications. Moreover, a set of assumptions is regarded as important in proportion to our ability to find *interpretations* for it in terms of investigations in the natural sciences or in other branches of mathematics. We shall return to this point.

2. A very desirable, and historically significant, property of axioms is their *independence*. A set of assumptions is *independent* if it is impossible to deduce any one of the axioms from the others. If a set of axioms is independent, it is possible to make a sharp distinction *in that system* between assumptions and theorems. And unless we know that two propositions are independent, we are unable to say whether we are entertaining different and alternate possibilities or simply the same possibility in a different form.

The question whether the axioms and postulates of Euclid are independent is historically of great interest. To the many attempts to answer it we owe some of the greatest advances that have been made in mathematics, physics, and philosophy. As we have indicated in a previous chapter, mathematicians have tried for more than two thousand years to deduce the parallel postulate from the other assumptions of Euclid. The basis for their doing so was their conviction that all his assumptions except the one about parallel lines were "self-evidently true." Consequently, they believed it was a serious blemish that any non-self-evident proposition should be taken as an axiom. They did not succeed in deducing Postulate 5 from the others without assuming some other proposition not included in the original assumptions of Euclid. But what did their lack of success prove—did it prove that Postulate 5 could not be deduced from the others? It certainly did not. But it turned some inquirers' minds to search for the reason of the lack of success. It led some mathematicians to look for a proof that the parallel postulate was independent of the others.

The proof was finally discovered. We have seen that demonstra·
tive proof consists in pointing out that certain axioms imply certain
theorems. Such an alleged implication is denied if we can show
that it is possible for the theorems to be false and the axioms to be
true. By developing a possible system of geometry in which Euclid's
parallel postulate is denied while the other axioms are retained,
Lobatchevsky was able to show that the parallel postulate cannot
be a logical consequence of the other axioms. It will be seen that
this proof illustrates the form of the logical principle we have discussed as the inconsistent triad. If a set of (consistent) propositions
P imply another proposition Q, then the propositions consisting of
P together with the contradictory (or contrary) of Q must be inconsistent with each other. If the inconsistency, shown by finding two
contradictory propositions, appears in the set of axioms, the task
is completed: Q is not independent of P. If the inconsistency does
not appear in the set of axioms, then it must be possible to deduce
by valid reasoning one or more theorems which contradict either
some of the axioms or some other theorem validly derived. If, on
the other hand, P does not imply Q, the set of propositions P together with the contradictory of Q is a consistent set, and no contradictions can ever be discovered.[2]

Let us indicate summarily the essence of one type of non-Euclidean geometry. Euclid's Postulate 5 is equivalent to the assumption
that through a point outside of a given line only one line may be
drawn parallel to the given line. In the Lobachevskian geometry
this is replaced by the assumption that through a point outside of a
line more than one parallel may be drawn to it. From this assumption and the other assumptions of Euclid a host of theorems may
be obtained, some of which are identical with the theorems of
Euclid, while others are contradictories of these. Thus the propositions. *The base angles of an isosceles triangle are equal* and *Two*

[2] The history of non-Euclidean geometry began when a clear perception of
this simple logical principle was attained. Saccheri, an Italian mathematician
of the eighteenth century, already possessed it, and by making an assumption
contrary to that of Euclid's parallel postulate obtained many theorems of what
is now known as non-Euclidean geometry. But for some unexplained reason he
came to the conclusion that such a geometry was self-contradictory—perhaps because many of the theorems he obtained were formal contradictories of the
theorems of Euclid. If that was his reason for rejecting non-Euclidean geometry,
he overlooked the possibility that both Euclidean and non-Euclidean geometries may be self-consistent, although the two systems are incompatible with each
other. The discovery of non-Euclidean geometry must be attributed, therefore,
to Lobachevsky and Bolyai, who wrote in the first half of the nineteenth century. Still another kind of non-Euclidean geometry was discovered by Riemann.

lines which are parallel to a third are parallel to each other are common to Euclid and Lobachevsky. On the other hand, the propositions *The sum of the angles of a triangle is equal to two right angles* and *The area of a circle is* πr^2 are correct only in Euclid.

3. Here the reader may protest: "I don't yet see that the parallel postulate has been proved to be independent of the others. You have shown that by assuming a contradictory postulate a host of theorems differing from that of Euclid may be obtained. But you have not yet shown that such a new set of postulates is *consistent*. And unless you do that, you have no good reason for supposing that a non-Euclidean geometry is really possible."

This is quite right. The fact that after any finite number of theorems have been derived from a non-Euclidean set of assumptions no contradiction has turned up proves nothing about the consistency of that set. For a contradiction *may* appear after a larger number of theorems have been obtained. And the same objection can be raised no matter how large is the number of theorems deduced. The reader's protest expresses clearly how closely connected are the problems of the independence and the consistency of a set of propositions.

We may, however, be permitted to ask the reader a question in return. "You think non-Euclidean geometries have not been proved to be consistent, and that since they lack such proof their very possibility is endangered. But what basis have you for believing that Euclidean geometry is self-consistent? It is true that after thousands of years of studying it, mathematicians have not discovered any contradictions in it. But you surely will not accept *that* as a proof. The Euclidean and non-Euclidean geometries seem, in this respect, to be in the same boat."

Let us try to resolve the reader's perplexity by turning once more to our miniature mathematical system, and face similar problems with regard to it. Are the seven axioms independent? Are they consistent with one another?

Mathematicians have found only one way of answering the second question. The method consists in discovering a *set of entities which will embody the relations of our set of abstract axioms*. On the assumption that these entities themselves are free from contradiction and that they in fact fully embody the axioms, the latter are shown to involve no inconsistencies.

We will illustrate the use of this method. Let the integers 0 to 6 inclusive be arranged in distinct groups of three each, as follows:

0	1	2	3	4	5	6
1	2	3	4	5	6	0
3	4	5	6	0	1	2

We now regard these seven integers as the elements of the class *S*. Every column of integers will then represent an *l-class*. On this interpretation, as a little reflection shows, every one of the seven axioms in our set is verified. The axioms are therefore consistent.

It must be emphasized, however, that this method merely shifts the difficulty. For the question still remains whether the set of entities and our method of interpretation are consistent. To this question no completely satisfactory answer seems at present available. We have, however, a certain amount of confidence that since the Euclidean axioms have enabled us to deal so adequately with the properties and relations of physical bodies, Euclidean geometry as a logical system is also consistent, because we assume that nothing occupying spatial and temporal position can be self-contradictory. Since non-Euclidean geometries have been shown to correspond, element for element, to Euclidean geometry in accordance with definite transformation formulae, it follows that if a contradiction could appear in non-Euclidean geometry, a corresponding contradiction would of necessity have to occur in the geometry of Euclid.[3]

We return once more to the problem of independence of axioms, and shall illustrate the problem by means of our miniature system. Is Axiom 7' independent of the others? The answer is yes if the first six axioms, together with any assumption incompatible with

---

[3] The assumptions required for other branches of mathematics are shown to be consistent in a similar way. However, complications enter. Mathematics as a system of propositions has advanced much beyond the achievements of Euclid. Mathematicians have shown that all the higher branches of mathematics, such as higher algebra, analysis, geometry, and so on, may be interpreted as studying the relations between whole numbers (integers); and that they require no fundamental notions other than those employed in arithmetic. This achievement has been called the arithmetization of mathematics, and is due largely to such men as Weierstrass, Dedekind, and Hilbert. An even further step in the analysis of mathematical ideas was made when arithmetic itself was shown to require no fundamental notions except those of logic, such as "class," "member of a class," "implies," and so on. This work has been accomplished largely through the efforts of Cantor, Frege, Peano, Whitehead, and Russell, and has received its most adequate expression in the *Principia Mathematica* of the last two men. As a consequence of a century of labor many, though not all, mathematicians are convinced that mathematics can be developed in terms of the ideas of pure logic. If this thesis is sound, the consistency of every branch of mathematics is dependent upon the consistency of the principles of formal logic. The question as to the consistency of any branch of mathematics is then reduced to the question whether logical principles themselves form a consistent system.

the seventh, form a consistent set. This condition is equivalent to finding an interpretation which will satisfy the first six axioms and fail to satisfy the seventh. Such an interpretation may be given in several ways, of which the following is one:

0	1	2	3	4	5	6	7	8	9	10	11	12
1	2	3	4	5	6	7	8	9	10	11	12	0
3	4	5	6	7	8	9	10	11	12	0	1	2
9	10	11	12	0	1	2	3	4	5	6	7	8

These thirteen numbers from 0 to 12 inclusive are the members of S. Each column of four numbers represents an *l-class* of S. Examination will show that all the axioms except the seventh are satisfied. This axiom is therefore independent of the first six. In a like manner we can show that each of the other assumptions is independent of the rest.

§ 6. MATHEMATICAL INDUCTION

"Aren't you, however, forgetting that induction takes place in mathematics?" the reader may protest. "You have been describing mathematics as a typical deductive science, in which all the theorems are necessary consequences of the axioms. But surely you are not going to overlook the method of proof known as mathematical induction?"

The reader has doubtless been ensnared by a word. There is indeed a method of *mathematical induction,* but the name is unfortunate, since it suggests some kinship with the methods of experimentation and verification of hypotheses employed in the natural sciences. But there is no such kinship, and mathematical induction is a purely demonstrative method.

Is it necessary, however, once more to caution the reader against the common error of confounding the temporal order of our discovering the propositions of a science and the order of their logical dependence? Everybody who has ever worked a problem in geometry knows that there is a preparatory "groping stage," in which we guess, speculate, draw auxiliary lines, and so on until, as the saying goes, we "hit upon" the proof. But no one will confuse that preparatory stage, however essential, with the proof finally achieved. Such an initial "groping" stage has indeed close kinship with human investigations in any field whatever. A process of tested guessing characterizes research in mathematics as well as research in the natural sciences.

The principle of mathematical induction may be stated as follows: If a property belongs to the number 1, and if when it belongs to n it can be proved to belong to $n + 1$, then it belongs to all the integers. Let us demonstrate, by its means, the theorem: For all integral values of n, $1 + 3 + 5 + 7 + \ldots (2n - 1) = n^2$.

This clearly is true for $n = 1$. Let us now show that if it holds for the integer n it holds for $(n + 1)$.

a. $1 + 3 + 5 + \ldots (2n - 1) = n^2$.

Adding $(2n - 1) + 2$ or $(2n + 1)$ to both sides, we get:

b. $1 + 3 + 5 + \ldots (2n - 1) + (2n + 1) = n^2 + (2n + 1) = (n + 1)^2$.

But b has the same form as a. Hence we have shown that if the theorem is true for the integer n it is true for $(n + 1)$. Now it is true for $n = 1$. Therefore it is true for $n = 1 + 1$ or 2; therefore it is true for $n = 2 + 1$ or 3, and so on for every integer which can be reached by successive additions of 1. The proof, therefore, is perfectly rigorous, deductive, and altogether formal. It makes no appeal to experiment. And the principle of mathematical induction, as modern researches show, is part of the very meaning of finite or "inductive" numbers.

§ 7. WHAT GENERALIZATION MEANS IN MATHEMATICS

In the preceding chapter we called attention to the changes in the meaning of words by the process of *generalization*. In mathematics, too, such processes take place, and reference is often made to the "modern generalization of number." It is easy to fall into error as to the sense in which "number" has in fact been generalized. Let us examine the matter.

The word "number" was originally restricted to the *integers* 1, 2, 3, and so on. Numbers, so understood, can be added and multiplied, and in some cases subtracted and divided. The abstract nature of integers may be expressed by means of a set of propositions which indicate what operations can be made upon integers, and what the relations are in which the operations stand to one another. For example, the following are some of the abstract properties of integers:

$$a + b = b + a$$
$$(a + b) + c = a + (b + c)$$
$$a \times b = b \times a$$
$$a \times (b + c) = a \times b + a \times c$$

Now on some of the integers, the operations *inverse* to multiplication and addition can be performed. Thus, $4 \times 3 = 12$; hence there is an integer x such that $x \times 3 = 12$: such a number x is the quotient of 12 *divided by* 3. But, unless we enlarge our conception of number, the inverse operation of division cannot *always* be formed. Thus, there is no integer x such that $x \times 3 = 5$. Consequently, in order that there should be no exceptions to the possibility of division, the fractions were introduced. They were also called numbers, and so the domain of number was increased in the interest of continuity and generality.

This was the first generalization of "number." Why were the fractions designated as numbers? The answer is simple, although it has been discovered only recently. It is because operations of addition, multiplication, and even division could be performed on them; and because the *formal relations* of integers to one another with respect to these operations are the same as the formal relations of fractions. In other words, integers and fractions form isomorphic systems.

But it must be pointed out that while addition or multiplication for integers is formally the same for fractions, nevertheless the differences are not thereby denied. Thus, the sign $+$ in $7 + 5 = 12$ and in $\frac{1}{2} + \frac{1}{3} = \frac{5}{6}$, while denoting formal properties common to the two cases, none the less denotes two distinct and different operations. The second is much more complex than the first. It is easy to confuse them because the same symbol is used to denote them both, but neither must we forget that the same symbol is applicable to the two cases because they have common elements of procedure.

Later on other "numbers" were discovered, when it was noticed that some of the previously defined numbers had square roots, cube roots, and so on, but others did not. Thus, the Pythagoreans proved that the diagonal of the square is incommensurable with its sides. In modern notation, this means that $\sqrt{2}$ cannot be expressed as the ratio of two integers. But why should the operation of extracting a root be legitimate only for some numbers (for example 4)? Why not permit the operation to be performed on every one of the previously defined numbers? Hence, in the interest of continuity of treatment and of generality, the *irrationals* were discovered, and they too were regarded as a "species of number."

Why? The answer is again simply: Because the operations upon them possess the formal properties of the operations upon integers and fractions.

Similar remarks, with only few qualifications, apply to the other "species of number" with which modern mathematics is familiar. Negative numbers, imaginary numbers, quaternions, transcendental numbers, matrices, have been introduced into the domain of number because continuity and universality of treatment demanded them. But they have been designated as "numbers" because they share certain abstract properties with the more familiar instances of mathematical entities.

Generality of treatment is thus an obvious goal of mathematics. But it is clearly a mistaken idea to suppose that the definition of "number" as applicable specifically to the cardinals 1, 2, 3, and so on, has in some sense been "extended" or "generalized" to apply to fractions, irrationals, and the rest. There is no generic definition of "number" of which the cardinals, ordinals, fractions, and so on are special instances *except in terms of the formal properties of certain "operations."* It is in virtue of the permanence or *invariance* of these formal properties that these entities are all "numbers."

This conclusion, so obvious when it is once pointed out, has been won only at the expense of tremendous labor by modern philosophers of mathematics. The source of many of the confusions in this subject is the frequent use of the same symbol to denote two essentially different ideas. Thus, the cardinal number 2 and the ratio $\frac{2}{1}$ are usually denoted by the same symbol 2; they denote, however, radically distinct ideas. But this danger from the symbolism of mathematics is undoubtedly outweighed by the great advantages it offers. It enables us to exhibit concisely the *structure* of mathematical propositions, and so makes possible our noting the precise analogies or isomorphisms in contexts that are in other respects very different from one another.

CHAPTER VIII

PROBABLE INFERENCE

§ 1. THE NATURE OF PROBABLE INFERENCE

In daily conversation "probability" is one of the most loosely used words, and in logical theory the correct analysis of the nature of probable inferences is one of the most disputed themes. Nevertheless, we make plans for births, marriages, deaths, holidays, commercial enterprises, friendships, and education on the basis of rational evidence whose weight can be recognized as probable and not conclusive. "Probability," Bishop Butler remarked, "is the very guide of life." The subject, therefore, needs to be examined in detail. The reader will keep his bearings more easily, however, if he recalls the definition of probable inference stated in the introductory chapter. That definition may serve as the Ariadne thread through the mazes of a long discussion. An inference is probable, we said, if it is one of a *class* of arguments such that the conclusions are true with a certain relative frequency when the premises are true.

The following incident occurs in Voltaire's story *Zadig:*

"One day, when he [Zadig] was walking near a little wood, he saw one of the queen's eunuchs running to meet him, followed by several officers, who appeared to be in the greatest uneasiness, and were running hither and thither like men bewildered and searching for some most precious object which they had lost.

" 'Young man,' said the chief eunuch to Zadig, 'have you seen the queen's dog?'

"Zadig modestly replied: 'It is a bitch, not a dog.'

" 'You are right,' said the eunuch.

" 'It is a very small spaniel,' added Zadig; 'it is not long since she has had a litter of puppies; she is lame in the left forefoot, and her ears are very long.'

" 'You have seen her, then?' said the chief eunuch, quite out of breath.

" 'No,' answered Zadig, 'I have never seen her, and never knew that the queen had a bitch.'

"Just at this very time, by one of those curious coincidences which are not uncommon, the finest horse in the king's stables had broken away from the hands of a groom in the plains of Babylon. The grand huntsman and all the other officers ran after him with as much anxiety as the chief of the eunuchs had displayed in his search after the queen's bitch. The grand huntsman accosted Zadig, and asked him if he had seen the king's horse pass that way.

" 'It is the horse,' said Zadig, 'which gallops best; he is five feet high, and has small hoofs; his tail is three and a half feet long; the bosses on his bit are of gold twenty-three carats fine; his shoes are silver of eleven pennyweights.'

" 'Which road did he take? Where is he?' asked the grand huntsman.

" 'I have not seen him,' answered Zadig, 'and I have never even heard anyone speak of him.'

"The grand huntsman and the chief eunuch had no doubt that Zadig had stolen the king's horse and the queen's bitch, so they caused him to be brought before the Assembly of the Grand Desterham, which condemned him to the knout, and to pass the rest of his life in Siberia. Scarcely had the sentence been pronounced, when the horse and the bitch were found. The judges were now under the disagreeable necessity of amending their judgment; but they condemned Zadig to pay four hundred ounces of gold for having said that he had not seen what he had seen. He was forced to pay his fine first, and afterwards he was allowed to plead his cause before the Council of the Grand Desterham, when he expressed himself in the following terms:

" 'Stars of justice, fathomless gulfs of wisdom, mirrors of truth, ye who have the gravity of lead, the strength of iron, the brilliance of the diamond, and a close affinity with gold, inasmuch as it is permitted me to speak before this august assembly, I swear to you by Ormuzd that I have never seen the queen's respected bitch, nor the sacred horse of the king of kings. Hear all that happened: I was walking towards the little wood where later on I met the venerable eunuch and the most illustrious grand huntsman. I saw on the sand the footprints of an animal, and easily decided that they were those of a little dog. Long and faintly marked furrows, imprinted where the sand was slightly raised between the footprints, told me that it was a bitch whose dugs were drooping, and that consequently she must have given birth to young ones only a few days before. Other marks of a different character, showing that the surface of the sand had been constantly grazed on either side of the front paws, informed me that she had very long ears; and, as I observed that the sand was always less deeply indented by one paw than by the other three, I gathered that the bitch belonging to our august queen was a little lame, if I may venture to say so.

" 'With respect to the horse of the king of kings, you must know that as I was walking along the roads in that same wood, I perceived the marks of a horse's shoes, all at equal distances. "There," I said to myself, "went a horse with a faultless gallop." The dust upon the trees, where the width of the road was not more than seven feet, was here and there rubbed off on both sides, three feet and a half away from the middle of the road. "This horse," said I, "has a tail three feet and a half long, which, by its movements to right and left, has whisked away the dust." I saw, where the trees formed a canopy five feet above the ground, leaves lately fallen from the boughs; and I concluded that the horse had touched them, and was therefore five feet high. As to his bit, it must be of gold twenty-three carats fine, for he had rubbed its bosses against a touchstone, the properties of which I had ascertained. Lastly, I inferred from the marks that his shoes left upon stones of another kind, that he was shod with silver of eleven pennyweights in quality.' " [1]

This miniature detective story is a fair representative of the sort of inferences which are employed in many practical problems and in many fields of scientific research. Why do we regard Zadig's conclusions as *reasonably well founded,* even though the evidence for them is not *absolutely complete?*

The argument that the queen's dog had passed by may be formulated as follows:

1. These marks on the sand have a determinate shape. (This is a true proposition, asserting an *observed fact.*)
2. But, if a small dog has passed by, its footprints on the sand would be marks of this shape. (This is a proposition, expressing a *general rule* which is believed to be true.)
3. Therefore, a small dog has passed by. (This is the *inferred proposition.*)

[1] Translation by R. B. Boswell, 1910, pp. 58-60.

Now this argument is formally invalid. It would be valid if we knew not only that proposition 2 is true, but that the proposition 2′ *If a mark of this shape has been made on sand, then a small dog has produced them as its footprints* is also true. (The reader should restate the argument using 2′ instead of 2, and convince himself of the validity of the inference.) Proposition 2′ is the *converse* of 2. But, in general, although we may know the truth of a proposition such as 2, we do not know the truth of its converse. Indeed, we may know that while small dogs produce footprints of this shape, marks very similar to those observed may be produced in other ways. Zadig's conclusion clearly did not necessarily follow from his premises.

Nevertheless, his conclusion is highly *probable* on the premises. For the inference he made *from* the observed fact *to* the inferred proposition *by means* of the general rule, is one of *a class of inferences* in which the number of times true propositions are inferred from true premises is a very large fraction of the number of times such inferences are employed at all. In other words, Zadig *in some instance* may be wrong in inferring the proposition *A small dog has passed by* from the proposition asserting the markings in the sand. But if he, and other observers, were to make a very large number of such inferences, they would be right *much more frequently* than wrong.

We may now state the matter in a slightly different way. Zadig is led, by some reason or other, to study the markings on the road. He is able to establish as true the proposition *These marks on the sand have a determinate shape*. But he also has some ground for asserting the following proposition: *Marks on the sand having such a shape are produced, in a ratio* r *of the time, by small dogs.* Now while nothing follows *necessarily* from these propositions, he may conclude, with *probability*, that *A small dog has passed by*. The conclusion is probable on the evidence, because a fraction r of the time when such an inference is employed, the conclusion is discovered to be true when the premises are true. In any one instance the conclusion (the inferred fact) of such an argument may be false even though the premise is true. But a series of such inferences would yield true conclusions with a perhaps calculable relative frequency r. The numerical value of r cannot always be obtained, and we may have to be satisfied with more or less trustworthy impressions as to its magnitude. But though the evidence for our estimate may be unreliable, the meaning of our judgment of probability is clear. When r is zero, the argument is worthless; when it is 1 the inference is altogether conclusive; when it is greater than ½, the argument leads us aright more often than not.

We must now consider the probability of hypotheses. Observation of magnetized bars of iron, needles, nails, and the like shows that magnets have two unlike poles such that unlike poles attract and like poles repel one another. We also observe that metals are not all equally magnetizable, and that the best metal magnets loose their magnetic properties with lapse of time. How may we explain this? One way of doing so is to assume that all metal substances are composed of small particles, each a *permanent* magnet with two poles, and each capable of rotating around a fixed center. It can be shown that in one arrangement of these particles the opposite poles will neutralize each other completely, so that the entire bar will display no magnetic properties; but in another arrangement, only *some* of these small particles will neutralize one another, so that the entire bar will show magnetic properties. The changes in the relative position of these small permanent magnets, and the ease of their rotation around their fixed centers, will then explain why a metal bar acquires or loses magnetic properties.

Now we have already seen that this hypothesis as to the nature of magnetism is not *demonstrated* when it is shown that its consequences agree with observation. For other theories may also explain the phenomena of magnetism. Moreover, we cannot be sure that some of the logical consequences of our assumption may not turn out to be in disagreement with observation. Nevertheless, our assumption or hypothesis as to the nature of magnetism can be said to be probable in the same sense in which Zadig's conclusions were probable.

We can throw our argument into the familiar form of the hypothetical syllogism *This, that, and the other metal bars exhibit phenomena of magnetism under specified conditions* (true proposition, asserting *observed facts*); but if each metal is composed of *imperceptibly small permanent magnets free to rotate around a fixed axis, then these metals will exhibit magnetic properties under the stated conditions* (general rule); therefore, each metal is composed of permanent magnets, and so on (inferred proposition). We notice again that as it is stated the argument is invalid. Nevertheless, the conclusion is *probable* on the evidence supplied by the premises, because in a series of such inferences the conclusion is true with a considerable relative frequency when the premises are true.

"But hold on!" the reader may protest. "What do you mean by

saying that the conclusion is true a certain fraction of the time that the premises are true? How do you *ever* know that the *conclusion* is true? Aren't the permanent magnets which compose the metal bars imperceptibly small, and doesn't that make it simply impossible ever to establish the truth of the conclusion? And in that case, can we ever determine the relative frequency of its truth?"

The answer to this objection is based on the distinction between the meaning of a proposition and the evidence in favor of its truth. The meaning of probability in general may be definite, even though in some cases we do not have enough evidence to determine its specific numerical value. The difficulty here pointed out has its analogue elsewhere. Thus the question What is a sphere? may and must be answered independently of and before the question whether in a given case the object examined is in fact a sphere.

The analysis of the probability of propositions which cannot be *directly* verified is much more complicated than we have indicated so far. In such cases the argument depends upon the fact that the theory has as its logical consequences propositions which *may* be directly verified, and which lead to the observation of phenomena *other* than those for which the theory was originally proposed. As we shall see in a later chapter, the evidence upon which a theory is probable consists of *samplings* made from all the necessary consequences of the theory. For the present example, the theory that all metals are composed of small permanent magnets has as one consequence, among others, that hammering or heating a magnet should make it lose its magnetic properties, and this inferred fact is directly observable. A more complete form of the argument may therefore be stated as follows *This, that, and other metals exhibit magnetic properties under specified conditions* (the observed fact); *but, if these metals are composed of small permanent magnets, and so on, then they should exhibit magnetic properties under specified conditions* (general rule); *therefore, each metal is composed of permanent magnets,* and so on (the inferred fact, or theory, not capable of direct verification). However, if metal bars are composed of permanent magnets, then hammering or heating a magnetized needle will make it lose its magnetic properties (*inferred fact,* directly verifiable). The purpose of the deductive elaboration of the theory is to supply us with as many verifiable consequences of it as possible. The argument *for* the theory thus proceeds *from* a proposition known to be true, *to* other propositions directly verifiable, *via* the theory which is not directly verifiable. The argument is now more complicated, but this does not alter the nature of the inference employed. The theory is probable on the evidence, because the argument for it belongs to a *class* of arguments in which the relative frequency r of the truth of the conclusion when the premise is true is not necessarily 1.

We must, however, analyze still more complicated cases of inferences that are recognized as probable. But before we do so, let us state explicitly the essential characteristics of probable inferences. Some of these characteristics we have already noted; others are stated in anticipation of later discussions.

1. Probable inference, like all inference, is based upon certain relations between propositions. No proposition is probable *in itself*. A proposition is probable in relation to other propositions which serve as evidence for it.

2. Whether a proposition has or has not a degree of probability on definite evidence, does not depend on the state of mind of the person who entertains the proposition. Questions of probability, like questions of validity, are to be decided entirely on objective considerations, not on the basis of whether we *feel an impulse* to accept a conclusion or not.

3. An inference is probable only in so far as it belongs to a definite class of inferences in which the frequency of the conclusions being true is a determinate ratio of the frequency of the premises being true. This is the same as saying that the very *meaning* of probability involves *relative frequencies*.

4. Since the probability of a proposition is not an intrinsic character of it, the same proposition may have *different* degrees of probability, in accordance with the evidence which is marshaled in its support.

5. The evidence which may be marshaled in support of a proposition may have different degrees of relevance. In general, that evidence is chosen for a proposition which will make the degree of probability of that proposition as great as possible. But the relevance of the evidence cannot be determined on formal grounds alone.

6. While the meaning of the *measure* of the probability of an inference is the relative frequency with which that type of inference will lead to true conclusions from true premises, it is true that in most cases, as we shall see, the definite numerical value of the probability is not known.

In comparison to the number of cases in which we judge a proposition to be probable on the basis of certain evidence, it is relatively infrequently that we are in a position to determine the exact numerical degree of such probability. But this does not annul the analysis of probability we have given, since we may very well know what probability is *in general* without having adequate evidence in a given case on the basis of which to determine what the numerical value is.

§ 2. THE MATHEMATICS OR CALCULUS OF PROBABILITY

The modern study of probability began when the Chevalier de Méré, a famous gamester of the seventeenth century, consulted his friend, the saintly Pascal, on how best to lay his bets in games with dice. And most discussions of probability center around questions to which numerical answers can be given: What is the probability of getting three heads in four throws with a coin? What is the probability of getting seven with a pair of dice? Problems of this kind, as well as those of a more complicated nature, have been studied by mathematicians. At present, practically every branch of physics and some branches of chemistry and biology find it necessary to employ the calculus of probability. We must consider the simpler problems of this nature in some detail, and note the limitations of the mathematical approach.

Let us begin with the limitations. Mathematics is a discipline which studies the necessary consequences of any set of assumptions. And so conceived, mathematics is not concerned with the truth or falsity of the premises whose consequences it explores. In this respect, logic and mathematics are indistinguishable.

It follows that no purely mathematical theory can determine the degree of probability of any proposition which deals with actual matters of fact. It can determine the probability of a proposition when certain assumptions are explicitly made concerning it. It can tell us what are the necessary consequences of these assumptions; but it cannot determine, and is not concerned with, the truth or falsity of those assumptions. Consequently, *the theory of probability can be purely mathematical only if it is restricted to questions of necessary inference.* This is the case if the theory of probability is viewed as a part of pure mathematics. We shall make a brief study of its elementary theorems, in part because tradition has become fixed in this respect, and in part because the nature of scientific method is illuminated through the use of the rigorous theorems of the calculus of probability in the study of probable inference.

Let us begin with a very simple problem. What is meant by the "mathematical probability" of obtaining a head when a coin is tossed? Let us employ the usual terminology. Instead of discussing the probability of the *proposition: This coin will fall head uppermost,* we shall talk of the probability of the *event* "getting a head," or simply "heads." "Heads" and "tails" are referred to as the *possible events* or *possible alternatives.* If we are interested in getting a head, "heads" is said to be the *favorable event,* all the others the *unfavorable events.* The mathematical probability is then defined as the fraction whose numerator is the number of possible favorable events and whose denominator is the number of possible events (the sum of the number of favorable and unfavorable events), *provided that all the possible events are equiprobable* (equally probable). If, therefore, a coin has 2 faces which can fall in no other way except to yield heads or tails, and if the 2 faces are also equiprobable, the probability of getting a head is $\frac{1}{2}$. In general, if f is the number of favorable events, u the number of unfavorable ones, and if the events are equiprobable, the probability of the favorable event is defined as $\frac{f}{f + u}$. It is clear that this is always a proper fraction, having values between 0 and 1 inclusive; a probability of 0 indicates that the event is impossible, a probability of 1 that it will necessarily take place.

The condition that the possible events must be equiprobable is of fundamental importance, but very difficult to define. It has been the source of serious errors, some of which we shall examine later. What is meant, roughly, is that one possibility should occur as frequently as any other; and it has often been maintained that two possibilities are equally probable when we know no reason why one rather than the other should occur. Nevertheless, whatever may be the difficulties in determining the equiprobability of a set of alternatives, it is not the mathematician's business to find the criteria of equiprobability, since his concern is with the necessary consequences of such an assumption irrespective of its truth or falsity. The importance of this condition will be clear if we ask for the probability of getting a six with a die. We can argue as follows: there are 2 possibilities, getting a six, and getting other-than-a-six; one of them is favorable; consequently, the probability is $\frac{1}{2}$. This answer, however, may be false unless we make the material assumption that these 2 alternatives are equiprobable. This material assumption is generally not made, because the possibility of getting other than a six is assumed to be made up of 5 subsidiary alternatives—getting a one, getting a two, and so on—each of which is equiprobable with getting a six. Hence if the 6 sides are assumed as equiprobable, the probability of getting a six with a die is $\frac{1}{6}$.

The main burden of the calculus of probability is to determine the probability of a complex event from a knowledge of the probability of its component events. We therefore require further definitions. Two events are said to be *independent* if the occurrence of one is not affected by the occurrence or nonoccurrence of the other. The assertion that two events are in fact independent is a *material assumption* which must be explicitly stated. Many serious errors arise in applying the calculus when the independence of events is assumed without adequate ground, or when this condition is completely neglected.

The Probability of a Joint Occurrence

What is the probability of getting 2 heads in tossing a coin twice (or 2 coins once)? This is a complex event, whose components are: 1 head on the first throw, and 1 head on the second. If the events are independent, and if the probability of getting a head on each throw is $\frac{1}{2}$, the calculus of probability demonstrates that the probability of the *joint occurrence* of heads on each throw is the *product* of the probability of heads on each throw: that is, the probability of getting two heads is $\frac{1}{2} \times \frac{1}{2}$, or $\frac{1}{4}$. We can see why this result is a necessary consequence of the assumptions if we enumerate all the possible events in throwing the coin twice. These are: *HH, HT, TH, TT*, in which the order of letters in any one group indicates one possible sequence of heads and tails. There are, therefore, on the assumptions made, 4 equiprobable possibilities; only 1, *HH*, is favorable. Consequently, the probability of getting 2 heads is $\frac{1}{4}$, in agreement with the previous result. In general, if a and b are two independent events, $P(a)$ the probability of the first, and $P(b)$ the probability of the second, the probability of their joint occurrence is $P(ab) = P(a) \times P(b)$.

Care must be taken, when calculating the probability of complex events, to enumerate all the possible alternatives. If we require the probability of getting *at least* 1 head in 2 throws with a coin, the enumeration of the alternatives shows 3 favorable events. Hence the probability of at least 1 head is $\frac{3}{4}$. Eminent scientists have erred by failing to note all the alternatives. According to D'Alembert, for example, the probability of at least 1 head is $\frac{2}{3}$. He enumerated the possibilities as *H, TH, TT*, for he argued that if a head comes uppermost on the first throw, it is not necessary to continue throwing in order to get at least 1 head. But this analysis is faulty, since the possibilities he enumerated are not equiprobable: the first alternative may be regarded as including two distinct cases that are equiprobable with the others.

The probability of the joint occurrence of two events may sometimes be calculated even if the events are not completely independent. Suppose an urn containing 3 white and 2 black balls, and assume all the balls equiprobable in drawing them from the urn one at a time. What is the probability of getting 2 white balls in succession in the first 2 drawings if the balls are not replaced after they have been drawn? Now the probability of drawing a white ball is $\frac{3}{5}$. If a white ball is drawn and not replaced, there remain 2 white and 2 black balls in the urn. Hence the probability of getting a second white ball *if the first ball drawn has been white* is $\frac{2}{4}$. It follows therefore that the probability of getting 2 white balls under these conditions is $\frac{3}{5} \times \frac{2}{4}$, or $\frac{3}{10}$.[2] In general, if $P(a)$ is the probability of event a, and $P_a(b)$ the probability of event b when a has occurred, the probability of the joint occurrence of a and b is $P(ab) = P(a) \times P_a(b)$.

The Probability of Disjunctive Events

We sometimes require not the probability of the joint occurrence of two events, but the probability that *either one* of the events will occur. For this purpose we define *strictly alternative* or *disjunctive events*. Two events are disjunctive if both cannot simultaneously occur (if one does occur, the other cannot). In tossing a coin, the possibilities (heads and tails) are assumed to be disjunctive. It is demonstrable that the probability that either one of two disjunctive events occurs is the *sum* of the probabilities of each. What is the probability of getting either 2 heads or 2 tails in tossing a coin twice, on the assumption that the probability of heads is $\frac{1}{2}$ and that the tosses are independent? Now the probability of getting 2 heads is the product of the probabilities of 1 head on the first throw and 1 head on the second, or $\frac{1}{4}$; similarly, the probability of 2 tails is $\frac{1}{4}$. Hence the probability of either 2 heads or 2 tails is $\frac{1}{4} + \frac{1}{4}$, or $\frac{1}{2}$. The same result is obtained by applying directly the defini-

[2] This result conforms to the definition of mathematical probability. For the total number of ways of drawing 2 balls from a collection of 5 (that is, the number of combinations of 5 balls, 2 at a time) is $\frac{5 \times 4}{1 \times 2}$, or 10. And the number of ways of drawing 2 white balls from a collection of 3 whites is $\frac{3 \times 2}{1 \times 2}$, or 3; this is the number of favorable events. The probability of getting 2 white balls under these conditions is therefore 3/10, as before.

tion of probability to the four possible events *HH, HT, TH, TT.*
Two of these are favorable to either 2 heads or 2 tails; consequently,
the required probability is $\frac{2}{4}$, or $\frac{1}{2}$. In general, if $P(a)$ and $P(b)$
are the respective probabilities of two exclusive events a and b, the
probability of obtaining either is $P(a + b) = P(a) + P(b)$.

These two theorems, the product theorem for independent events
and the addition theorem for exclusive events, are fundamental in
the calculus of probability. In terms of them and their extensions
more complicated problems can be solved easily. Let us suppose we
make one drawing from each of two urns. The first contains 8 white
and 2 black balls, the second contains 6 white and 4 black balls.
The balls are assumed to be equiprobable. What is the probability
that when we draw a ball from each urn, *at least one* of the balls
is white? The probability of a white ball from the first urn is $\frac{8}{10}$,
and of a white ball from the second urn is $\frac{6}{10}$. It is tempting to
add these fractions in order to obtain the probability of a white
ball from either urn. But this would be an error. The answer would
be greater than 1, which is absurd. And indeed we cannot simply
add in this case, because the events are not exclusive. But we may
calculate the result as follows: The probability of not getting a
white ball (that is, of getting a black) from the first urn is $\frac{2}{10}$; and
of not getting a white ball from the second is $\frac{4}{10}$. Therefore, assuming the drawings to be independent, the probability of getting
a white neither from the first nor from the second urn is $\frac{2}{10} \times \frac{4}{10}$,
or $\frac{8}{100}$. Consequently, since we must either get no white ball from
either urn or at least 1 white ball from either, the probability of
getting at least 1 white ball is $1 - \frac{8}{100}$ or $\frac{92}{100}$.

What is the probability of getting just 3 heads in tossing 5 coins,
assuming that heads and tails are equiprobable on each coin, and
that the ways the coins fall are independent of one another? This
problem will introduce us to an important formula in the calculus
of probabilities. We may perhaps reason as follows: Since 5 coins
are thrown, and the probabilities of getting a head on each is $\frac{1}{2}$,
the probability of getting heads is $\frac{1}{2} \times \frac{1}{2} \times \frac{1}{2}$, or $\frac{1}{8}$; but we
want just 3 heads, and therefore the other 2 coins must fall tails,
the probability of which is $\frac{1}{2} \times \frac{1}{2}$, or $\frac{1}{4}$; hence, we may conclude,
the probability of getting *just* 3 heads (that is, 3 heads and 2 tails)
is $\frac{1}{8} \times \frac{1}{4}$, or $\frac{1}{32}$. This result, however, is not correct. This may
be seen quite readily if we write out all the possible ways in which
the five coins can fall, and then apply directly the definition of
probability to these equiprobable alternatives.

The possible alternatives are:

HHHHH   1 possible way of getting 5 heads, 0 tails

HHHHT
HHHTH
HHTHH   5 possible ways of getting 4 heads, 1 tail
HTHHH
THHHH

HHHTT
HHTHT
HTHHT
THHHT
HHTTH   10 possible ways of getting 3 heads, 2 tails
HTTHH
TTHHH
HTHTH
THTHH
THHTH

HHTTT
HTHTT
HTTHT
HTTTH
THTTH   10 possible ways of getting 2 heads, 3 tails
TTHTH
TTTHH
TTHHT
THHTT
THTHT

HTTTT
THTTT
TTHTT   5 possible ways of getting 1 head, 4 tails
TTTHT
TTTTH

TTTTT   1 possible way of getting 0 heads, 5 tails.

There are therefore 32 equiprobable possibilities, 10 of which are favorable to the event. The probability of getting 3 heads and 2 tails is $^{10}/_{32}$, a result ten times as large as the one obtained by the incorrect method.

We can understand now, however, why that method is incorrect. For that method failed to take into account the different orders or arrangements in which 3 heads and 2 tails can occur. We must therefore have some way of evaluating the number of different arrangements which can be made of 5 letters, 3 of which are of one kind and 2 of which are of another kind. Readers who are familiar with the theory of combinations will have no difficulty in evaluating this and similar numbers. However, readers who are unacquainted with this branch of arithmetic need not despair, for there is a very simple formula which will yield the required probabilities easily. For the number of possibilities favorable to each category of complex event (that is, 1 for 5 heads, 0 tails; 5 for 4 heads, 1 tail, and so on) is nothing other than the appropriate coefficient in the expansion of the binomial $(a + b)^5 = a^5 + 5a^4b + 10a^3b^2 + 10a^2b^3 + 5ab^4 + b^5$.

In general, then, it is rigorously demonstrable that if p is the probability of an event, q the probability of its *sole exclusive alternative*, then the probability of a complex event with n components is obtained by selecting the appropriate term in the expansion of the binomial $(p + q)^n$. This binomial expansion can be performed quite simply. It is: $(p + q)^n = p^n + \frac{n}{1} p^{n-1}q + \frac{n(n-1)}{1 \times 2} p^{n-2}q^2 + \frac{n(n-1)\,(n-2)}{1 \times 2 \times 3} p^{n-3}q^3 + \cdots + q^n$.

We shall consider one further illustration of the binomial formula. An urn contains 2 white and 1 red balls, and we are to make 4 drawings from the urn, replacing the ball after each drawing. We are allowed to assume that the balls are equally probable, and that the contents of the urn are thoroughly mixed after each drawing, so that the drawings are independent. What is the probability of getting 3 white balls and 1 red? The probability of drawing a white ball is $p = \frac{2}{3}$, and of drawing a red ball is $q = \frac{1}{3}$. To obtain the required answer, we need only expand $(p + q)^4 = p^4 + 4p^3q + 6p^2q^2 + 4pq^3 + q^4$, and substitute the indicated numerical values in the term which represents the probability of getting 3 white and 1 red balls. This term is $4p^3q$, and the required probability is $4 \times (\frac{2}{3})^3 \times (\frac{1}{3})$, or $\frac{32}{81}$.

§ 3. INTERPRETATIONS OF PROBABILITY

This brief discussion of the calculus of probability does not exhaust the interesting theorems it contains. We must, however, resume the discussion of the *logic* of probable inference. But we must repeat a former warning. The mathematical theory of probability studies the necessary consequences of our assumptions about a set of alternative possibilities; it cannot inform us as to the probability of any actual event. The question very naturally arises, therefore, how the probability of such events is to be determined. Under what circumstances may the theorems of the calculus of probability be applied?

Probability as a Measure of Belief

The analysis of probable inference which we discussed at the beginning of this chapter is not the usual interpretation. The probability of an event has been commonly identified with the *strength of belief* in the event taking place. Probability means, according to De Morgan, "the state of mind with respect to an assertion, a coming event, or any other matter on which absolute knowledge does not exist." The expression, "It is more probable than improbable," means, according to him, "I believe that it will happen more than I believe that it will not happen." [3] An omniscient being would never employ probable inferences, since every proposition would be known to be certainly true or certainly false. Beings lacking omniscience must rely on probabilities, since their knowledge is incomplete, and probability measures their ignorance. When we *feel altogether sure* that an event will take place, its probability is 1; when our *belief in its impossibility is overwhelming,* its probability is 0; when our *belief is intermediate* between the certainty of its occurrence and the certainty of its nonoccurrence, the probability is some fraction intermediate between 1 and 0.

On this interpretation of what probability is, the calculus of probability may be employed only when our ignorance is equally distributed between several alternatives. As we have seen, the mathematical theory can answer the question, "What is the probability of 3 heads with a coin tossed 3 times?" only when information is supplied concerning (1) the number of alternative ways in which the coin can fall, (2) the equiprobability of these alternatives, and (3) the independence of the different throws. On the psychological theory of probability as a measure of belief or expectation, this information is obtained quite simply. For this theory employs a famous criterion called the *principle of insufficient reason* or the *principle of indifference.* According to this principle: *If there is no known reason for predicating of our subject one rather than another of several alternatives, then relatively to such knowledge the assertions of each of these alternatives have an equal probability.* And if there is no known reason for believing that two events are independent rather than dependent, it is just as probable that they are independent as it is that they are not. Two alternatives are equally probable if there is "perfect indecision, belief inclining neither way." When we are completely ignorant about 2 alternatives, the probability of 1 of them occurring must, on this view, be $\frac{1}{2}$. If, then, we are shown a strange coin, since we can have no reason for believing that one face is more likely to come up than the other,

[3] *Formal Logic,* Chap. IX.

we must say the probability of heads is the same as the probability of tails.

It is difficult to believe, however, that this interpretation does justice to the foundations of probability. In the first place, our ability to predict successfully and control portions of the flux of things by means of probable inferences (for example, in thermodynamics and statistical mechanics) is altogether inexplicable if such inferences rest on nothing but our ignorance or the strength of our beliefs. It would be suicidal for an insurance company to conduct its business on the basis of estimating the feeling of expectation which its officers may have.

In the second place, if probability is a measure of belief, whose belief are we to measure? That beliefs about the same event vary considerably in intensity with different people is notorious. All of us have sufficiently mercurial temperaments so that our beliefs at some time and with respect to some things run the entire gamut from despair to certitude for very trivial reasons indeed. Which state of expectation shall be taken as a measure of probability?

Thirdly, since probabilities can be added and multiplied, beliefs would have to be combinable in a corresponding manner. But in fact no operations of addition of beliefs can be found, and beliefs cannot be measured, as our discussion of the principles of measurement will show.

Finally, the psychological theory of probability can be shown to lead to absurd results—unless indeed the range of its application is considerably restricted. Thus suppose we know that the volume of a unit mass of some substance lies between 2 and 4. On this interpretation of probability, it is just as probable that the specific volume lies between 2 and 3 as between 3 and 4. But the specific density is inversely proportional to the specific volume, so that if the volume is v, the density is $1/v$. Hence the density of this substance must lie between $1/2$ and $1/4$ (that is, between $4/8$ and $2/8$) and therefore it is just as likely that it will lie between $1/2$ and $3/8$ as between $3/8$ and $1/4$. This, however, is equivalent to saying that it is just as likely that the *specific volume* will lie between 2 and $8/3$ as between $8/3$ and 4. And this contradicts our first result.

Probability as Relative Frequency

Difficulties of this nature have led to the interpretation of probability as the *relative frequency* with which an event will occur in a class of events. Thus when we say that the probability of a given coin falling heads is $1/2$, we mean that as the number of throws increases indefinitely (in the long run) the ratio between the number of heads and the total number of throws will be about (that is, will not materially differ from) $\frac{1}{2}$. Such a statement is of course an assumption or hypothesis as to the actual course of nature, and therefore needs factual evidence. Such evidence may be rational (in the sense of deduction from previous knowledge as to the constitution of things) or statistical. We may know that pennies are symmetrical and from our knowledge of mechanics infer that the forces making a penny fall head are bound to balance those which make it fall tail. Or we may rely on purely empirical observation as evidence that in the long run neither head nor tail predominates. In the physical sciences, such as meteorology or genetics, and also in practical affairs, such as insurance, we rely on both kinds of evidence. But the statistical evidence is not only indispensable but also apt to be more prominent. We must not, however, completely identify the meaning of a hypothesis with the actual amount of statistical evidence for it available at any given time. A hypothesis as to the nature of things asserts something in regard to all possible phenomena or members of a given class. It can therefore never be completely proved by any number of finite observations. But if we have several hypotheses, the one that agrees best with observable truths that are statistically formulated is naturally preferable.

From this point of view we can understand more clearly the function of the mathematical theory of probability. Suppose we start with the hypothesis that the probability of a male birth is $\frac{1}{2}$. The calculus of probability may then be used to deduce and predict the frequency with which families with 2 male children or families with 2 children of opposite sexes should in the long run occur. Now it may happen that in some particular community *all* the children born during one year are girls. Will this disprove the assumption that the probability of a male birth is $\frac{1}{2}$? Not at all! The calculus shows that on our assumption such an occurrence is *extremely improbable* but not impossible. However, the calculus may also show that such an actual "exceptional" occurrence is in greater conformity with (or would be *less improbable* than) some other assumption. A large number of repetitions of "exceptional" occurrences may thus increase the probability of some other hypotheses, and diminish the probability of our original one. Thus the hypothesis that the probability of a male child is $^{105}\!/_{205}$ is more constant with actual statistical observations.

The calculus of probabilities thus systematizes our experiences on the simplest available assumptions that will also explain apparent exceptions. Of course no hypothesis concerning the probability of an event can be absolutely refuted by a finite number of observations, since even very large discrepancies from theoretically most probable results are not impossible. But statistical results can show some hypotheses to be more improbable than others.

On this view probability is not concerned with the strength of subjective feelings but is grounded in the nature of classes of events, and objective data are needed to determine their probability. We must note, however, that on this view the probability of a unique event is meaningless. When we appear to be talking of the probability of singular events, we must be understood to be speaking elliptically of that phase of the event which it has in common with other possible events of a certain kind. Hence, when we say that the probability of a head with a *given* coin on a *definite* toss is $\frac{1}{2}$, what we must mean is that in a *long series* of such throws heads will turn up about half the time. When we say that in tossing a coin twice, the probability of 2 heads is $\frac{1}{4}$, what we must mean is that in *a long series* of sets of 2 throws each, sets which contain 2 heads are approximately $\frac{1}{4}$ of all the sets.

An immediate corollary from these remarks is a caution against what is known as the "gambler's fallacy." Suppose we enter a game played with a coin assumed to be "fair," that is, for which the probability of heads is $\frac{1}{2}$ and the tosses are independent. Suppose there is a run of 20 heads in succession and we wish to bet on the next throw. What is the probability that the next throw is a head? Many players cannot resist the conclusion that the probability is *less* than $\frac{1}{2}$, on the ground, presumably, that heads and tails must "even up" if the coin is fair. But this conclusion is erroneous, and all gambler's systems devised to make winnings secure when playing with *fair* instruments are inevitably fatal to those who employ them. For if the coin is indeed fair, the 20 heads which have already turned up do not affect the results of the 21st throw; when we say the probability of heads on the 21st throw is $\frac{1}{2}$, we are talking elliptically of a *large series* of throws. On the other hand, if the coin is not fair, but loaded to favor heads, then clearly the probability of heads on the 21st throw is *greater,* and not less, than $\frac{1}{2}$. Laplace tells a story of a man about to become a father. As the date of his wife's delivery approached, he noticed that during the preceding month more girls were born in the community than boys. He therefore placed large bets giving odds favoring the birth of a son.

4. We must note, finally, that no event is probable intrinsically,

but only in terms of its membership in certain classes or series of events. The probability of heads with a coin tossed by hand may be ½; the probability of heads with this same coin shaken in a cup may be altogether different. The event "heads" is here referred to two different classes. And in general the class of events to which a specified event belongs must be explicitly noted in evaluating its probability.

The frequency theory of probability as stated so far has had certain objections urged against it. It does not *seem* capable of interpreting what we mean by the probability of a theory being true, or by the probability of propositions which deal with singular events. We often declare that the heliocentric theory is more probable than the geocentric theory. What does this mean on the frequency theory? And we repeatedly assert propositions like the following: *It is probable that it will rain tonight; It is improbable that Hercules was a historical figure; It is probable that even if Napoleon had been victorious at Waterloo, he would have been unable to remain Emperor of France for much longer.* Such statements are not easily interpreted on the ordinary form of the frequency theory. But these objections are really not fatal, and can be answered by altering the technical expression of the frequency theory.

Probability as the Truth-Frequency of Types of Arguments

This brings us back to the analysis of probable inference we have outlined at the beginning of this chapter—a third interpretation of probability due to Charles Peirce. We have already indicated the objective foundations of probability on this view. We now wish to exhibit the scope of this interpretation.

Suppose a street railway company desires to obtain a city franchise, and decides on bribery as the most effective way of persuading the city fathers to grant it. Great care must be taken, however, for if an alderman genuinely filled with civic virtue were to be approached, the whole game might be spoilt. Should the company approach Alderman A? Now the following facts, believed to be relevant, may be known about Mr. A:

1. He is an alderman, and that means a professional politician.
2. He is a jovial Irishman, ready to see the point of a joke.
3. He is a devout Catholic, and professes high moral principles.
4. He owns real estate, and is suspected of sharp practices in connection with it.
5. He is a member of the local school board, and offers prizes to children for devoted school service.

6. He is not on record as having ever protested against corrup·
tion in public office.

Is it probable that he will accept payment for his vote if the
bribe is proffered in a proper manner? Let us consider the first
item. If that were the sole circumstance known about Mr. A, the
truth-frequency theory would interpret the probability of Mr.
A's accepting a bribe in the following way. Consider the class of *true*
propositions n, obtained from the expression "X is a politician,"
by giving particular values to the variable X. Consider also the
class of propositions n_t, obtained by giving the same values to X
in the expression "X is a politician and X is a bribe-taker." Some
of the resulting propositions of the second set are true, others are
false. Then the limiting value of the ratio $\dfrac{n_t}{n}$ is defined as the probability that any given individual, say Mr. A, will take bribes, on
the evidence that he is a politician. That is, the probability of a
proposition being true is the relative frequency with which a class
of inferences yield true conclusions from true premises. In general,
we do not know the precise numerical value of this ratio. In that
case we say that a conclusion is probable on the evidence if the class
of such inferences lead to true conclusions *more often than not*.

But what if the evidence for a proposition is more complicated
than that we have so far considered? In that case the *analysis* of the
argument is more complicated: but the *interpretation* of the probable inference remains the same. If we were to consider the first two
items about Mr. A, the class of propositions n would be obtained
from the expression "X is a politician, and X is a jovial Irishman," while the class n_t would be obtained from "X is a politician,
and X is a jovial Irishman, and X is a bribe-taker." The limiting
value of the ratio $\dfrac{n_t}{n}$ would again define the probability of Mr. A's
being a bribe-taker on the evidence that he was a jovial Irish politician. Similar considerations apply if we were to take as evidence
all of the six true propositions known about Mr. A.

In most cases, as we have already said, the numerical value of
the measure of probability is not known. In those cases we must be
content with more or less vague impressions, and sometimes with
sheer guesses, as to its magnitude. Very often, too, the evidence may
be so complex that a numerical evaluation of the truth-frequency
becomes impossible on practical grounds. This, however, is not fatal
to this interpretation, since we can reason on indeterminate ratios

as well as we can on determinate ones. The great merit of the truth-frequency theory lies (1) in the success with which it can interpret definite numerical probabilities as well as the indeterminate ones, and (2) in its ability to give an objective reading to the probability of propositions dealing with singular events.

1. The truth-frequency theory can take over all the theorems of the calculus of probability, and accept the statistical foundation for probability, simply by making a few verbal changes in the terminology. Instead of talking about *events,* such as "heads," the truth-frequency theory discusses the *proposition This coin will fall head uppermost on the next throw.* Instead of talking about a *class of events,* this theory discusses a *class of inferences.* For it is very clear that the relative frequency with which *This coin falls head uppermost on toss X* is true, or when *This coin is thrown under specific conditions on toss X* is true, must be the same as the relative frequency with which the event "heads" occurs in a series of tosses with the coin. In the same manner, independent, exclusive, and complex events are discussed in terms of independent, exclusive, and compound propositions.

2. The probability of actual singular events is evaluated by the truth-frequency theory in terms of the *kind of evidence* which is supplied for each. And the probative force of evidence depends upon objective matters of fact. To say *It is probable it will rain tonight* means that the truth of propositions stating the present behavior of the barometer, the changes in temperature, the cloudiness of the sky, and so on, is *in fact* accompanied, with a certain relative frequency, by the truth of propositions stating the occurrence of rainfall within a determinate number of hours.[4]

A final caution will help us to avoid frequent confusions on this point. Just as it is meaningless to speak of a body at rest or in mo-

[4] It may be worth repeating that on the view of probability here advanced, the question of the truth of a proposition concerned with a single event (for example, Caesar's crossing the Rubicon) or of a theory (for example, the Copernican one), is equivalent to the question: With what frequency are propositions or theories of a certain class true if there is as much evidence for them as there is for the proposition or theory being considered? Hence on this view a theory highly probable on one set of evidence may cease to be so as the evidence is increased. This, however, follows not from the subjectivity but from the relative character of probability. Indeed, the reason that the psychological interpretation of probability has held the field so long is the mistaken prejudice that all relativity is psychological. It has been, perhaps, a dim recognition of the relative character of probability which has militated against the common form of the frequency theory. For to speak of the probability of an event generally carries the suggestion that the probability is an intrinsic characteristic of the event itself.

tion except in reference to some other body, so it is meaningless to speak of the probability of an event occurring, or a set of propositions being true, except relative to certain evidence or material assumptions. If despite that we all do often speak of some bodies being at rest, it is because we so usually assume our earth as a reference body that it is not generally necessary to mention it. So in philosophy when we speak of all material propositions or theories as only probable, we understand this in reference to the whole body of available relevant knowledge as evidence.

This removes a difficulty often felt in regard to the probability of philosophical theories as to the total world. "Universes," as Peirce puts it, "are not as plentiful as blackberries." But logically the actual world is one of a class of possible ones, and the probability of any theory in respect to it is the relative frequency with which, according to our estimate, theories of the given type are true on the sort of evidence actually available.

The specific difficulties encountered in the study of probable inferences lie in analyzing the great variety of such inferences into their components, in evaluating the probative force of each, and in determining whether the components are independent of one another. That is not a task for an elementary book. We shall, however, have occasion to study more complicated forms of probable inferences in a later chapter.

CHAPTER IX

SOME PROBLEMS OF LOGIC

§ 1. THE PARADOX OF INFERENCE

A richer understanding of the nature of formal logic can be obtained if we consider some critical onslaughts upon it. Our discussions of traditional logic as well as those of generalized or modern logic and mathematics have made clear that in every valid argument the conclusion *necessarily* follows from the premises. At the same time, we have indicated that the conclusion is not merely a *verbal* transformation of the premises: more than a knowledge of language is needed to prove a theorem in geometry or to determine the weight of evidence for a given proposition. As a consequence, many students have been led to serious doubt as to the usefulness or the validity of formal logic.

On the one hand, it has been said, since the conclusion necessarily follows from the premises, the conclusion must be "contained" in the premises. If the conclusion were not "contained" in the premises, it would be quite arbitrary whether we inferred one rather than another, perhaps incompatible, proposition from them; and "validity" would be a meaningless sound. On the other hand, it has been said, the conclusion must be different from the premises, and a valid inference should advance us to something "new" or "novel"; if it did not, an inference would be useless. This "paradox of inference" may be stated in the following form: *If in an inference the conclusion is not contained in the premise, it cannot be valid; and if the conclusion is not different from the premises, it is useless; but the conclusion cannot be contained in the premises and also possess novelty; hence inferences cannot be both valid and useful.*

This criticism of formal logic, although it has been often urged, is based upon several confusions. We must examine what is meant when it is said that the conclusion "is contained" in the premises, and that the conclusion represents something "novel." The questions are closely connected. Let us consider the second one first.

1. It is essential to distinguish the psychological novelty which a conclusion may have from any logical novelty it may be supposed to have. A conclusion may be surprising or unexpected even though it is correctly implied by the premises. Certainly to most men all the consequences of Euclid's assumptions are not present to their minds when they contemplate the assumptions. Even in less complex arguments psychological novelty is very frequently the rule. The following is a frequently cited story of Thackeray's. "An old abbé, talking among a party of intimate friends, happened to say, 'A priest has strange experiences; why, ladies, my first penitent was a murderer.' Upon this, the principal nobleman of the neighborhood enters the room. 'Ah, Abbé, here you are; do you know, ladies, I was the Abbé's first penitent, and I promise you my confession astonished him!' " The reader may add that the conclusion of the syllogism no doubt surprised the ladies. In a puzzle invented by C. L. Dodgson about two clocks, the unexpectedness of the conclusion from premises freely granted is clearly illustrated. "Which is better, a clock that is right only once a year, or a clock that is right twice every day? 'The latter,' you reply, 'unquestionably.' Very good, now attend. I have two clocks: one doesn't go *at all,* and the other loses a minute every day: which would you prefer? 'The losing one,' you answer, 'without doubt.' Now observe; the one which loses a minute a day has to lose twelve hours, or 720 minutes, before it is right, and is therefore right about once every two *years,* whereas the other is evidently right as often as the time it points to comes around, which happens twice a day. So you've contradicted yourself *once."*

It may therefore be granted as a well-attested fact about human minds that the conclusion of an argument is not in general known to them when they inspect or believe the premises, especially if a long chain of inferences is required to reach the conclusion. And it may well be that if it were otherwise, we would not perform explicit inferences, and that deduction would be unnecessary. *But this has nothing to do with the validity of an inference.* An inference may be valid even though the conclusion is quite familiar, and to teachers of geometry the cogency of the demonstration of the Pythagorean theorem has not disappeared simply because they know exactly what is coming next at each step of the proof. If the reader, unlike Euclid, "immediately sees" that the second part of his Proposition 29—If a straight line falls on two parallel lines, it makes the interior angles on the same side equal to two right angles—asserts precisely the same state of affairs as does his Postulate 5—If a straight line falling on two straight lines makes the interior angles on the same side less than two right angles, the two straight lines, if produced, meet on that side—he will not need an elaborate demonstration, as did Euclid, for the theorem. Nevertheless, the theorem is a necessary consequence of the assumption.

The question of *psychological* novelty is, therefore, not one for logic. On the other hand, by *logical* novelty must be meant the logical independence of what is said to be the "conclusion" from its "premises." And it is clear that if the argument is to be valid, the conclusion cannot, so long as it is dependent upon the premises, possess logical novelty.

2. We must now examine what is meant when it is said that the conclusion "is contained" in the premises. In the first place, "to be contained" is clearly a *spatial* metaphor, and it surely cannot be meant that the conclusion is contained or is present in the premises as a desk is in a room, or even as a chicken is in an egg. In the second place, we have already disposed of the view that the conclusion is psychologically or explicitly present to our minds when we entertain the premises from which we infer it. What meaning, then, can we assign to the assertion that the conclusion is contained in the premises? Simply this: The conclusion in a valid argument is *implied by* the premises. And the paradox disappears when it is once seen that the relation of implication between propositions is of such unique type that only confusion is courted when it is replaced by some analogous relation which has some of its formal properties.

Some further remarks may remove any lingering perplexity in the reader. Propositions imply one another, and our inferences are valid in virtue of such *objective* relations of implication. We may *make* inferences; we do not make, but only *discover*, implications. *Which* of the propositions implied by a set of assumptions we *do* infer, is of course not logically determined. That depends upon our extralogical interests and our intellectual skill.

It is convenient also, in this connection, to distinguish between the *conventional meaning* of a proposition, and the propositions it implies. In one sense, of course, such a distinction is quite gratuitous, since after we discover some of the implied propositions they are taken as constituting part of the *meaning* of the premises. Thus, having discovered that Euclid's axioms imply that the angle sum of a triangle is equal to two right angles, we often regard this theorem as characterizing the full import of the axioms. Nevertheless, although no sharp or final line of division can be drawn between what is the agreed or conventional meaning of a proposition and its logical consequences, such a distinction is recognized in practice. The tyro in geometry understands in some measure what is meant by saying that through a point outside a line only one parallel can be drawn to it, even though he may not know to what other proposition he is committed when he accepts this one. Let us then agree to designate as *conventional meaning* that minimum of meaning which is required if a group of inquirers can be said to address themselves to the *same* proposition. Thus, the conventional meaning of *All men are mortal* may be that the class of men is included in the class of mortals. In such a case, the meaning of the proposition *All immortals are non-men* is not a part of its conventional meaning, but is the meaning of a proposition *implied* by it.

This distinction is useful for the purpose of stating clearly the answer to the paradox. Since only the conventional meaning of the premise is necessarily before the reasoner's mind, the conventional meanings of some of the implied propositions may be absent, so that when these are found to be implied by a set of premises, a feeling of novelty may result. On the other hand, from the point of view of the relations between conventional meanings, the meaning of the implied propositions is always connected with ("contained in") the meaning of the premises.

The thesis that the conclusion of an inference is essentially connected with its premises, so that the latter could not be true if the former were false, has sometimes been understood to preclude the possibility of physical change or physical novelty. An adequate discussion of this question would lead us into metaphysics. But the reader should have no difficulty in rejecting such an interpretation if he remembers that the relations of implication hold not in virtue of the premises being empirically true, but in virtue of the logical relations between premises and conclusion. These relations are applicable to a changing world—indeed, we know of change only in relation to certain relative constants. The question whether there is any constancy in the physical world involves empirical as well as logical considerations. But *if* any proposition in physical science turns out to be true in fact, it reveals certain structural identities which are common characteristics of different or successive states.

§ 2. IS THE SYLLOGISM A *Petitio Principii?*

A somewhat different attack on the usefulness of formal logic has been made since the days of Aristotle. It has been leveled specifically against the syllogism. However, if the charge is well founded, it is fatal to the value of all deductive reasoning. But it is sufficient to examine the specific form of the criticism. John Stuart Mill, who has renewed the ancient charge upon the syllogism, although he believed he was replying to it, has stated it as follows:

"We have now to inquire, whether the syllogistic process, that of reasoning from generals to particulars, is, or is not, a process of inference; a progress from the known to the unknown: a means of coming to a knowledge of something which we did not know before.

"Logicians have been remarkably unanimous in their mode of answering this question. It is universally allowed that a syllogism is vicious if there be anything more in the conclusion than was assumed in the premises. But this is, in fact, to say, that nothing ever was, or can be, proved by syllogism, which was not known, or assumed to be known, before. . . .

"It must be granted that in every syllogism, considered as an argument to prove the conclusion, there is a *petitio principii.* When we say,

> All men are mortal,
> Socrates is a man,
> therefore
> Socrates is mortal;

it is unanswerably urged by the adversaries of the syllogistic theory, that the proposition, Socrates is mortal, is presupposed in the more general assumption, All men are mortal: that we cannot be assured of the mortality of all men, unless we are already certain of the mortality of every individual man: that if it be still doubtful whether Socrates, or any other individual we choose to name, be mortal or not, the same degree of uncertainty must hang over the assertion, All men are mortal: that the general principle, instead of being given as evidence of the particular case, cannot itself be taken for true without exception, until every shadow of doubt which could affect any case comprised with it, is dispelled by evidence *aliundè;* and then what remains for the syllogism to prove? That, in short, no reasoning from generals to particulars can, as such, prove anything: since from a general principle we cannot infer any particulars, but those which the principle itself assumes as known." [1]

In order to understand this criticism the reader must distinguish the charge that the premises of a syllogism could not be true unless the conclusion were also true from the charge that we must *know* the truth of the conclusion in order to establish the truth of one or other of the premises. The first charge, the reader will realize, is perfectly harmless. It is not a criticism of the syllogism, but is a statement of the conditions of validity for any deductive inference. It is the second charge which is serious and to which we must address ourselves. It raises the pertinent question of whether any part of the evidence employed to establish the *truth* of a proposition is, in turn, established by evidence of which that *very* proposition is a part. The syllogism begs the question, the criticism runs, because the premises advanced as evidence for the conclusion can be advanced only if the conclusion is known to be true. This charge may therefore be summed up in the following dilemma: If *all* the facts of the premises have been examined, the syllogism is needless; if some have not been, it is a *petitio*. But either all the facts have been examined or some have not. Therefore, the syllogism is either useless or circular. This charge, rightly understood, is not leveled at the validity of deductive inferences as such.

The question, then, is whether the universal premise of a syllogism can ever be asserted as true without examining all of its instances, and if it cannot be asserted as true, whether the syllogism is therefore useless. Now there are undoubtedly some cases when a universal proposition is established by examining all its instances. Thus, when we assert *All the known planets revolve around the sun* the evidence for it is that *Mercury revolves around the sun, Venus revolves around the sun,* and so on for all the known planets. A universal so obtained is called an *enumerative* universal, and may with justice be considered as merely summarizing neatly such a collection of singular propositions. If, then, we were to argue that Jupiter revolves around the sun because all known planets do so and Jupiter is a known planet, the charge that we are arguing in a circle would be justified.

Is it the case, however, that enumerative universals are the typical universals employed in inquiry? Does the proposition *All men are mortal* merely summarize the collection: *The man Adam is mortal, The man Abel is mortal,* and so on, down the line? As we shall see in the sequel, such a view is an absurd interpretation of scientific

---

[1] *A System of Logic*, 1875, 2 vols., Vol. I, p. 210. The first edition was published in 1843.

method. At this place we can only suggest alternative views. In the first place, a universal may express a resolution to act in certain ways that may have been made independently of any specific occasion to which it nevertheless applies. Thus it may be a rule that *All policemen shall be at least five feet eight inches in height,* and we may know that this rule is and will be enforced without knowing any members of the present or a future police force. If in such a case we infer that Smith is at least five feet eight because he is on the police force, the argument is not circular.

But secondly, and this is the important case, a universal proposition may be advanced as a hypothesis in order to discover the solution of some practical problem or to unify our knowledge. In such a case, the universal is not known to be *certainly* true. Nevertheless, the evidence for it may be more adequate and stronger than for any individual proposition that is a verifiable consequence of it but which is not included in the antecedent evidence for the theory. Thus one consequence of Newtonian physics is that a pair of double stars will revolve around their common center of gravity in elliptic orbits. But Newtonian physics is established with considerable security without first examining double stars; and the evidence for the theory may be greater than that for the existence of such elliptic orbits even if we try to examine double stars directly. The inference that double stars do move on such orbits is therefore not circular. The conclusion is, indeed, not certain, since the theory is not certainly true. But only a mistaken idea of science, such as Mill's, which demands absolute certitude in matters of fact, would reject it as useless for that reason. Similarly, we infer the mortality of any living man from the premise *All men are mortal* without basing this premise upon an enumeration of dead men. For we know that *All men have organic bodies* and *All organic bodies disintegrate with time* are supported by evidence of a far-reaching character which itself does not rest in turn upon an examination of the mortality of any one human being.

It is interesting to consider Mill's attempted defense of the syllogism. According to him, when we infer that the Duke of Wellington is mortal (he was alive when Mill was writing) from the premises *All men are mortal* and *The Duke is a man* the major premise is not the real basis for the inference. He says:

"Assuming that the proposition, The Duke of Wellington is mortal, is immediately an inference from the proposition, All men are mortal; whence do we derive our knowledge of that general truth? Of course from observation. Now, all which man can observe are individual cases. From these all general truths must be drawn, and into these they may be again resolved; for a general truth is but an aggregate of particular truths; a comprehensive expression, by which an indefinite number of individual facts are affirmed or denied at once. But a general proposition is not merely a compendious form for recording and preserving in the memory a number of particular facts, all of which have been observed. Generalization is not a process of mere naming, it is also a process of inference. From instances which have been observed, we feel warranted in concluding, that what we found true in those instances, holds in all similar ones, past, present, and future, however numerous they may be. We then, by that valuable contrivance of language which enables us to speak of many as if they were one, record all that we have observed, together with all that we infer from observations, in one concise expression; and have thus only one proposition, instead of an endless number, to remember or to communicate. The results of many observations and inferences, and instructions for making innumerable inferences in unforeseen cases, are compressed into one short sentence. . . .

"If, from our experience of John, Thomas, etc., who once were living, but are now dead, we are entitled to conclude that all human beings are mortal, we might surely without any logical inconsequence have concluded at once from those instances, that the Duke of Wellington is mortal. The mortality of John, Thomas, and others is, after all, the whole evidence we have for the mortality of the Duke of Wellington. Not one iota is added to the proof by interpolating a general proposition. . . . Not only *may* we reason from particular to particular without passing through generals, but we perpetually do so reason." [2]

Thus, on Mill's view, the charge of *petitio* against the syllogism is quashed simply by denying that the premises of the syllogism are the true basis for the conclusion, and by insisting that the conclusion is not part of the data from which the universal premise is inferred. It will not have escaped the reader, however, that Mill's attempt to defend the syllogism culminates in regarding an inference as valid when it is not so without a further premise. Why may we infer from the death of John, Thomas, and the rest that the Duke of Wellington is mortal? Because, says Mill, what was true in those instances holds in all similar ones. If, however, we state

[2] *A System of Logic*, 1875, 2 vols., Vol. I, p. 210. The first edition was published in 1843.

this argument formally, we find, lo and behold! a syllogism: *What is true for the case of John, Thomas, and so on is true for all similar instances; but John, Thomas, and so on died; therefore the Duke, being a similar instance, is mortal.* And the major premise of this syllogism cannot, even on Mill's view, be regarded as simply an aggregate of particular propositions. In many cases, such as the theory of gravitation, universals cannot possibly be conceived as being memoranda for singular propositions. In such cases the absolute indispensability of universal propositions is even more evident than in the simple illustrations given by Mill. But we are trespassing on a discussion which we must reserve until later.

We may therefore summarize the discussion of the syllogism as a *petitio:*

1. The charge that the syllogism is a *petitio principii* is significant only if we are interested in the evidence for the *material* truth of premises and conclusion. Even if this charge were sustained, the syllogism as a mode of valid inference would not be impugned.

2. Those universal premises which express our resolutions, commands, laws, may be asserted without examining all the possible instances to which they may be applied.

3. Universal premises may be asserted as probably true on evidence which does not contain as parts every verifiable consequence of those premises.

And it is simply not true that every universal proposition is a shorthand device for summarizing a collection of previously known singular propositions.

§ 3. THE LAWS OF THOUGHT

Logic has often been defined as the study of the "laws of thought." And in particular three principles—the principle of identity, the principle of contradiction, and the principle of excluded middle—have been taken as the necessary, and sometimes as the sufficient, conditions for valid thinking. We wish to examine these principles, discuss whether they are indeed laws of thought, and indicate finally the nature of logical principles.

The three principles mentioned have been formulated in several ways. One formulation of them, in the order stated above, is *If anything is A it is A; nothing can be both A and not A; anything must be either A or not A.* It is preferable, however, to consider the following alternative formulation first. The *principle of identity* asserts that: *If any proposition is true, it is true.* The *principle of contradiction* asserts that: *No proposition can be both true and false.* The *principle of excluded middle* states that: *Any proposition must be either true or false.*

It will doubtless strike the reader that in either formulation none of the principles asserts anything about anybody's *thoughts.* In the second formulation, which we shall take as particularly relevant to logic, the so-called laws of thought state something about *propositions.* The principle of contradiction, for example, does not say that we cannot *think* a proposition to be both true and false. If it did assert that, it would be most certainly false, as the fact that men often believe contradictory propositions clearly shows. There is no psychological impossibility, unfortunately, to think confusedly and inconsistently. If, therefore, these principles are representative of logical principles, we must conclude that the subject matter of logic is not human thoughts at all. On the other hand, if the qualification is made that the laws of thought do not refer to human thinking as a process in time, but to the conditions of valid thinking, the reply is much the same. The conditions of valid thinking are themselves not thoughts. In fact, as the reader knows, logic studies the relations between sets of propositions in virtue of which some limitation is placed upon the possible truth or falsity of one set by the possible truth or falsity of another set.

But after our lengthy discussion of many principles of logic, it should also be clear that while these three "laws of thought" state essential logical properties of propositions, they are not an *exhaustive* statement of logical principles. The principle of the syllogism, the principles of tautology, simplification, absorption, and others discussed in Chapter VI have an equal claim with the traditional three to belong to the foundations of logic. It may be thought, perhaps, that all the other logical principles may be derived from these three by a chain of logical steps. This, however, would be a mistake. The so-called laws of thought are not a sufficient basis from which to deduce all the other logical principles.

It is also an error to suppose that any one of the three "laws" may be deduced logically from the others without assuming it in the process of deduction. Into these matters we cannot go in further detail. But the reader will recall our previous discussion of demonstrability. Even if the other principles of logic could be derived from the traditional three, that would not make these more important, or more certain, than any of the others.

Criticisms of the Three "Laws"

The significance of the three "laws of thought" may be made more evident if we consider some criticisms which have been made of them.

1. It has been denied, for example, that the *principle of identity* is universally true, because a proposition may be true at one time and false at another. Thus it is said that *The sun is shining* may be true today but false tomorrow, and perhaps even later on the same day. The objection, however, arises from a confusion. The expression, "The sun is shining," does not fully express the proposition which is judged true or false. There is an implicit time and place reference, which is suppressed (because it is taken for granted) in the expression, but which is essential in the proposition judged. As it stands, therefore, the expression is a *propositional function* (and not a proposition) of the form *The sun is shining at (place) x on (time) y.* If we supply that reference, as in the expression *The sun is shining at New York on January 1, 1932, the proposition cannot be true on one day and false on another.* We must distinguish, therefore, the time and place *in* predication (the time and place reference *in* the proposition) from the time and place *of* predication (the time and place *at* which a position is judged). The truth or falsity of a proposition is independent of the time and place *of* predication, so that it is correct to say of a proposition that "once true, always true, once false, always false."

2. Similarly, the universality of the *principle of contradiction* has been denied on the ground that in some cases two apparently contradictory propositions may both be true. Thus it is said *The floor is wet* and *The floor is not wet* may both be true; also *This penny has a circular shape* and *This penny has an elliptical shape* (where the subject is the same penny) may both be true. This apparent violation of the principle of contradiction may be resolved as was the criticism of the principle of identity. In the first pair of expressions the time *in* predication is not specified; in the second pair, the place *in* predication, the place at which the penny presents the shape, is omitted. If these omissions are supplied, in neither of the pairs are the propositions contradictories.

Another objection has arisen from a consideration of what have been known traditionally as *sophisms,* which play an important rôle in modern logic. Suppose a man asserts, "I am lying." If he is speaking the truth, "I am lying" is true. But in that case, the man is not speaking the truth, so that "I am lying" is false. But in that case he *is* speaking the truth, and "I am lying" is true, and so on, *ad infinitum*. Here seems to be a proposition which is both true and false.

Common sense will easily dispose of this difficulty by recognizing that the man who says, "I am lying," and says nothing else, has not *asserted* anything, and therefore has not committed himself to any proposition. The difficulty arises from confusing a group of words which form a *sentence* with a *proposition*, which alone is true or false. The sentence, "I am lying," would indicate a proposition only if it referred to some *other* assertion of the speaker, which would thus be characterized as a lie. In such a case the paradox obviously vanishes.

The recognition of the fact that the sentence, "I am lying," is not a complete and independent proposition, but can only serve as such if it points to some other proposition, is at the basis of an elaborate and carefully worked-out doctrine known as the *theory of types*. According to the theory of types the assertion, "I am lying," is a proposition only if it has as its own subject matter a collection of propositions which do *not* include the proposition *I am lying*. This proposition is then of different type from those which it is *about*, and cannot, without contradiction, be regarded as asserting anything about propositions which are of the *same* type as itself. In other words, "I am lying" must be interpreted as, "There is a proposition which I am affirming and which is false." But this assertion itself cannot be any one of the propositions referred to. If the speaker subsequently wishes to deny that he was lying, the proposition expressing the denial must be of a *higher* type than "*I am lying.*" In this way, propositions can be arranged in hierarchies or types. so that any proposition may be about a proposition of a lower type, but never about a proposition of the same or a higher type. The principle used to avoid such contradictions has been named the *vicious-circle principle,* and has been stated as follows: *Whatever involves* all *of a collection must not be one of the collection.*

3. Finally, the *principle of excluded middle* has been challenged on the ground that another alternative is possible to the truth or falsity of a proposition. Thus, it is claimed that it is not necessary that one of the following two propositions be true: *He is older than his brother* and *He is younger than his brother* for there is the alternative that *He is as old as his brother.* But the objection confuses the contrary of a proposition with its contradictory. The contradictory of *He is older than his brother* is not *He is younger*

than his brother, but *He is not older than his brother.* To this pair of contradictories the principle of excluded middle does apply.

Another objection has been made on the ground that things change, often insensibly, so that the line between the truth and the falsity of a proposition is difficult to draw, even if it is not altogether arbitrary. Thus it is said *He is mature* and *He is not mature* are formal contradictories, and yet we cannot decide which one of them is true. This objection does not deny the principle, since the latter simply states that one of a pair of contradictories must be true, but does not tell us which one. It is true, however, that "maturity" may denote a vaguely defined character, so that it may be difficult to draw a line between maturity and the lack of it. But in such cases, because there is a region of indetermination in the application of our concepts we must either make further distinctions as to what is meant by "maturity," or agree upon some conventional standard, such as age, which will fix the denotation of the concept.

Finally, it has been said that to the two alternatives *true* and *false,* there is a third, the *meaningless.* Thus, according to Mill, "Abracadabra is a second intention," is neither true nor false, but meaningless. To which the proper reply is that the principle of excluded middle is applicable only to propositions, and that a meaningless expression is not a possible object to which the principle may be applied. However, the question of what constitutes a meaningful expression is a large one, and we cannot more than suggest some of the problems. Is, "Wisdom has a low electrical resistance," either true or false—is it a proposition? In what sense may we deny that a number has weight? Such questions lead to a discussion of the categories or types of being and the general conditions of significance.

§ 4. THE BASIS OF LOGICAL PRINCIPLES
IN THE NATURE OF THINGS

We turn now to the first formulation of the three so-called laws of thought. This formulation is an obvious counterpart of the propositional formulation. And it expresses, perhaps even more clearly, that their subject matter is certain *general or generic traits of all things whatsoever.* And the same may be said of *all* the principles of logic. From this point of view, logic may be regarded as the study of the most general, the most pervasive characters of both whatever is and whatever may be. From what has already been said, however, the reader will recognize that the principle of identity (If anything is *A,* it is *A*) does not deny the possibility of change and does *not* affirm that if a poker is hot it will always remain hot. It *does* say that anything whatsoever in some definite context and occasion has some determinate character. If a poker is hot here and now, then it is hot, and not, in this one of its aspects, something else. If the coin has a round shape at this time and from this point of view, then the shape cannot also be not round. And if evenness or oddness can be significantly predicated of a number, then such a number must be either odd or even.

The insight that logical principles express the most general nature of things was first clearly expressed by Aristotle. At the same time he recognized that since the general nature of things is the ground for the correctness or incorrectness of reasoning, that general nature is also expressed in the principles of logic or inference. According to him, therefore, logic studies the nature of anything that is; "it investigates being as being." It is differentiated from other sciences because while the other disciplines examine the properties which distinguish one subject matter from another, logic studies those truths which hold for everything that is, and not for some special subdivision of what is apart from the others. As a consequence, logical principles must be formal—they represent the common characters of any subject matter, and they cannot be employed to differentiate one subject matter from another. Instead of regarding the abstractions of logic as a fault, we must regard them as a virtue. For we require to know only the most general characters of a subject matter (that which it has in common with everything else) in order to reason upon it validly. We need not encumber our thought with useless intellectual baggage if we reason intelligently. As principles of being, logical principles are universally applicable. As principles of inference, they must be accepted by all, on pain of stultifying all thought. Logical principles, therefore, are not independent of questions of truth. For when we draw a conclusion from the premises correctly we are tacitly recognizing the truth of the proposition, which is grounded in the general nature of things, that the premises do imply the conclusion. (We must mention in passing that this view of the nature of logic is not accepted by all thinkers.)

It is important, however, to be clear about the sense in which logical principles are principles of being. As has been noted before, it has often been supposed that logical principles are "better known" or "more certain" than any other principles. Whether this is so or not is not the significant fact about the principles. Logical principles are involved in every proof, and in that sense every proof depends upon them *whether we know them explicitly or not, or whether we have confidence in them or not.* We have already pointed out that the fundamental assumptions in a system need not be more familiar than the theorems. That we know logical principles at all, is not a consequence or a condition of their expressing pervasive characters of whatever is.

It has also been supposed that we can prove logical principles to be necessarily true by showing that they are involved in every reflective inquiry. This also is an error, if by proof is meant what is ordinarily understood by proof. Logical principles in their full generality cannot be proved, since every such attempted proof must assume some or all of them. That which is required in every proof cannot itself be demonstrated. Nevertheless, logical principles are confirmed and exhibited in every inference that we draw, in every investigation which we successfully bring to a close. They are discovered to hold in every analysis which we undertake. They are inescapable, because any attempt to disregard them reduces our thoughts and words to confusion and gibberish.

It has also been supposed that because logical principles are first principles in the sense that every subject matter verifies them, they are prior to existence and condition it. Now there is no doubt that every significant proposition, if true, limits the subject matter, and prohibits something else to be true. In this sense, and only in this sense, do logical principles condition existence. It is an error, however, to suppose that logical principles are prior to existence in the sense that logical principles were *first in time.* On this point Aristotle himself has said all that needs to be said: "The fact of the being of a man carries with it the truth of the proposition that he is, and the implication is reciprocal: for if a man is, the proposition wherein we allege that he is is true, and conversely, if the proposition wherein we allege that he is is true, then he is. The true proposition, however, is in no way the cause of the being of the man, but the fact of the man's being does seem somehow to be the cause of the truth of the proposition, for the truth or falsity of the proposition depends on the fact of the man's being or not being." [3] The priority of logic lies simply in its expression of the utmost generality possible.

[3] *Categoriae*, Chap. 12, in *Works*, ed. by W. D. Ross, 1928, Vol. I, p. 14b.

EXAMPLES OF DEMONSTRATION

§ 1. WHAT DOES A DEMONSTRATION ESTABLISH?

According to an age-old tale, Hiero, the tyrant of Syracuse, commanded a votive crown of pure gold to be placed in a temple of the immortal gods. But gossip concerning the goldsmith led him to suspect that silver had been mixed in its construction, and he requested Archimedes to determine, without injuring the crown, whether or not this was the case. While taking a bath, Archimedes noticed that his limbs were unusually light when in the water, and that in proportion as his body was immersed in the tub, water ran out of it. A method of resolving the problem forthwith became evident to him, and leaping out of the tub in great joy, he returned home naked, shouting as he ran, "Eureka! Eureka!"

The reader may know that the solution of the problem depends on the proposition: *A solid denser than water will, when immersed, suffer a loss in weight equal to the weight of the displaced water.* But how can we, or how did Archimedes, demonstrate the truth of this key proposition? The incident in the bath cannot be regarded as conclusive evidence for it, even though it may have *suggested* the proposition to Archimedes.

How would the reader go about demonstrating it? If he is empirically minded and very modern, he may perhaps believe that all that is necessary is to make a series of careful measurements on the weight of bodies in and out of the water by suspending them from a spring balance. Archimedes, however, was too wise a scientist, too well acquainted with the requirements of a *demonstration,* to do any such thing. For in the first place the confirmation of the proposition by measurement would never be more than *approximate.* No two measurements will yield exactly the same weight lost

[1] To be read by more advanced students after Chapter I.

by the solid, or show that the weight lost is precisely equal to the weight of the displaced water. And in the second place, no number of measurements can show that the proposition is true *for all possible cases*—for the unexamined instances which occurred in the past, as well as for the instances when a solid will fall into water in some distant future. How can one be sure, on the evidence supplied by such measurements, that if the solid exceeds a definite size, or if the quantity of water is increased sufficiently, the relation asserted by the proposition will still hold? The reader will agree that the method of experimental confirmation cannot guarantee that exceptions may not occur.

How, then, did Archimedes *prove* this proposition? Fortunately, the demonstration he found adequate is included in the extant portions of his treatise *On Floating Bodies*. It has been for centuries a model of what a demonstration should be, and has served as inspiration for the work of such men as Kepler and Galileo. It consists in exhibiting necessary relations between the *nature* or *definition of fluids* and the *nature of the behavior of solids* immersed in them. Let us examine it in detail, and so discover for ourselves the essential features of deductive reasoning.

Archimedes begins his treatise with a postulate, or assumption, which serves to define the nature of fluids. He then demonstrates six propositions by means of this postulate and the theorems of geometry which have already been demonstrated in treatises on that subject. In order to prove the seventh proposition, however, only the postulate and two of the preceding propositions are required. We shall simply state these, and then reproduce the demonstration of the seventh theorem. (We shall omit quotation marks here and abridge somewhat.)

The *postulate* reads: Let it be supposed that a fluid is of such a character that, in all uniform and continuous positions of its parts, the portion that suffers the lesser pressure is driven along by that which suffers the greater pressure. And each part of the liquid suffers pressure from the portion perpendicularly above it if the latter be sinking or suffer pressure from another portion.

Proposition 3. Solids which have the same density as a fluid will, if let down into it, be immersed so that they do not project above the surface but do not sink lower.

Proposition 6. If a solid lighter than a fluid be forcibly immersed in it, the solid will be driven upwards by a force equal to the difference between its weight and the weight of the fluid displaced.

Proposition 7 and its proof are as follows: A solid denser than a fluid will, if placed in it, descend to the bottom of the fluid; and the solid will, when weighed in the fluid, be lighter than its true weight by the weight of the fluid displaced.

Proof. 1. The first part of the proposition is obvious, since the part of the fluid immediately under the solid will be under greater pressure than the parts of the fluid under this part; and therefore these other parts will give way until the solid reaches bottom.

2. Let A be a solid heavier than the same volume of the fluid, and let $(G + H)$ represent its weight, while G represents the weight of the same volume of the fluid.

Take a solid, B, lighter than the same volume of the fluid, and such that the weight of B is G, while the weight of the same volume of the fluid is $(G + H)$. (That is, B is to be so chosen that its volume is equal to that volume of the fluid which is equal in weight to the body A.)

Let A and B be now combined into one solid and immersed. Then, since $(A + B)$ will be of the same weight as the same volume of fluid, both weights being equal to $(G + H) + G$, it follows that $(A + B)$ will remain stationary in the fluid.

Therefore the force which causes A by itself to sink must be equal to the upward force exerted by the fluid on B by itself. This latter is equal to the difference between $(G + H)$ and G. Hence A is depressed by a force equal to H, i.e., its weight in the fluid is H, or the difference between $(G + H)$ and G.

The reader should examine this proof carefully and repeatedly. When he has, let him consider the following questions.

1. In what sense does the "proof" demonstrate the proposition, assuming that it is conclusive?

2. Is the proof conclusive?

3. Upon what factors or aspects of the subject matter does the conclusiveness depend?

These questions must be squarely met if we are to avoid confusion concerning the philosophy of proof.

1. If the proof is cogent, then for all possible solids and for all fluids *conforming to the conditions stated in the postulate,* the relations specified in the proposition *must* hold. No exceptions to the proposition are possible, and no empirical examination of liquids is required in order that we be certain of this. The proposition can be asserted without fear of contradiction by any future experiment—*if the postulate is assumed.* But this qualifying "if" clause is

extremely important. It reminds us that we have *not* proved the proposition to be *materially* true. We have not shown that in any *actual* volume of water a denser solid will sink to the bottom—*unless,* indeed, the actual water is a fluid for which the postulate is true. What we have shown, therefore, is that *if* water is a fluid whose nature is expressed in part by the postulate, *then* the further relations stated in the proposition will of necessity be predicable of it. But the proof does not show, and does not claim to show, that water is in fact such a liquid.

Now Archimedes may have believed that it was "self-evident" that the postulate was true for all fluids. If he did, he was assuredly mistaken. As we shall have occasion to see repeatedly, and as we have already pointed out, the apparent self-evidence of a proposition is not conclusive evidence for its truth. But whether he did so believe or not, the truth or falsity of the postulate plays no part in the *demonstration*. The foregoing proof, to repeat, does *not* demonstrate the material truth of the proposition. What sort of evidence is required for the material truth of the proposition is considered in Chapters VIII, XI, XIII and XIV. Here we must make it perfectly plain that the *only* sense in which the proof, if conclusive, can be said to demonstrate is that it reveals a necessary connection between the defining properties of fluids and solids and their other properties. *The demonstration uncovers relations of implication between propositions,* and does nothing else. Whether any actual fluid does embody the properties stated by the postulate is not decided by the proof.

The reader will also note that the volume of the liquid and the size of the solid immersed in it play no part in the proof, because the proposition follows from the assumption concerning liquids *as such,* not from assumptions concerning liquids and solids of a certain volume. A proposition is demonstrated, therefore, if the premises *imply* the proposition, or, in other words, if the proposition is a necessary consequence of the premises.

2. It is time to proceed to the second question: Is the proof conclusive? Before the reader commits himself, let us remind him that the proof is conclusive only if the proposition is a necessary consequence of the premises. A proof is *not* conclusive if *other* premises are required besides those explicitly stated. How, then, can we be sure that no premises other than those stated are needed to imply the proposition? There is only one way to find out. We must break up the demonstration above into a series of implications, each of

which is to require no assumptions other than those explicitly granted. Let us therefore analyze the proof in some detail.

The first part of the proof may be put as follows:

1. The part of the liquid which suffers greater pressure than other parts moves out of the way the parts which are under lower pressure.
   Postulate

   The part of the fluid immediately beneath the solid suffers greater pressure than the parts of the fluid under this part.
   The solid is by hypothesis denser than the liquid.

   ∴ The part of the fluid immediately beneath the solid moves out of the way the parts underneath itself.

The second part of the proof can be stated as follows. We shall letter each step as a convenience for reference.

2. a. The weight of A is equal to $(G+H)$.
   The weight of B is equal to G.
   ∴ The weight of $(A+B)$ is equal to $(G+H)+G$.
   Hypothesis
   Hypothesis
   The weight of a body is equal to the arithmetical sum of the weights of its parts, that is, the property of weight is assumed to be additive.

   b. The volume of A is equal to the volume of fluid weighing G.
   The volume of B is equal to the volume of fluid weighing $(G+H)$.
   ∴ The volume of $(A+B)$ is equal to the volume of fluid weighing $(G+H)+G$.
   Hypothesis

   Hypothesis

   The volume of a body is equal to the arithmetical sum of the volumes of its parts, that is, the property of volume is assumed to be additive. Furthermore, the density of the fluid must be assumed to be constant.

   c. $(G+H)+G$ is the weight of the fluid equal in volume to the volume of $(A+B)$.
   The weight of $(A+B)$ is equal to $(G+H)+G$.
   ∴ The weight of $(A+B)$ is equal to the weight of the fluid whose volume is $(A+B)$
   Conclusion of 2 b

   Conclusion of 2 a

   or
   $(A+B)$ has the same density as the fluid.

   d. Solids which have the same density as a fluid will, if let down into it, be immersed so that they do not project above the surface but do not sink lower.
   Proposition 3

   $(A+B)$ has the same density as the fluid, and is let down into it.
   Conclusion of 2 c

∴ $(A + B)$ will not project above the surface nor sink lower

or

$(A + B)$ will remain stationary in the fluid.

e. If a solid lighter than a fluid be forcibly immersed in it, then the solid will be driven upwards by a force equal to the difference between its weight and the weight of the fluid displaced.   *Proposition 6*

B is a solid lighter than the fluid and forcibly immersed in it.   *Hypothesis*

∴ B is driven upwards by a force equal to the difference between its weight and the weight of the displaced fluid.

f. G is the weight of B.   *Hypothesis*

$(G + H)$ is the weight of the fluid displaced by B.   *Hypothesis*

∴ The difference between the weight of B and the weight of the displaced fluid, is the difference between G and $(G + H)$, or H.

g. The difference between the weight of B and the weight of the displaced fluid is H.   *Conclusion of 2 f*

B is driven upwards by a force equal to the difference between its weight and the weight of the displaced fluid.   *Conclusion of 2 e*

∴ B is driven upwards by a force H.

h. $(A + B)$ remains stationary in the fluid.   *Conclusion of 2 d*

B is driven upwards by a force H.   *Conclusion of 2 g*

∴ A is depressed by a force H *The forces acting on a body in the same straight line can*

or   *be added algebraically. This*

The weight of A in the fluid is equal to H.   *is an assumption concerning the additive nature of forces.*

The entire demonstration, we now see, can be analyzed into a number of distinct steps. The demonstration is conclusive, therefore, if each distinct step is conclusive. In this way we discover that the proposition cannot be demonstrated if we assume *only* the postulate. We require in addition four other assumptions concerning the additive nature of weights, volumes, and forces, and the constancy of density in a fluid. Archimedes did not state them explicitly, and in so far as he did not do so the proof is *not* conclusive. These assumptions, however, are of so general a nature that in almost all physical inquiries they are silently taken for granted. Nevertheless, it is very important that we note them explicitly, for without them or their equivalents we cannot prove the hydrostatic principle of Archimedes. Moreover, in some branches of modern physics evidence has been found for doubting the universal truth of several of them. The careful enumeration of all the premises or assumptions of an argument is of extraordinary value in the development of the sciences.

3. We are prepared now to answer the third question: Upon what factors or aspects of the subject matter does the conclusiveness of the demonstration depend? We have seen that the demonstration is conclusive if each step is conclusive. Why, then, is each step conclusive? We have already discussed the answer in the introductory chapter. Each step is conclusive because if the premises in that step are true the conclusion of the step *must also* be true: the relations between premises and conclusion are such that it is not possible to find a universe in which the premises of *this form* are true and the conclusion false.

§ 2. SOME FALLACIOUS DEMONSTRATIONS

We can see more clearly the need for the careful analysis of inferences if we examine two further examples of historically famous inferences.

1. The first is an attempt to improve upon Euclid. Euclid began his great work *The Elements* (of geometry) with twenty-three definitions, five axioms (which were unproved assumptions common to all the sciences), and five postulates (which were unproved propositions relating solely to geometry). The fifth postulate (Book I) is a proposition about parallel lines, but Euclid did not find it necessary to employ it until he came to the twenty-ninth proposition of his first book. Now while the other axioms and postulates struck Euclid's successors as "self-evident," the fifth postulate seemed to require proof. As Proclus, a mathematician of the fifth century, remarked, ". . . the fact that, when the right angles are lessened, the straight lines converge is true and necessary; but the statement that, since they converge more and more as they are produced, they will sometimes meet is plausible but not necessary, in the absence of some argument showing that this is true in the case of straight lines." [2] That the fifth postulate was stated without proof has been for centuries regarded as a blemish in the *Elements,* and many attempts have been made to demonstrate it.

We shall examine a proof by Ptolemy, as reported by Proclus. But we must first state the relevant definitions and postulates of Euclid. Parallel straight lines, according to him (Definition 23), are

2 *The Thirteen Books of Euclid's Elements,* tr. by Sir T. L. Heath, 1926 **3** vols., Vol. I, p. 203.

"straight lines which, being in the same plane and being produced indefinitely in both directions, do not meet one another in either direction." The following are the five postulates:

Postulate 1. "To draw a straight line from any point to any point."

Postulate 2. "To produce a finite straight line continuously in a straight line."

Postulate 3. "To describe a circle with any center and distance."

Postulate 4. "All right angles are equal to one another."

Postulate 5. "If a straight line falling on two straight lines make the interior angles on the same side less than two right angles, the two straight lines, if produced indefinitely, meet on that side on which are the angles less than the two right angles."

Euclid introduced this last postulate in order to demonstrate Proposition 29: "A straight line falling on parallel straight lines makes the alternate angles equal to one another, the exterior angle equal to the interior and opposite angle, and the interior angles on the same side equal to two right angles." Ptolemy tried to prove the parallel postulate by first proving Proposition 29 without its aid, and then showing that the postulate was a consequence of this theorem. We reproduce his attempted proof for the theorem:

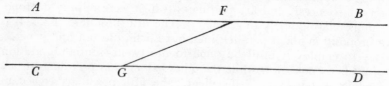

"The straight line which cuts the parallels must make the sum of the interior angles on the same side equal to, greater than, or less than two right angles.

"Let AB, CD be parallel, and let FG meet them. I say (1) that FG does not make the interior angles on the same side greater than two right angles.

"For, if the angles AFG, CGF are greater than two right angles the remaining angles BFG, DGF are less than two right angles.

"But the same two angles are also greater than two right angles; for AF, CG are no more parallel than FB, GD, so that, if the straight line falling on AF, CG makes the interior angles greater than two right angles, the straight line falling on FB, GD will also make the interior angles greater than two right angles.

"But the same angles are also less than two right angles; for the four angles *AFG, CGF, BFG, DGF* are equal to four right angles: which is impossible.

"Similarly (2) we can show that the straight line falling on the parallels does not make the interior angles on the same side less than two right angles.

"But (3), if it makes them neither greater nor less than two right angles, it can only make the interior angles on the same side *equal* to two right angles." [3]

Is Ptolemy's proof valid? Does Proposition 29 follow necessarily from the axioms and postulates, omitting Postulate 5? Let us examine carefully the reasoning we have italicized above. Ptolemy argues that if we suppose angles *AFG, CGF,* are greater than two right angles, we must also suppose angles *BFG, DGF,* to be greater (as well as less) than two right angles, because *whatever is true of the interior angles on one side of the transversal* FG *to the parallel lines is necessarily true at the same time of the interior angles on the other side.* But this assumption is *not* included among the postulates. Ptolemy defends it by asserting that *AF, CG,* are no more parallel in one direction than *FB, GD,* are in the other. However, this simply amounts to saying that *through the point* F *only one parallel can be drawn to the line* CD. And this assumption is precisely *equivalent* to Postulate 5 which he is trying to prove.[4]

Ptolemy's proof, therefore, is unsuccessful, and a more careful analysis of his reasoning could have shown him that this was so. As a matter of fact, we know that Postulate 5 cannot be shown to be a necessary consequence of the remaining postulates. For it can be *demonstrated* that Postulate 5 is *independent* of the others. We discuss the method of proving independence in Chapter VIII. The reader should note at present that a rigorous analysis of an argument into a series of steps makes possible the discovery of all the assumptions required to validate the proof. A recognition of what assumptions we are making, and a readiness to consider all possible alternatives to them, is the one outstanding trait of the method of science. It is the only safeguard we can erect against intellectual dogmatism and arrogance.

2. The second example of a historically significant "proof" is the attempt to demonstrate an important proposition in elementary algebra. The reader is doubtless familiar with the rule that the

[3] *The Thirteen Books of Euclid's Elements,* tr. by Sir T. L. Heath, 1926, 3 vols., Vol. I, p. 205.
[4] *Ibid.,* p. 206.

product of two negative integers is always positive, thus: $(-3) \times (-4) = (+12)$. Can this proposition be demonstrated? Of course a demonstration is possible only if other propositions are assumed as premises. It turns out that algebra too may be developed systematically on the basis of axioms concerning the addition and multiplication of quantities. Our question must therefore be put as follows: Can the proposition that the product of two negatives is positive be shown to be a logical consequence of the assumptions concerning the addition and multiplication of *positive* numbers alone?

Unfortunately, the systematic exposition of algebra is highly abstract, requiring considerable intellectual maturity for its com-

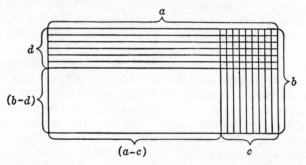

prehension, so that beginners are introduced to the subject as if it were simply a collection of rules. However, proofs are sometimes attempted of the important rules, and the following argument is frequently offered in support of the proposition concerning the product of two negative numbers. The argument tries to show that the rule for multiplying negative numbers is a necessary consequence of the rules for multiplying and adding positive ones.

The accompanying rectangle has sides equal to a and b respectively. Its area, in accordance with a theorem in plane geometry, is ab. The area of the smaller, unshaded rectangle, with sides equal to $(a-c)$ and $(b-d)$ respectively, is equal to $(a-c)(b-d)$. Let us now express this last area in terms of the large rectangle and the smaller, shaded ones. An examination of the figure shows that the area of the unshaded figure may be obtained by first *subtracting* from the large rectangle the vertically shaded rectangle (its area is bc) as well as the horizontally shaded rectangle (its area is ad), and then *adding* the rectangle shaded both ways (its area is cd). Hence we may write equation 1: $(a-c)(b-d) = ab - bc - ad + cd$.

Let us now give to both a and b the value zero. Then we get equation 2: $(0-c)(0-d) = 0.0 - 0.c - 0.d + cd$; or equation 3: $(-c)(-d) = (+cd)$. In general, the proof concludes, the product of two negatives is positive.

But is the proof valid? The reader will see easily that it is not. For equation 1 was developed on the assumption that a and b are *not* equal to zero. We cannot obtain equation 3 from equation 1 unless we make the *additional* assumption that equation 1 will be true for *all possible values* of a and b. But this addition is equivalent to the assumption that *all the laws which hold for the addition and multiplication of positive numbers are also true for negative ones.* And it is just this assumption which was being demonstrated.

We know, in fact, that the rules of operation upon negative numbers are *independent* of the rules for positive ones. Once more the value of analyzing an argument into a series of steps becomes evident. Just as the study of the assumptions required to prove Euclid's Postulate 5 led Lobatchevsky and Bolyai to the discovery of non-Euclidean geometries, so an examination of the fundamental rules of algebra led to the discovery by Sir William R. Hamilton and H. G. Grassmann of different algebraic systems. Without non-Euclidean geometries and the more general algebras, the advances of modern physics would hardly have been possible. It is well to note the far-reaching consequences of the method which insists on exhibiting all the assumptions required in demonstrations, and studies impartially the alternatives to such assumptions. The significance for civilization of logical method cannot be made clearer than by a contemplation of its rôle in the history of science.

EXERCISES

CHAPTER I: THE SUBJECT MATTER OF LOGIC

1. Is it on the basis of immediate knowledge or on evidence that you know
   a. that there is a center to the earth?
   b. that there is a king of Italy?
   c. that you have lungs with which you breathe?
   d. that there is a Belgian Congo?
   e. that there is a country called Tibet between India and China?

2. What evidence have you for the belief that a remote ancestor of yours must have lived in 2000 B.C.? or that Washington, Napoleon, King Arthur, King David, Homer, or Moses lived on this earth?

3. Prove that $5 + 2 = 7$. Formulate all the assumptions involved in this proof. (See Poincaré, *The Foundations of Science*, pp. 34-42.)

4. What is meant by saying that logic is formal?

5. Examine the proof that:
   $$a^2 - b^2 = (a + b)(a - b)$$
   What fundamental assumptions are involved?

6. State the propositions necessary to prove
   a. that the earth is round,
   b. that it revolves around its axis and also around the sun.

7. What evidence is there that under the present Constitution a President of the United States might be elected by a minority vote?

8. Are the following arguments valid?
   a. San Francisco is west of New York.
      Peking is west of San Francisco.
      Berlin is west of Peking.
      ∴ Berlin is west of San Francisco.
   b. A is to the right of B.
      B is to the right of C.
      ∴ A is to the right of C.
      Is this true of people sitting in a circle?

9. Is the following a valid argument simply because premises and conclusion are true?
   a. Fish live in water.
      Monkeys are not fish.
      ∴ Monkeys do not live in the water.

b. Compare with:
Fish live in water.
Whales are not fish.
∴ Whales do not live in the water.

10. Examine the following as to their validity:

a. All lions are fierce.
Some lions do not drink coffee.
∴ Some creatures that drink coffee are not fierce.

b. Some pillows are soft.
No pokers are soft.
∴ Some pokers are not pillows.

c. No bankrupts are rich.
Some merchants are not bankrupts.
∴ Some merchants are rich.

d. No emperors are dentists.
All dentists are dreaded by children.
∴ No emperors are dreaded by children.

e. All the clever boys got prizes.
All the hard-working boys got prizes.
∴ All the clever boys were hard-working.

f. All liberals hold these opinions.
He holds these opinions.
∴ He is a liberal.

11. Discuss the following as to their validity:

a. If war is declared, the enemy country will be invaded.
But war is not declared.
∴ The enemy country will not be invaded.

b. If a number is divisible by 4, it is even.
It is not even.
∴ It is not divisible by 4.

c. If the street is sprinkled, there is no dust in the air.
The street is not sprinkled.
∴ There is dust in the air.

d. Either the child is ill or it is spoiled.
But the child is ill.
∴ It is not spoiled.

e. If he fulfills his election promises, he will be a popular mayor.
He will be a popular mayor.
∴ He will fulfill his election promises.

f. If he was born in Paris, he cannot become a cabinet officer.
He was born in Paris.
∴ He cannot become a cabinet officer.

g. Either he is indifferent or he is forgetful.
He is not forgetful.
∴ He is indifferent.

12. Examine the following arguments:

a. Ninety-nine Cretans in a hundred are liars.
Epimenides is a Cretan.
∴ Epimenides is a liar.

b. Minos, Sarpedon, Rhadamantus, Deucalion, and Epimenides are all the Cretans I know.
They were all atrocious liars.
∴ Pretty much all Cretans must have been liars.
c. All the beans taken from bag A are white.
These beans are white.
∴ These beans are from bag A.

13. Distinguish between inference and implication.

14. What is the difference between logic and grammar, logic and psychology, logic and physics?

15. In Book IV, Chapter XVII of his Essay Concerning Human Understanding, Locke comments as follows upon the value of the study of formal logic:

"If syllogisms must be taken for the only proper instrument of reason and means of knowledge, it will follow that, before Aristotle, there was not one man that did or could know anything by reason; and that, since the invention of syllogisms, there is not one of ten thousand that doth. But God has not been so sparing to men to make them barely two-legged creatures, and left it to Aristotle to make them rational."

Examine the force of this jibe against Aristotle.

For further study: L. S. Stebbing, Modern Introduction to Logic, 1930, Chap. I; John Dewey, How We Think, new ed., 1933, Pt. II; John Venn, Principles of Empirical or Inductive Logic, 2d ed., Chap. 5, Sec. 1.

CHAPTER II: THE ANALYSIS OF PROPOSITIONS

1. Classify the following propositions:

a. A bird in the hand is worth two in the bush.
b. Truth crushed to earth will rise again.
c. Six is the first perfect number.
d. All the king's horsemen could not put Humpty Dumpty together again.
e. Never will the dead speak.
f. There is nothing in the contract which prevents you from going.
g. Many men labor in vain.
h. Most adults are married.
i. Eight out of every thousand soldiers were killed.
j. Youth is always full of hope.
k. Few trees bear fruit.
l. My coat is on the chair.
m. A few eminent men had distinguished sons.
n. Few eminent men had distinguished sons.
o. Not a few eminent men had distinguished sons.
p. A few facts are better than much rhetoric.
q. One or the other of the members of the committee must have divulged the secret.
r. Literacy is a necessary but not a sufficient condition for voting.
s. Being without funds is a necessary but not a sufficient condition for obtaining help.
t. The virtuous alone are happy.
u. Only the unemployed are lazy.

v. None but foreigners are ill-treated.
w. All students except freshmen are welcome.
x. No one is admitted unless on business.
y. All but the wounded went hungry

2. Exhibit the logical structure of the following arguments:

a. "For we assumed that the world had no beginning in time, then an eternity must have elapsed up to every given point of time, and therefore an infinite series of successive states of things must have passed in the world. The infinity of a series, however, consists in this, that it never can be completed by means of a successive synthesis. Hence an infinite past series of worlds is impossible, and the beginning of the world is a necessary condition of its existence." (This is part of Kant's proof (in his first antinomy) of the thesis that the world had a beginning in time.) 1

b. "Every compound substance in the world consists of simple parts, and nothing exists anywhere but the simple, or what is composed of it.

"For let us assume that compound substances did not consist of simple parts, then if all composition is removed in thought, there would be no compound part, and (as no simple parts are admitted) no simple parts either, that is, there would remain nothing, and there would therefore be no substance at all. Either, therefore, it is impossible to remove all composition in thought, or, after its removal, there must remain something that exists without composition, that is, the simple. In the former case the compound could not itself consist of substances (because with them composition is only an accidental relation of substances, which substances, as permanent beings, must subsist without it). As this contradicts the supposition, there remains only the second view, namely, that the substantial compounds in the world consist of simple parts.

"It follows as an immediate consequence that all the things in the world are simple beings, that their composition is only an external condition, and that, though we are unable to remove these elementary substances from their state of composition and isolate them, reason must conceive them as the first subjects of all composition, and therefore, antecedently to it, as simple beings." (This is part of the proof in Kant's second antinomy.) 2

c. Proof of God's existence: "Whatever is in motion is moved by another: and it is clear to the sense that something, the sun for instance, is in motion. Therefore it is set in motion by something else moving it. Now that which moves it is itself either moved or not. If it be not moved, then the point is proved that we must needs postulate an immovable mover: and this we call God. If, however, it be moved, it is moved by another mover. Either, therefore, we must proceed to infinity, or we must come to an immovable mover. But it is not possible to proceed to infinity. Therefore it is necessary to postulate an immovable mover." 3

3. Discuss the existential import of these propositions:

a. The present King of France is bald.
b. A square circle is a contradiction in terms.
c. The fifth root of a quadratic equation is an integer.

1 *Critique of Pure Reason*, tr. by Max Müller, p. 344.
2 *Ibid.*, pp. 353-54.
3 St. Thomas Aquinas, *Summa contra Gentiles*, tr. by the English Dominican Fathers.

4. What is the distinction between a proposition and a sentence; between a proposition and a judgment?

5. What assumptions, statable as propositions, are involved in the following:

   a. Beware of the dog!
   b. Take your hats off!
   c. May the Lord have mercy on your soul!
   d. Will you join the dance?

6. Arrange the following terms in order of increasing intension: animal, organic being, vertebrate, man, body, featherless biped. What can you say about their extensions?

7. Distinguish between the subjective intension, the connotation, and the comprehension of: circle, man.

8. Which terms are distributed in the propositions in example 1?

9. Classify the following propositions:

   a. Unless he comes soon, we shall not wait.
   b. Either he is drunk or sober.
   c. He sold his horse in town.
   d. Either he answers all the questions, or he will fail to pass.

10. Distinguish between the following with respect to form:

   a. Newton is a physicist.
   b. All Englishmen are good-natured.
   c. Smith is older than Brown.
   d. This leaf is green.
   e. He gave a book to his daughter for her birthday.

11. Express the following as general propositions:

   a. Only the brave deserve the fair.
   b. Some men are teetotalers.
   c. All but children are admitted.
   d. No mathematician is musical.
   e. Some soldiers are not wounded.

For further study on existential import of propositions:

J. N. Keynes, *Formal Logic*, 4 Ed., p. 210 ff.
W. E. Johnson, *Logic*, Part I, Chap. IX.

On the analysis of propositions by contemporary logicians, see:

B. Russell, *Introduction to Mathematical Philosophy*, Chaps. XV, XVI, XVII; also, "Philosophy of Logical Atomism" in *Monist*, Vols. XXVIII and XXIX.

On the significance of negation, see

J. Royce, in Hasting's *Encyclopaedia of Religion and Ethics*, Article on Negation.
R. Demos, *Journal of Philosophy*, 1932. Article "Non-Being."
F. H. Bradley, *Principles of Logic*, Bk. I, Chap. 3.

On disjunction, see

F. H. Bradley, *Principles of Logic*, Bk. I, Chap. 4.

CHAPTER III. THE RELATIONS BETWEEN PROPOSITIONS

1. If *All giraffes have long necks* is true, what may be inferred concerning the following?

    a. No giraffes have short necks.
    b. No giraffes have long necks.
    c. Most giraffes have long necks.
    d. Thirty per cent of the giraffes have not long necks.
    e. All long-necked animals are giraffes.
    f. No short-necked animals are giraffes.
    g. All animals which are not giraffes have short necks.

2. If *No mammals weigh less than ten pounds* is false, what may be inferred concerning the following?

    a. All mammals weigh not less than ten pounds.
    b. All mammals weigh less than ten pounds.
    c. Few mammals weigh less than ten pounds.
    d. No animals weighing less than ten pounds are mammals.
    e. Some mammals do not weigh less than ten pounds.
    f. Some mammals weigh not less than ten pounds.
    g. All animals weighing not less than ten pounds are mammals.
    h. No nonmammalian animals weigh less than ten pounds.

3. If *Most men die young* is true, what may be inferred concerning the following?

    a. Some men do not die young.
    b. Some men die old.
    c. All men die young.
    d. All men die old.
    e. Most of those dying young are men.
    f. Some of those dying old are not men.
    g. Few creatures which are not men die old.

4. If *Some of the American population have no savings* is false, what may be inferred concerning the following?

    a. Forty per cent of the American population have savings.
    b. Some of the American population have savings.
    c. All of the American population have savings.
    d. No part of the American population has any savings.
    e. Some people who have no savings belong to the American population.
    f. Some of the non-American population have savings.
    g. Some people who have savings do not belong to the American population.

5. What information about "mortals" may be obtained from *All Struldbrugs are immortal?*

6. What information about "noncapitalists" may be obtained from *No capitalists are far-sighted?*

7. What information about "a solid body" can be derived from *No bodies which are not solids are crystals?* (Jevons.)

8. Examine the following:

   a. If *All = lateral △ are = angular,* then *All △ with = angles have = sides.*

   b. If *All pacifists are social radicals,* then *All social radicals are pacifists.*

   c. If *All wealthy men are generous,* then *All poor men are niggardly.*

   d. If *Few old men do not desire immortality,* then *Few of those who desire immortality are not old men.*

   e. If *Heat expands bodies,* then *Cold contracts bodies.* (Jevons.)

   f. If *A false balance is abominative to the Lord,* then *A just weight is His delight.* (Jevons.)

9. State equivalent propositions for the following:

   a. If the treasury was not full, the taxgatherers were to blame.

   b. Through any three points not in a straight line a circle may be described.

   c. It is false to say that only the notorious prosper in life.

10. What can be inferred from *The <s at the base of an isosceles △ are equal* by obversion, conversion, and contraposition? (Jevons.)

11. Are the following equivalent?

   a. All who were there talked sense.

   b. All who talked nonsense were away. (De Morgan.)

12. Is the obverse of *No numbers are both odd and even, All numbers are either odd or even?*

13. "When I was a boy I have seen plenty of people puzzled by the following: An elderly nun was often visited by a young gentleman, and the worthy superior thought it necessary to ask who it was. 'A near relation,' said the nun. 'But what relation?' said the superior. 'Oh, madam,' said the nun, 'very near, indeed; for his mother was my mother's only child.' The superior saw that this was very close, and did not trouble herself to disentangle it. And a good many people on whom it was proposed used to study and bother to find out what the name of the connexion was." (De Morgan.) What was it?

14. What is the opposition between each pair of the following?

   a. None but Democrats voted against the proposal.

   b. Amongst those who voted against the proposal were some Democrats.

   c. It is untrue that those who voted against the motion were all Democrats.

15. What is the contradictory of each of the following?

   a. Few men are wealthy.

   b. Denmark was not the only nation to remain neutral.

   c. Forty per cent of the population is in dire want.

   d. "You can fool some of the people all of the time, or all of the people some of the time; but you can't fool all of the people all of the time." (Abraham Lincoln.)

   e. The King of Utopia did not die on Tuesday last.

16. Give a contrary of each of the following:

   a. He was the tallest man in the German army.

   b. Descartes was certain of his own existence.

17. Prove that if two propositions are equivalent their contradictories are equivalent.

18. If *p, q, r, s,* are *any* propositions such that *p* and *q* are *contradictories* of one another, *r* and *s* are *contradictories* of one another, and *p* and *r* are *contraries* of one another, what is the relation of *s* to *p*, *q* to *r*, and *s* to *q*?

19. Give the contrapositive and inverse of each of the following:

 a. Whom the gods wish to destroy they first make mad.

 b. All are not saints that go to church.

20. *All that love virtue love angling.* Arrange the following propositions in the three following groups: (a) Those which can be inferred from the proposition above; (b) those which are consistent with it but which cannot be inferred from it; and (c) those which are inconsistent with it.

 a. None that love not virtue love angling.

 b. All that love angling love virtue.

 c. All that love not angling love virtue.

 d. None that love not angling love virtue.

 e. Some that love not virtue love angling.

 f. Some that love not virtue love not angling.

 g. Some that love not angling love virtue.

 h. Some that love not angling love not virtue.

21. A denies that *None but the native-born are citizens;* B denies that *None but citizens are native-born.* Which of the five class relations between "native-born" and "citizens" must they agree in *rejecting* and which may they agree in *accepting?*

22. Give the contrapositive and contradictory of each of the following:

 a. If any nation prospers under a protective tariff, its citizens reject all arguments in favor of free trade.

 b. If all men are mortal, then none of us will live to know his great-grandchildren.

23. Are the following contradictories?

 a. When there is thunder there is lightning and it either rains or hails.

 b. Sometimes when it thunders either there is no lightning or no rain or no hail.

24. Examine: If anyone is punished, he should be responsible for his actions. Hence, if some lunatics are not responsible for their actions, they should not be punished.

25. What is the logical relation between each of the propositions in the following pairs:

 a. Ten is greater than five.
    Five is less than ten.

 b. All angels fear to tread there.
    Some who fear to tread there are angels.

 c. Seven plus five equals twelve.
    The base angles of an isosceles triangle are equal.

 d. Smith is older than Brown.
    Smith is younger than Brown.

 e. This book is not in English.
    This book is not in French.

 f. No crocodiles shed tears.
    Some crocodiles shed tears.

g. The base angles of an isosceles triangle are equal.
   The base angles of an equilateral triangle are equal.

For further study on the relations between propositions, see:

W. E. Johnson, *Logic*, Part I, Chaps. III, IX.
E. J. Nelson, *Monist*, 1932, "The Square of Opposition."
J. N. Keynes, *Formal Logic*, 4 ed. Appendix C, Chaps. II, IV, and V.

CHAPTER IV: THE CATEGORICAL SYLLOGISM

1. The first four axioms of the categorical syllogism are not independent of one another. Prove the second, third, and fourth by assuming the first axiom, together with the general principle of contraposition as well as the processes of conversion and obversion.

Example: Proof of Axiom 2. Suppose p and q are the premises and r the conclusion of a syllogism in which a term N is distributed in r but not in p. Now by the general principle of contraposition, the *contradictory* of r, together with p, must imply the *contradictory* of q. The term N will now be the middle term of the new syllogism. But since N is, by hypothesis, distributed in r, it will not be distributed in the contradictory of r; since if a term is distributed in one proposition, it is not distributed in its contradictory. Hence the middle term of the new syllogism is not distributed. It follows that a syllogism violating Axiom 2 implicitly violates Axiom 1.

2. Given that the major term is distributed in the premises and undistributed in the conclusion of a valid syllogism. Determine the syllogism.

3. Prove that, if three propositions involving three terms, each of which occurs in two of the propositions, are together incompatible, (a) each term is distributed at least once, and (b) one and only one of the propositions is negative.

4. Examine the validity of the following argument which sometimes appears in mathematical texts: "A magnitude required for the solution of a problem must satisfy a particular equation; since the magnitude x satisfies this equation, it is the magnitude required."

5. Is the following argument valid?

No P is M.
No S is M.
∴ Some non-S is P.

6. Is it possible to construct an *invalid* syllogism in which the major premise is *universal negative*, the minor premise *affirmative*, and the conclusion *particular negative?*

7. How many more distributed terms may there be in the premises of a valid syllogism than in the conclusion?

8. What can be determined respecting a valid syllogism under each of the following conditions?

a. Only one term is distributed, and that one only once.
b. Only one term is distributed, and that one twice.
c. Two terms only are distributed, each only once.
d. Two terms only are distributed, each twice.

9. In what cases will contradictory major premises both yield conclusions when

combined with the same *minor?* How are the conclusions related? Are there any cases in which contradictory *minor* premises both yield conclusions when combined with the same *major?*

10. Do c and d of the following propositions follow from a and b?

a. All just actions are praiseworthy.
b. No unjust actions are expedient.
c. Some inexpedient actions are not praiseworthy.
d. Not all praiseworthy actions are inexpedient.

11. Prove that any mood valid in both the second figure and the third figure is valid also in the first figure and the fourth figure.

12. Show that any given mood may be *directly* reduced to any other mood, provided that (a) the latter contains neither a strengthened premise nor a weakened conclusion; and (b) if the conclusion of the former is universal, the conclusion of the latter is also universal.

13. Construct a valid sorites consisting of five propositions and having *Some acorns do not grow into oaks* as its first premise. What is the mood and figure of each of the distinct syllogisms into which the sorites may be resolved?

14. Whatever P and Q may stand for, we can show *a priori* that: Some P is Q, for everything that is both P and Q is Q, and everything that is both P and Q is P, therefore some P is Q. Examine this paradox.

15. In what figures is the mood *AEE* valid? (Jevons.)

16. If the major term of a syllogism be the predicate of the major premise, what do we know about the minor premise? (Jevons.)

17. Prove that O cannot be a premise in the first or fourth figure; and that it cannot be the major in the second, or the minor in the third. (Jevons.)

18. If the middle term is distributed in both premises, what can we infer as to the conclusion? (Jevons.)

19. Show that if the conclusion of a syllogism be a universal proposition, the middle term can be distributed but once in the premises. (Jevons.)

20. Prove that when the minor term is predicate in the premise, the conclusion cannot be an A proposition. (Jevons.)

21. Prove that the major premise of a syllogism whose conclusion is negative can never be an I proposition. (Jevons.)

22. If the major term be universal in the premise and particular in the conclusion (which is not weakened), determine the mood and figure.

23. If the minor premise of a syllogism be O, what is the figure and mood?

24. Examine the validity of the following syllogisms:

a. None but whites are civilized; the ancient Germans were whites; therefore they were civilized. (Whately.)

b. None but civilized people are whites; the Gauls were whites; therefore they were civilized. (Whately.)

c. All books of literature are subject to error; and they are all of man's invention; hence all things of man's invention are subject to error. (Jevons.)

25. Show that if either of two given propositions will suffice to expand a given enthymeme of the first or second order, the two propositions are equivalent provided neither is a strengthened premise.

26. Prove special rules for the sorites:

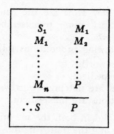

a. Only one negative premise, and that one must be the last.

b. Only one particular premise and that one must be the first.

27. Construct a valid sorites of five propositions in which: Some *A* is not *B:* is the first premise.

28. Complete: Opponents of Robespierre declared in the Convention that he had identified his own enemies with those of the state. This he denied, adding, "And the proof is that you still live."

29. Examine the following as to their validity:

a. No Frenchmen like plum pudding.
   All Englishmen like plum pudding.
   ∴ Englishmen are not Frenchmen.

b. No pigs can fly.
   All pigs are greedy.
   ∴ Some greedy creatures cannot fly.

c. Nothing intelligible ever puzzles me.
   Logic puzzles me.
   ∴ Logic is unintelligible.

d. No bald creatures need a hairbrush.
   No lizards have hair.
   ∴ No lizards need a hairbrush.

e. All lions are fierce.
   Some lions do not drink coffee.
   ∴ Some creatures that drink coffee are not fierce.

f. No fossil can be crossed in love.
   An oyster can be crossed in love.
   ∴ Oysters are not fossils.

g. Some pillows are soft.
   No pokers are soft.
   ∴ Some pokers are not pillows.

h. No fish suckles its young.
   The whale suckles its young.
   ∴ The whale is no fish.

i. No ducks waltz.
   No officers ever decline to waltz.
   All my poultry are ducks.
   ∴ My poultry are not officers.

j. All babies are illogical.
   No one is despised who can manage a crocodile.

Illogical persons are despised.

∴. No babies can manage crocodiles.

For further study:

A. De Morgan, *Transactions of the Cambridge Philosophical Society,* Vols. 8, 9, 10, series of papers "On the Syllogism."

Wm. P. Montague, *Ways of Knowing,* pp. 93 to 99.

CHAPTER V: HYPOTHETICAL, ALTERNATIVE, AND DISJUNCTIVE SYLLOGISMS

1. Examine the following:

a. If all men were capable of perfection, some would have attained it. But no men have attained perfection.

∴. No men are capable of perfection.

b. If you needed food, I would give you money. But since you do not care to work, you cannot need food.

∴. I will give you no money.

2. What may be inferred from the following?

a. He always stays in when it rains, but he often goes out when it is cold.

b. Either luck is with us or the robbers have been frightened away.

c. Either the robbers have not been frightened away or our jewels are gone.

3. Examine:

a. If I am fated to be drowned now, there is no use in my struggling; if not, there is no need of it.

But either I am fated to drown now or I am not.

∴. It is either useless or needless for me to struggle against it.

b. Patriotism and humanitarianism must be either incompatible or inseparable.

But although family affection and humanitarianism are compatible, either may exist without the other.

∴. Family affection may exist without patriotism.

4. If *P*, then *Q;* and if *R*, then *S*. But *Q* and *S* cannot both be true. Prove that *P* and *R* cannot both be true. (De Morgan.)

5. Examine:

a. "Either our soul, said they [the ancient philosophers], perishes with the body, and thus, having no feeling, we shall be incapable of any evil; or if the soul survives the body, it will be more happy than it was in the body; therefore death is not to be feared." (*The Port Royal Logic,* tr. by T. S. Baynes.)

b. If Abraham was justified, it must have been either by faith or by works. Now he was not justified by faith (according to James) nor by works (according to Paul).

∴. Abraham was not justified.

c. If the Mosaic account of the cosmogony is strictly correct, the sun was not created till the fourth day. And if the sun was not created till the fourth day, it could not have been the cause of the alternation of day and night for the first three days. But either the word "day" is used in Scripture in a different sense to that in which it is commonly accepted now, or else the sun must have been the cause of the alternation of day and night for the first three days. Hence either the Mosaic account of the cosmogony is not strictly correct, or else the word "day" is used in Scripture in a different sense to that in which it is commonly accepted now. (Keynes.)

d. Everyone is either well informed of the facts or already convinced on the subject.

No one can be at the same time both already convinced on the subject and amenable to argument.

∴ Only those who are well informed of the facts are amenable to argument.

e. Poetry must be either true or false: if the latter, it is misleading; if the former, it is disguised history and savors of imposture as trying to pass itself off for more than it is.

Some philosophers have, therefore, wisely excluded poetry from the ideal commonwealth. (Keynes.)

f. You say that there is no rule without an exception. I answer that, in that case, what you have just said must have an exception, and so prove that you have contradicted yourself. (Keynes.)

g. If all the accused were innocent, some at least would have been acquitted; but since none have been acquitted, none were innocent.

h. Given that A is B, to prove that B is A. Now B (like everything else) is either A or $not\text{-}A$. If B is $not\text{-}A$, then by our first premise we have the syllogism, A is B, B is $not\text{-}A$, hence A is $not\text{-}A$, which is absurd. Therefore B is A. (Keynes, after Jastrow.)

i. If all the soldiers had been English, they would not all have run away; but some did run away; hence some of them at least were not English. (Keynes.)

6. Examine:

a. Logic is indeed worthy of being cultivated, if Aristotle is to be regarded as infallible; but he is not. Logic, therefore, is not worthy of being cultivated (Whately.)

b. We are bound to set apart one day in seven for religious duties, if the fourth commandment is obligatory on us: but we are bound to set apart one day in seven for religious duties: and hence, it appears that the fourth commandment is obligatory on us. (Whately.)

c. "He [Robert Simson] used to sit at his open window on the ground floor, . . . deep in geometry. . . . Here he would be accosted by beggars, to whom he generally gave a trifle, he roused himself to hear a few words of the story, made his donation, and instantly dropped down into his depths. Some wags one day stopped a mendicant who was on his way to the window with 'Now, my man, do as we tell you, and you will get something from that gentleman, and a shilling from us besides. You will go and say you are in distress, he will ask you who you are, and you will say you are Robert Simson, son of John Simson of Kirktonhill.' The man did as he was told; Simson quietly gave him a coin, and dropped off. The wags watched a little, and saw him rouse himself again, and exclaim 'Robert Simson, son of John Simson of Kirktonhill! why, that is myself. That man must be an impostor.'" (De Morgan.)

7. Analyze the argument in the following:

Which is better, a clock that is right only once a year, or a clock that is right twice every day? "The latter," you reply, "unquestionably." Very good, now attend.

I have two clocks: one doesn't go *at all*, and the other loses a minute every day: which would you prefer? "The losing one," you answer, "without a doubt." Now observe: the one which loses a minute a day has to lose 12 hours or 720 minutes, before it is right, whereas the other is evidently right as often as the time it points to comes round, which happens twice a day.

So you've contradicted yourself *once*.

"Ah, but," you say, "what's the use of its being right twice a day, if I can't tell when the time comes?"

Why, suppose the clock points to 8 o'clock, don't you see that the clock is right *at* eight o'clock? Consequently, when 8 o'clock comes round your clock is right.

"Yes, I see *that*," you reply.

Very good, then you've contradicted yourself *twice:* now get out of the difficulty as best you can, and don't contradict yourself again if you can help it.

You *might* go on to ask, "How am I to know when 8 o'clock *does* come? My clock will not tell." Be patient. You know that when 8 o'clock comes your clock is right; very good; then your rule is this: Keep your eye fixed on your clock, and the *very moment it is right* it will be 8 o'clock. "But—," you say. There, that'll do; the more you argue, the farther you get from the point, so it will be as well to stop. (Lewis Carroll.)

For further study, see:

J. Venn, *Empirical Logic*, Chap. X.

J. N. Keynes, *Formal Logic*, 4 ed. Appendix C, Chap. V, for a discussion of more complicated forms of agreement.

CHAPTER VI: GENERALIZED OR MATHEMATICAL LOGIC

1. State whether the relation in each of the following is transitive, intransitive, symmetrical, asymmetrical, one-one, one-many, or many-many.

a. He is the shortest man in the army.
b. Joseph had the same parents as Benjamin.
c. Adam is the ancestor of all of us.
d. Impatience is not the characteristic of a good teacher.
e. Smith is a next-door neighbor of Jones.
f. Russia was defeated by Japan.
g. Romeo is the lover of Juliet.
h. The ticket agent is on speaking-terms with many notables.
i. Brown is an employee of Jackson.

2. Discuss the following:

"It is a profoundly erroneous truism, repeated by all copybooks and by eminent people when they are making speeches, that we should cultivate the habit of thinking of what we are doing. The precise opposite is the case. Civilization advances by extending the number of important operations which we can perform without thinking about them. Operations of thought are like cavalry charges in battle—they are strictly limited in number, they require fresh horses, and must only be made at decisive moments." [4]

3. State the following expressions in words and simplify:

a. $ad + \bar{a}\bar{c}d$.
b. $a\bar{d} + a\bar{e} + \bar{a}b + \bar{a}c + \bar{a}e + \bar{b}c + \bar{b}\bar{d} + \bar{b}\bar{e} + \bar{b}\bar{e} + \bar{c}\bar{d} + \bar{c}\bar{e}$. (Keynes.)

4. Show that:

a. $bc + \bar{b}d + cd$ is equivalent to $bc + \bar{b}d$. (Keynes.)
b. $ab + ac + bc + \bar{a}b + \bar{a}b\bar{c} + c = \bar{a} + b + c$.

5. Give the contradictories of the following terms:

a. $ab + bc + cd$.
b. $ab + \bar{b}c + \bar{c}d$. (Keynes.)

6. Give the contradictory of each of the following:

a. Flowering plants are either endogens or exogens, but not both.
b. Flowering plants are vascular, and either endogens or exogens but not both. (Keynes.)

7. What are some of the difficulties in employing everyday language for special scientific purposes?

8. Consult a large dictionary and discover what changes have occurred in the meaning of the following words: kind, manuscript, watch, genus, doctor.

9. What is meant by a class?

10. What is meant by the logical sum of two classes; by the logical product of two classes?

11. What is meant by saying that one of two classes is included in the other?

12. What is the null-class, and what relations hold between it and every other class?

13. State the following symbolically:

a. Only the perseverant succeed.
b. Some professors are not gray-haired.
c. None but the young are capable of heroism.
d. All logic books contain misprints.
e. No athletes live long.

14. Prove symbolically the following:

a. All a's are b's; therefore all non-b's are non-a's.
b. No a's are b's; therefore all a's are non-b's.
c. Some a's are b's; therefore some b's are a's.
d. Some a's are not b's; therefore some non-b's are not non-a's.

15. State the following propositions symbolically:

a. If p implies q, and q implies r, then p implies r.
b. If p and q imply r, then p and not-r imply not-q.
c. If either p or q implies r, then either p implies r or q implies r.

For further study:

On the logic of relations:

B. Russell, *Principles of Mathematics*, Chaps. II and IX.

On the algebra of logic:

L. Couturat, *Algebra of Logic*.

[4] A. N. Whitehead, *Introduction to Mathematics*, 1911, p. 61.

A. N. Whitehead, *Universal Algebra*, Bk. I, Chap. I and Book II.

C. I. Lewis, and Langford, *Symbolic Logic*.

R. M. Eaton, *Symbolism and Truth*, Chap. VII.

On the nature of symbols:

W. E. Johnson, *Logic*, Part II, Chap. III.

A. N. Whitehead, *An Introduction to Mathematics*, Chap. V.

R. M. Eaton, *Symbolism and Truth*, Chap. II.

CHAPTER VII: THE NATURE OF A LOGICAL OR MATHEMATICAL SYSTEM

1. How would you establish that the following postulates are *consistent?* Show also that they are *independent* of one another.

Postulate 1. If *a* and *b* are distinct elements of a class *K*, and $<$ an otherwise unspecified relation, then either $a < b$ or $b < a$.

Postulate 2. If $a < b$, then *a* and *b* are distinct.

Postulate 3. If $a < b$, then $b < c$, then $a < c$.[5]

2. Show that the set of operations (addition, multiplication, division, and subtraction) upon *integers* is isomorphic with the set of operations upon *fractions*.

3. Discuss the relation of algebra to analytic geometry with respect to isomorphism.

4. Prove that Aristotle's *dictum de omni et nullo* for the categorical syllogism is *equivalent* to the five axioms of validity stated in § 3 of Chapter IV.

5. Show that Axiom 1 for categorical syllogism (the middle term must be distributed at least once) is equivalent to Axiom 2 (no term can be distributed in the conclusion if it is not distributed in the premises).

6. "Write any odd number, say 35, on one card, and any even number, say 46, on another. Ask someone to give one of the cards to A and another to B, but not to tell you who has which. You undertake to tell A which number he was given. Ask A to multiply the number on his card by any even number, and B to multiply his by any odd number. Ask A and B to add their results and tell you what the sum is. If the sum is even, A was given the odd number; if the sum is odd, A was given the even number."[6] Demonstrate that this result will always hold.

7. Show that it is *impossible* to factor an integer into its *prime* factors in more than one way.

8. What is an axiom?

9. What is meant by saying that a proposition is self-evident?

10. What kinds of questions is logic in the position to ask and settle concerning a proposition?

11. Prove by mathematical induction:

$$1 + 2 + 3 + \ldots + n = \frac{n(n+1)}{2}$$

12. Read Chapters 6 and 7 in Whitehead's *Introduction to Mathematics*. Discuss the ways in which integral, rational, real, and imaginary numbers differ from one another.

[5] E. V. Huntington, *The Continuum*, 1917, p. 10.

[6] E. T. Bell, *Numerology*, 1933, p. 174.

For further study:

J. W. Young, *Fundamental Concepts of Algebra and Geometry*, Chaps. II, III, IV, and V.

R. D. Carmichael, *The Logic of Discovery*, Chaps. II, III, IV, V, VI.

A. N. Whitehead, *Introduction to Mathematics*

P. E. B. Jourdain, *The Nature of Mathematics.*

B. Russell, *Mysticism and Logic*, Chaps. IV and V.

CHAPTER VIII: PROBABLE INFERENCE

1. What is the probability that a coin will fall tails up 3 times in succession if the coin can fall with either face uppermost, each of which events is as probable as the other?

2. What is the probability of getting heads 3 times in 5 throws of a fair coin?

3. A purse contains 2 quarters, 3 dimes, and 6 nickels. Two coins are taken out at random. What is the probability that the 2 coins are:

a. The 2 quarters.

b. One dime and 1 nickel.

4. The probability that A will die within ten years is $9/100$; that B will, is $7/100$, and that C will, is $11/100$.

a. What is the probability that A will live for another ten years?

b. What is the probability that both A and B will live another ten years?

c. What is the probability that at least one of the three will live another ten years?

5. If 7 people seat themselves at random at a round table, what is the probability that 2 designated men will be neighbors? What is the probability if 3 people so seat themselves?

6. The probability of getting a head with a coin is $1/2$; of getting a six with a die is $1/6$; and of drawing a white ball from an urn is $3/5$. What is the probability, if these are independent events, that:

a. One of these events, and only 1, will happen?

b. Two, but not more than 2, of these events will happen?

c. That at least 1 will happen?

d. That at least 2 will happen?

e. That at most 1 will happen?

f. That at most 2 will happen?

7. One of two externally similar boxes contains 4 pens and 2 pencils; the other contains 5 pens and 3 pencils. A box is opened at random and an item taken out. What is the probability that it is a pen? If the contents of two boxes had been in one bag, what is the probability that an item taken at random from it would be a pen?

8. Examine the following argument:

"The world that we know contains a quantity of good which, though limited, is still far in excess of what could be expected in a purely mechanistic system.

"If the Universe were composed entirely of a vast number of elementary entities, particles of matter or electricity, or pulses of radiant energy, which preserved themselves and pushed and pulled one another about according to merely physical laws, we should expect that they would occasionally agglutinate into unified structures, which in turn, though far less frequently, might combine to form structures still more complex, and so on. But that any considerable number of these higher aggregates would come about by mere chance would itself be a chance almost infinitely small. Moreover, there would be a steady tendency for such aggregates, as soon as they were formed, to break down and dissipate the matter and energy that had been concentrated in them. . . .

"Now the serious atheist must take his world seriously and ask: What is the chance that all this ascent is, in a universe of descent, the result of chance? And of course by chance, as here used, we mean not absence of any causality, but absence of any causality except that recognized in physics. Thus it would be 'chance' if a bunch of little cards, each with a letter printed on it, when thrown up into the breeze, should fall so as to make a meaningful sentence like 'See the cat.' Each movement of each letter would be mechanically caused, but it would be a chance and a real chance, though a small one, that they would so fall. . . . Let the atheist lay the wager and name the odds that he will demand of us. Given the number of corpuscles, waves, or what not, that compose the universe, he is to bet that with only the types of mechanistic causality . . . that are recognized in physics, there would result, I will not say the cosmos that we actually have, but any cosmos with an equal quantity of significant structures and processes. He certainly will not bet with us on even terms, and I am afraid that the odds that he will feel bound to ask of us will be so heavy that they will make him sheepish, because it is, after all, the truth of his own theory on which he is betting.

"But what is the alternative to all this? Nothing so very terrible; merely the hypothesis that the kind of causality that we know best, the kind that we find in the only part of matter that we can experience directly and from within, the causality, in short, that operates in our lives and minds, is not an alien accident but an essential ingredient of the world that spawns us." [7]

9. Analyze the following arguments to exhibit their probable nature:

"Our visitor bore every mark of being an average commonplace British tradesman, obese, pompous, and slow. He wore rather baggy gray shepherd's check trousers, a not over-clean black frock-coat, unbuttoned in the front, and a drab waistcoat with a heavy brassy Albert chain, and a square pierced bit of metal dangling down as an ornament. A frayed top hat and a faded brown overcoat with a wrinkled velvet collar lay upon a chair besides him. Altogether, look as I would, there was nothing remarkable about the man save his blazing red head and the expression of extreme chagrin and discontent upon his features.

"Sherlock Holmes's quick eye took in my occupation, and he shook his head with a smile as he noticed my questioning glances. 'Beyond the obvious facts that he has at some time done manual labor, that he takes snuff, that he is a Freemason, that he has been in China, and that he has done a considerable amount of writing lately, I can deduce nothing else.'

"Mr. Jabez Wilson started up in his chair, with his forefinger upon the paper, but his eyes upon my companion.

"'How, in the name of good-fortune, did you know all that, Mr. Holmes?' he asked. 'How did you know, for example, that I did manual labor. It's as true as gospel, for I began as a ship's carpenter.'

[7] W. P. Montague, *Belief Unbound*, 1930, pp. 70-73.

" 'Your hands, my dear sir. Your right hand is quite a size larger than your left. You have worked with it, and the muscles are more developed.'

" 'Well, the snuff, then, and the Freemasonry?'

" 'I won't insult your intelligence by telling you how I read that, especially as, rather against the strict rules of your order, you use an arc-and-compass breast-pin.'

" 'Ah, of course, I forgot that. But the writing?'

" 'What else can be indicated by that right cuff so very shiny for five inches, and the left one with the smooth patch near the elbow where you rest it upon the desk.'

" 'Well, but China?'

" 'The fish which you have tattooed immediately above your right wrist could only have been done in China. I have made a small study of tattoo marks, and have even contributed to the literature of the subject. That trick of staining the fishes' scales of a delicate pink is quite peculiar to China. When, in addition, I see a Chinese coin hanging from your watch-chain, the matter becomes even more simple.' " [8]

10. Examine the following:

a. "In the controversies raised on the subject of Phrenology, the opponents of the system have considered that they disproved it by instancing decided exceptions to the phrenological allocations of faculties—cases of mathematicians with a small organ of number, or musicians with a small organ of tune. The facts supposed, however, are not conclusive against the system. For, in the first place, the disproof of the coincidence alleged, in respect of one or two faculties, or any number, would not disprove all the rest. But, in the second place, a few exceptions would not thoroughly disprove the alleged connexion; they would only disprove its unfailing uniformity. . . . For, if the coincidences of a certain distinguished mental aptitude—as number, music, colour—with the unusual size of a certain region of the head, were more frequent than it would be on mere chance, or in the absence of all connexion, he [the phrenologist] would be entitled to infer a relationship between the two." [9]

b. "The prevalence of the different forms of Christianity after the Reformation shows a coincidence with Race that chance would not account for. The Greek church was propagated principally in the Slavonic race; the Roman Catholic church coincides largely with the Celtic race; and the Protestant church has found very little footing out of the Teutonic races. From this coincidence must be presumed a positive affinity between the several forms and the mental peculiarities of the races." [10] (Bain.)

11. Point out the error in the following alleged "correction," written to the editor of a New York newspaper.

Sir:

Some little time ago a very interesting problem was propounded to your readers—a head being thrown in two flips of a coin, and an ace being cast in six throws of a die, which has the greatest probability of happening?

[8] Sir A. Conan Doyle, "The Red-Headed League," in *Adventures of Sherlock Holmes.*

[9] Alexander Bain, *Logic,* 2d ed., 1895, 2 vols., Vol. II, pp. 87-88.

[10] *Ibid.,* p. 88.

You have had several mathematical answers printed, but, strange to say, these answers are based on fallacies and are incorrect.

The chances with these two propositions are equal—that is, you have the same chance of casting an ace in six throws of a die as you have in turning up a head in two flips of a coin.

The chances of flipping a head in two throws of a coin are not one to two, or one to three, as given in two of your correspondents' answers, but it amounts to no chance at all. There are but two faces to a coin, therefore mathematically in every two throws a head must come up once. With the die the odds are: ace in one throw, five to nine; in two throws, four to two; in three throws, three to three; in four throws, two to four; in five throws, one to five, and in six throws no odds at all, because the ace, mathematically, is certain to come up.

12. What is probable inference?

13. Examine the following arguments:

a. From a bag of coffee a handful is taken out and found to have nine-tenths of the beans perfect. It is inferred that about nine-tenths of all the beans in the bag are probably perfect.

b. A man once landed at a seaport in a Turkish province; and as he walked up to the house he was to visit, he met a man on horseback surrounded by four horsemen holding a canopy over his head. Since the governor of the province was the only person the stranger could think of who would be so greatly honored, he inferred that the person he saw was the governor.

For further study:

C. S. Peirce, *Chance, Love, and Logic.* Part I, Chaps. 3, 4, 5, and 6. Also *Col lected Papers.* Vol. II, Chaps. 5, 6, 7, and 8.

M. R. Cohen, *Reason and Nature,* Bk. I, Chap. III, § 3 and § 4.

J. M. Keynes, *Treatise on Probability,* Part I.

J. Laird, *Knowledge, Belief and Opinion,* Chap. XVII.

CHAPTER IX: SOME PROBLEMS OF LOGIC

1. How would you distinguish between principles of logic and principles of physics?

2. How would you solve the following difficulties?

a. A barber is defined as one who shaves *all* those and *only* those who do *not* shave themselves. Does the barber shave himself?

b. A word standing for an adjective will be said to be *autologous* if it itself possesses the property denoted by it; it will be said to be *heterologous* otherwise. Thus the word "short" is itself short and is therefore autologous; the word "long" is not itself long and is heterologous.

Consider the word "heterologous." If it is autologous it has the property denoted by itself, and so is heterologous; if it is heterologous, it has not the property denoted by itself (that is, is *not* heterologous) and so is autologous. It seems then, that if it is, it isn't; and if it isn't, it is.

c. "The number of syllables in the English names of finite integers tends to increase as the integers grow larger, and must gradually increase indefinitely, since only a finite number of names can be made with a given finite number of syllables. Hence the names of some integers must consist of at least nineteen syllables, and among these there must be a least. Hence 'the least integer not nameable in fewer than nineteen syllables' must denote a definite integer; in fact, it denotes 111,777. But 'the least integer not nameable in fewer than nineteen syllables' is itself a name consisting of eighteen syllables; hence the least integer not nameable in fewer than nineteen syllables can be named in eighteen syllables, which is a contradiction.[11]

3. Analyze the following discussion of the "laws of thought":

"If they are principles of thinking, we have to consider how they may be applied to reality and with what success. If they are principles of being, we want exhaustive evidence that all reality obeys these laws, and must at least grapple with the paradox of Change. For the reality of Change seems flatly to defy them all. A thing that changes neither remains itself, nor is it incapable of assuming contrary attributes in time or even simultaneously. It both is and is not, and cannot strictly be said to 'be' either one thing or another. If the moving arrow ever 'were' at the points it passes through, if we were ever right in *saying* that it was, Zeno's inference would be inevitable that motion is impossible. . . ."[12]

4. Examine the following argument: The principle of contradiction does not hold, since according to it *animal* cannot both be vertebrate and invertebrate, although in fact some animals are vertebrate and some are not.

5. What is the alleged paradox of inference?

For further study:

J. Venn, *Empirical Logic,* Chaps. I, II, III.
M. R. Cohen, "Subject Matter of Formal Logic," in *Journal of Philosophy,* Vol. XV, 1918.
B. Bosanquet, *Essentials of Logic,* Chaps. I, II, III.
J. Dewey, "Notes on Logical Theory" in *Journal of Philosophy,* Vol. I, 1904.
C. S. Peirce, *Collected Papers,* Vol. II, Bk. I, Chap. I.

[11] A. N. Whitehead and Bertrand Russell, *Principia Mathematica,* 2d ed., 1925, 3 vols., Vol. I, p. 61.
[12] F. C. S. Schiller, *Formal Logic,* 1912, p. 117.

INDEX

Abélard, 96
Absorption, principle of, 124
Abstract, all propositions and systems are, 140
Added determinants, inference by, 73
Addition, logical, 122
Affirmative propositions, 36
A fortiori arguments, 77, 116
Alternative propositions, 45; equivalence to hypothetical and disjunctive propositions, 64-5; contradictory of, 69
Alternative syllogism, 100-1, 105
Antecedent, 8, 44; fallacy of denying, 99
Antilogism, 91-4
Apodosis, 8
Aristotelian sorites, 95
Aristotle, v, vi, vii, 17, 34, 76, 82, 87, 88, 110, 132, 177, 186, 187
Association, principle of, 124
Asymmetry, of relations, 114
Authenticity, of historical data, 326-9
Axioms, for categorical syllogism, 78-9; function of in system, 129-33; consistency and independence of, 143-7; fertility of, 143

Binomial theorem, and mathematical probability, 164
Bolyai, 144
Boole, George, 112
Bradley, F. H., 34
Butler, Bishop, 151

Cantor, Georg, 113, 146
Categorical propositions, 33-44; symbolical representation of, 124-5

Certainty, in logic, 19, 186
Change, and logic, 176
Classes, calculus of, 121-6
Commands, and propositions, 28
Commutation, principle of, 123
Complex conception, inference by, 74
Complex constructive dilemma, 106
Complex destructive dilemma, 106
Composition, principle of, 124
Compound propositions, 44-8; equivalence between, 63-5; opposition between, 68-75
Conclusion, 8
Conditional propositions, 33, 44
Conjunctive propositions, 46; their contradictories and equivalents, 69-70
Connexity, of relations, 114
Connotation of terms, 30-3
Consequent, 8, 44; fallacy of affirming, 98
Consistency of axioms, 143-7
Contradiction, principle of, 123, 181, 183-4
Contradictory propositions, 53, 55, 66, 68
Contradictory terms, 59
Contraposition, of categorical propositions, 59-60; of hypothetical propositions, 64
Contrary propositions, 55, 66, 71
Contrary terms, 59
Converse subaltern, 56, 66, 74
Conversion of propositions, 58-9; of relations, 63
Copernicus, 213
Copula, 30
Correlation, of relations, 115